PRAISE FOR *EVIL*

"A sober examination of a serious topic. Morrow is one of America's best essayists, and he treats his subject with the necessary sensitivity and openness to paradox."
—*National Review*

"Lance Morrow's *Evil* belongs at the top of the must-read lists."
—*The Richmond Times-Dispatch*

"Compassionate, wise and invaluable…highly readable and, dare one say of so unpalatable a topic, utterly compelling."
—Simon Winchester

"The superb essayist is not a dogmatist about evil, although he does believe Western society is dangerously dismissive of it. Instead, he teases out insights, like the parallel tracks run by evil and humor—the surprise, exaggeration and elusive nature of both."
—*Macleans*

"Morrow stalks his elusive quarry in its many incarnations—Hitler, bin Laden, Jack the Ripper, the Marquis de Sade, as well as Mike Myers' Dr. Evil—in an engaging, unflinching attempt to rethink the unthinkable."
—*Time*

EVIL

AN INVESTIGATION

LANCE MORROW

BASIC
BOOKS

A Member of the Perseus Books Group
New York

To Stefan Kanfer

Designed by Jeff Williams

The Library of Congress catalogued the hardcover edition as follows:
Morrow, Lance
   Evil : an ivestigation / Lance Morrow.
      p.   cm.
   ISBN 0-465-04754-8 (hc)
   1. Good and evil.   I. Title.
BJ1401.M66 2003
170—dc21

                                                                  2003009526

ISBN 0-465-04755-6 (pbk)

04 05 06 / 10 9 8 7 6 5 4 3 2 1

CONTENTS

INTRODUCTION

A DOZEN YEARS AGO, when evil seemed funnier than it does now, Ron Reagan, the son of former President Ronald Reagan, had a television talk show that he taped in Los Angeles.

One day, his booker called me at my office at *Time* magazine in New York and asked me to appear on the show. I had written a cover story for the magazine on the subject of evil. Ron Reagan wanted to do a program on the subject.

I demurred.

The booker used a merry, cajoling voice:

"Come on, Lance. It'll be fun. Think about it—EEEEEE-vul! Nothing's more fun than EEE-vul!"

And so I flew to Los Angeles, and checked into one of those threadbare budget hotels where cost-cutting syndicated television shows put up non-celebrity guests. They did send a limo, which brought me in due course to the studio.

Ron Reagan looked nothing like his father. He was lithe, with a birdlike alertness (he had studied to be a ballet dancer) and an air of affable inaccessibility—an elfin sweetness that, along with his name, was his marketable charm; a sweetness compounded by a remote something that might have suggested earlier hard times, of the neglected-children-of-celebrities variety. Or was it shyness?

The overall effect was of a bright adolescent unwillingly entertaining his parents' friends when his parents were late getting home from the country club.

My fellow guests on the show were 1) a judiciously slow-witted historian of religion who made a specialty of evil and Satan; and 2) the representative of the San Francisco Church of Satan—a dark-haired woman in her thirties named Karla LaVey, who was dressed in a black leather miniskirt and had the face of an angry pizza waitress. She was the eldest daughter of the Church of Satan founder, Anton LaVey. (The father died a few years after we did the Ron Reagan show, his poignantly tacky Church of Satan fell into disrepair, and Karla morphed it into the First Satanic Church, which now promises on its web site to "take Satanism into the 21st century" and offers, among other fiendish delights, a "BlackXmass party" ("Enjoy an evening of blasphemy and Christ-raping performances").

On the Ron Reagan show, Karla LaVey was incensed because I had written bad things about evil; we sat side by side in leather guest chairs, but she turned her back on me (as an angry waitress might) and addressed Ron Reagan, telling him irritably that I did not understand evil, and certainly did not understand, as it were, the positive side of evil—the black attractions.

In response to that, Ron Reagan, scintillating remotely, seemed confused, as if by a paradox (positive evil, did she say? Positive evil? *Whoa!!*) that he sensed was hilarious but also forbidden; in alarm at having to deal, on air, with the contradiction, he turned to the middle-aged historian, who sat on my other side like a lump of anthracite, flickering bluely from time to time.

I did not have much to offer. The woman from the Church of Satan held it against me that I was square and retrograde where evil was concerned, as if I had missed some exciting moral revolution: the good news about the Prince of Darkness.

I was bigoted against evil. I was a moral remnant of the age of Eisenhower.

She was right. People's views of evil tend to be generational, formed by particulars of personal and historical experience. The sixties' rebellion against authority introduced the idea of Satan as rock star; I am inclined to refer, in a more conventional way, to Auschwitz—to think of evil as bad, metaphysically negative, distinctly real: elusive, but real, not an ironic illusion or a remnant medieval misdirection, or a blunt instrument in the hands of primitive fundamentalists.

Evil is a strange, versatile, and dangerous word that can be used to describe a genocide or to incite one ("Let's kill all of the —s. They are evil."). Black magic envelopes the word—now you see it, now you don't. Many people do not believe evil exists. It is a subjective word, and yet describes objective realities—massacres, great wrongs, holocausts. Evil is the *ne plus ultra*, the doomsday word. Nothing can be eviler than evil. The Inuit have all those words for snow. It is difficult to find one suitable synonym in English for evil. Wickedness is close, but not the same.

My conclusion is that it is ultimately not possible to understand evil. Mine is a traditional point of view that echoes Augustine's line about evil, "Do not seek to know more than is appropriate," or repeats what William Langland wrote in *Piers Plowman,* at the time of the Black Death over 600 years ago: "If you want to know why God allowed the Devil to lead us astray . . . then your eyes ought to be in your arse."

I come at evil with this thought of Jung's in mind: ". . . paradox is one of our most valuable spiritual possessions, while uniformity of meaning is a sign of weakness. Hence a religion becomes inwardly impoverished when it loses or waters down its paradoxes; but their multiplication enriches because only the paradox comes anywhere near to comprehending the fulness of life.

yeah Antonine

Non-ambiguity and non-contradiction are one-sided and thus unsuited to express the incomprehensible."

But it is possible to describe evil. Evil is vivid and dramatic; some think that evil is the most interesting thing about human beings. (Evil and humor, perhaps.) The trouble comes in trying to understand evil. When people become frustrated in their effort to do so, they are inclined to say that because they do not understand evil, it does not exist—a somewhat self-important fallacy based on the thought that what I do not understand cannot be real. Evil has made a successful career over many centuries by persuading people that it does not exist.

In the mid-1990s, Andrew Delbanco wrote an elegant book called *The Death of Satan: How Americans Lost the Sense of Evil.* At the beginning of the new millennium, they seem to have found it again. It's best not to say good-bye to evil prematurely. We may have circled round to George Steiner's conceit: "We no longer believe in hell. We have created it here on earth."

Civilized society in any case does not escape the implications of evil simply by declaring that to speak of evil without irony is to be uncivilized. T. S. Eliot wrote:

The world turns and the world changes
But one thing does not change
However you disguise it, this one thing does not change
The perpetual struggle of good and evil.

But evil evolves. It has a talent for adaptation. It keeps up with history and technology. The word "evil"—and the idea of evil—have become pertinent from a new angle. A door has opened into another dimension. The idea of evil has to be rethought in that dimension, under new conditions. A lively awareness of evil, once part of any healthy mind, must be re-installed in the consciousness of the West. Without an awareness of evil, people

,become confused; they fail to anticipate its ruthless possibilities. In the new instantaneous global dimension, it may be catastrophic not to think clearly about evil, not to be aware of what it is capable of doing.

It is amusing to ask why one person might be more qualified than another to discuss evil. The mystery of evil, with us from the beginning, remains essentially intact, so one must operate on the premise that the discussion is still open to laymen. I am not qualified to pronounce definitively on evil. Who is? An archbishop? A saint? A murderer? Anthropologist? Sociologist? Psychiatrist? Who, except one of the monsters or one of his victims, can claim professional expertise?

If I have a choice between consulting a theologian, a philosopher, or a policeman on the workings of evil, I talk first to the policeman, on the theory that he has wider experience of the subject than the others do, and might be less apt to lose his way in theory.

I suppose I would also try to talk to a torturer, though it might not be worth it. A torturer forces people to tell the truth. But the torturer himself seldom tells the truth. His work destroys his ability even to recognize any truth that matters; he recovers it only if, by some grace, he comes to feel the need to be forgiven. Which happens, in rare cases.

Everyone knows about evil as everyone knows about the weather; meteorologists know more. There are, however, no evilologists; the study of evil is not a scientific discipline, but rather a tabloid branch of the humanities, a matter of experience, reading, understanding, interpretation, and a certain appalled fascination, which, if taken over a line, may turn into the sort of obsession that has pale adolescents playing Dungeons and Dragons in the basement.

A few years ago, a 15-year-old girl from an upper-middle-class family, a classmate of my younger son's at a Jesuit school in New

York City, participated in a grisly murder in Central Park. My son knew the girl—her name was Daphne, and he told me everyone knew that she was trouble, but no one knew how much. She and a 16-year-old drinking companion stabbed a man to death one night, then disemboweled him and threw him into the Central Park Lake. My son and I tried to make sense of the murder. Here was an act, close to home, that did not seem explainable except by using the word "evil"—which of course may not, in itself, have explained much at all but simply assigned the event we did not understand to a prestigious metaphysical abyss.

Curious—it was the grisly detail of the disemboweling that seemed to carry the murder over into the territory of evil—even though the young murderers, disconcertingly practical, disemboweled their victim mainly in order to make him sink. Perfectly sensible. A few nights after my troubled and theologically clumsy discussions about the murder with my son, I happened to be reading Mark Twain's *Life on the Mississippi,* and to my surprise, came upon Twain's true account of a traveler set upon by a bandit, who robbed the traveler, shot him dead, and then disemboweled him and threw the body into a river. A few pages on, a similar murder: A man killed, disemboweled, and thrown into another river! In the light of these literary precedents, which I stumbled on by coincidence, I began to wonder ruefully whether Daphne's deed was truly evil or was, rather, part of a venerable American tradition. One learns to respect, if that is the word, the continuity of evil.

I have spent time as a journalist in arguably evil places, notably Bosnia in the mid-nineties. But my real interest in evil derives from my lamentable instinct to moralize and from a sort of naïve lifelong astonishment that people are capable of doing the things they sometimes do—from isolated personal acts like Daphne's murder to genocides.

When the Ron Reagan show was over, the woman from the Church of Satan refused to shake my hand, but tugged at her miniskirt and turned away. Ron Reagan thanked me as if he had already forgotten who I was. The merry booker shimmered onto the set, all smiles, bearing my thank-you present, my fee—a cellophane-covered basket containing little jars of jam and five blueberry muffins, which, he promised, were delicious.

The limo returned me to the hotel. I slept fitfully—the room smelled overpoweringly of disinfectant—and in the morning, I carried the muffins through the metal detectors and flew back to New York, where I ate them. They were indeed delicious.

Evil is the most powerful word in the language, and the most elusive.

The Ron Reagan show, I decided, represented an amiably American approach to the subject. The woman from the Church of Satan was, in a way, hilariously more wholesome and retrograde than, in her view, I was. Her proselytizing diabolism marched down Main Street in a Welcome Wagon sort of way, as if she had the American compulsion to turn nutty ideas into cults, to erect tents and sell peanuts. What seemed so American was her perverted entrepreneurial sense of evil's possibilities; she was thinking out of the box, she was opening up new territory. She saw evil as an opportunity, a new product. She was Satan's own Aimee Semple MacPherson, or P. T. Barnum; she could have been a shill for the Bhagwan Shree Rajneesh. America can turn exotic supernatural wonders into products and performances. There is much to be said for evil as a marketing tool.

But America never accepted evil as part of its deeper theological scheme; the nation was founded under divine sponsorship, and whatever evils attended the American unfolding (slavery, the extirpation of the Indians) did not permanently stain that essential virtue; the American idea is to leave the damage behind, and not look back; every evil will be transcended as the nation goes on, reinventing itself in better and more prosperous ways. Evils are disposable. Americans are Emersonians, and Henry James was right when he said of Emerson, "A ripe unconsciousness of evil is the sweetest sign by which we know him."

So, thousands of years of human experience with the *mysterium iniquitatis*—from Eden and the serpent through the rise and fall of civilizations, through the khans and Caligula and eons of atrocity and torture and treachery and annihilation, of genocide, infanticide, parricide, suicide, homicide—belonged elsewhere, either in the dumpster of the past, or in foreign countries, beyond the seas. The distillate of American evil, at that moment, arrived as the Emersonian sweetness of a Los Angeles talk show with Ronald Reagan's son: ripe unconsciousness indeed—unconsciousness as ripe as an apple.

In the early 1990s, when I was on the Ron Reagan show, evil seemed more playful than it does now—less potent, less real. The Soviet Union and its satellite regimes—what Ron Reagan's father had called the "evil empire"—had collapsed, poof! as if all of it (Stalin, the Gulags, so many deaths, the Great Terror) had been a mirage. There clung to the idea of evil that air of metaphysical sassiness and rebellion and outrageousness—fun, as the booker said—that belonged to adolescents from privileged neighborhoods affronting their parents, turning evil into a punk aesthetic, a Marilyn Manson performance, the idea being that the dark and forbidden vibes were the passionate ones, authentic ones, and evil was something you could revel in and play with, as you do when you are young, full of energy, and lashing at restraints. Evil was ironic, meaning it was "evil," with quotation marks around it; just as irony turns on the thought that the pea is not under the shell where you think it is, then "evil" could be merely a dark and fun surprise. If your parents condemned it, then evil had the attraction and frisson of the forbidden. Evil was an Oedipal gesture—a generational reversal of values.

But it seemed as if the somewhat recreational view of evil as a generational revolt and as something of a hoot gave way, just after the turn of the millennium, to the more deeply sinister tradition. Two seraphically lovely boys in Florida, the King brothers, aged 12 and 13—as beautiful in their way as the elusively diabolic brother and sister in Henry James's "The Turn of the Screw"—beat their father to death with an aluminum baseball bat while he dozed on a BarcaLounger because they said he interfered with their social lives, which included the older boy's sexual relationship with an older man.

In New Hampshire, almost in the same news cycle, two teenaged boys knocked one evening at the door of a couple, both of them professors at Dartmouth. The boys said they were conducting an environmental survey as a project for school, and once inside the house, they drew hunting knives and murdered the professors, stabbing them repeatedly, even stabbing them in the face (a difficult thing to do, one would think—and an especially disturbing violation of a taboo against face mutilation beyond the fundamental big taboo against murder). The boys had hoped to steal enough money to finance an adventure trip to Australia—as if they were Tom and Huck lighting out for the territory.

And there was Columbine.

Oedipus the King—the son of Laius and Jocasta—killed his father by accident, by inadvertence. The King brothers in Florida killed their father, apparently, in a paroxysm of blank moral stupidity, not by accident but by intention, on purpose, and because, terrifyingly, they did not know that they should not. It seemed a good idea at the time. Aristotle said that tragedy means that someone kills, or does something terrible to, a person closely related. Did the King boys' evil rise to the level of tragedy? Is it possible that evil is not always tragic, but as Hannah Arendt would have it (she was framing evil in the infinitely larger context of the Holocaust), "banal"? Arendt's admirable insight caught the ordinariness of evil—the unthinking routines through which it may operate. She might have been struck by this detail: The King boys, found guilty, complained that their sentencing hearing (the younger boy was sentenced to seven years, the older to eight) was going on too long and was forcing them to miss their favorite morning television shows, which they watched in the common room of the jail.

The King brothers' malignantly hermetic version of American childhood—the secret club, Our Gang—seemed a twenty-first-century travesty of Huck and Tom. If Twain gave a sense of American déjà vu to the Central Park murder, the story of Huck and Tom played with a more complicated, contrary resonance against the young Kings' patricide. In the brutal, alcoholic shadows of Twain's long-ago sun-freckled nostalgia, the crimes against nature went in the other direction: It was Huck's father who tried to kill his son.

Huckleberry Finn is one of the most interesting treatments of the subject of American evil. Huck, who speaks a language close to the dialect of slaves, is the unprotected outcast son of the town drunk, and confronts an entire anthology of American evils—child abuse, for example, in the form of his father's bestial and even murderous drunkenness and rage. Pap Finn sleeps with the town's pigs. He might be the embodiment of some kind of evil, except that he never rises to the standard of intelligent malevolence that classic evil expects of one of its own.

Or the psychotic blood feud in which the Grangerfords and Shepherdsons, aristocratic, civilized folk, kill one another off down the generations, even systematically executing one another's children.

In his treatment of race and racism, Twain addresses not just the evil of slavecatchers or the cruelty of overseers, but, far worse, the vast, smug unknowingness, the evil obliviousness of seemingly innocent people. When Tom gets off the steamboat downriver and he reports that there was an accident on the boat—a boiler exploded—the woman asks, "Anyone hurt?" Tom answers, "No, M'am. A couple of niggers killed." The woman replies, "Oh, thank heavens, because you know, sometimes people do get hurt."

The theme of an evil kind of innocence—the ignorant innocence of the powerful—runs through the American story and reasserts itself from time to time in a certain obliviousness in, for example, the area of foreign policy.

The King brothers' patricide and the New Hampshire professor-murders were sensational, exceptional cases—the news reports of them merging with the usual violent imagery of movies and television and popular music. It is not that the novel vileness of those crimes coalesced into a defining trend; it was simply part of a complex cultural picture, a vast and multifaceted, multicultural nation, its sense of itself organized day to day and week to week by the media.

A certain flippancy about evil flourishes in peacetime and a good economy. Not so long ago the television weatherman, speaking of the ski slopes, would deplore the "evil snow conditions." Quentin Tarantino's 1994 movie *Pulp Fiction* managed to find humor in John Travolta's character accidentally blowing off the head of someone sitting in the back seat of a car. A movie character called "Dr. Evil" in Mike Myers' Austin Power movies would spoof conventions of villainy, in a way suggesting that evil has become so domesticated, such a convention of entertainment (like the touchingly simple James Bond movies Dr. Evil spoofed) as to be funny. This was a new and different banality of

evil—not the banality that Arendt meant when she wrote of
Adolf Eichmann's bureaucracy of death but, rather, evil reduced
to goofy harmlessness. What's funny about "Dr. Evil," among
other things, is the cluelessness of his malevolence—his bur-
lesque inconsequence, his peevish impotence. He thinks that one
million dollars ("one meee-leee-own doe-lars!") would be an
enormous ransom to extort from the world. Dr. Evil's confederate hears that, and rolls his one good eye in disgust.

But then there came a crack in history, September 11, 2001,
and George W. Bush's "Axis of Evil," and all that followed. The
idea of evil regained some of its sinister prestige and seriousness.

Not all, however. In enlightened political conversation, the
word "evil" had been disreputable for a long time—and still is,
to a large extent, despite 9/11. The word "evil," in many minds,
still smacks of an atavistic, superstitious, and even medieval
simplism, of a fundamentalist mindset that might be inclined to
burn witches or to reject the teaching of evolution in the public
schools—or, it may be, to use terms like "the axis of evil"
(didn't we get rid of Reagan?) as the language of international
diplomacy.

Is evil a great dark forest that we behold, or is it thousands of
individual sprouts of wickedness, which we sort out the way a
forester would differentiate among maple, spruce, oak, birch,
pine, cedar, elm, hickory, hornbeam, ash, palm, gingko, acacia,
fig, and so on?

Evil is fundamentally a problem about the hedgehog and
fox—the archetypal mindsets on monism and pluralism that Isa-
iah Berlin described in his famous essay on Tolstoy, quoting a
fragment of ancient Greek poetry that said, enigmatically: "The
fox knows many things; the hedgehog knows one big thing."

Can evil be spoken of as One Big Thing? Or is it to be seen,
more sanely perhaps, as Many Things?

The secular, educated, cosmopolitan instinct is a fox; it tends to shun the word "evil" and, as an optimist and creature of the Enlightenment, approaches the world's horrors as individual problems that can be solved (we hope) in a systematic way. People who use the word "evil" are apt to be hedgehogs. But to alter Scott Fitzgerald's formulation, the test of a first-rate mind may be the ability to think like a fox and a hedgehog simultaneously, without losing the ability to function. The intelligent mind is bifocal, capable of seeing evil in both modes. Evil appears in an immense and subtle variety of forms—including, sometimes, the form of apparent good. The task is to recognize evil for what it is, and yet to respond to it with discernment. See comprehensively, as a hedgehog does, but respond discriminately, flexibly, as a fox does, without the dogmatism that makes zealots stupid and prompts them, from time to time, to burn people at the stake.

I

THE GLOBALIZATION
OF EVIL

GEORGE W. BUSH and his critics use the word "evil" in ways
that suggest both sides are fighting the last war, talking about a
world that no longer exists; or rather, both sides fail to see what
evil has become in the world that exists now.

The word needs serious parsing.

It is possible that neither side in the debate about evil quite
knows what it was talking about. President Bush uses the word in
an aggressively in-your-face born-again manner that takes its resonance from a long Judeo-Christian tradition of radical evil
embodied in heroically diabolical figures: personalized evil of the
kind insinuated by the sauntering Tempter in the first scene of
the Book of Job, when God and Satan speculate like racing touts
about whether Job can go a mile and a quarter on a muddy track.
In Bush's usage, evil has the perverse prestige of John Milton's
defiant Lucifer. Evil emanates, implicitly, from a devilish intelligence with horns and a tail, an absolutely malevolent personality,

God's rival in the cosmos, condemned to lose the fight (eventually), but nonetheless powerful in the world.

Bush's critics, hearing the word, go ironic, and put evil into quotes. They mock Bush for what they see as a primitive and frightening use of a medieval term that should probably be banished from civilized discourse in a multicultural world.

Evil, such critics say, is, in any case, such an elusive term that it can only cause mischief in human affairs, and has a way of evaporating—or turning into something else as time passes. But even if evil is elusive and even if the term is used brainlessly, evil is still there—a mystery, a black hole into which reason and sunshine vanish, but nonetheless there. Talk to the children in Sierra Leone whose hands have been chopped off by the rebels there. It is as fatuous to deny the existence of evil as it is to toss the word around irresponsibly. The children of the Enlightenment sometimes have an inadequate understanding of the possibilities of the Endarkenment. The question is not whether evil exists, but how it exists, how it works.

Go back 40 years to the controversy that surrounded Hannah Arendt's *Eichmann in Jerusalem,* a study of the Adolf Eichmann trial in which she coined the phrase "the banality of evil." Arendt did not seem satisfied with the term, and afterward wrote in a letter to a friend (the great scholar of Jewish mysticism Gershom Scholem): "Today I think that evil in every instance is only extreme, never radical: it has no depth, and therefore has nothing demonic about it. Evil can lay waste the entire world, like a fungus, growing rampant on the surface." This was what W. H. Auden meant: "Evil is unspectacular and always human,/ And shares our bed and eats at our own table." Always human, but evil nonetheless.

The truth about evil that needs attention now is that shallow, deadly, fungus quality: Nice people—especially in a tiny, multicultural world in which different civilizations inhabit different centuries—are often moved to evil deeds, like blowing up the Other. Do not bother to demonize people as being inherently evil. That's not how it works. Instead, we should view evil as opportunistic, passing like an electrical current through the world and through people; or wandering like an infection that takes up residence in individuals or cultures from time to time.

Distance once helped to dampen the effects of human wickedness; and of course, weapons once had limited range. But evil has burst into a new dimension. The globalization, democratization, and miniaturization of the instruments of destruction (nuclear weapons or their diabolical chemical-biological stepbrothers) mean a quantum leap in the delivery systems of evil. This levels the playing field, so to speak—and the level field has fungus on it. Every tinhorn with a chemistry set becomes a potential world-historical force with more discretionary destructive power at hand than the great old monsters from Caligula to Hitler ever had. In the new dimension, micro-evil (the dark impulse to rape or murder, say) and macro-evil (the urge to genocide) achieve an ominous reunion in any bid for the apocalyptic gesture.

That's the real evil that is going around.

Evil has a wandering, fluid quality; it drifts like thought. Evil is not systematic (although the Nazis bureaucratized and industrialized it for a time, since that was their style) but rather, when it is between jobs, is organic and Protean and given to flowing from place to place along the channels of least resistance.

Evil seeks its opportunities and settles in like a parasite where it finds conditions welcoming. It adopts the local language and customs; it infests the lifeforms and takes them over, in rather the way that insanity may enter the previously wholesome life and displace the person who lived there before. This is the model of demonic possession, dramatized in the Gospel stories of Christ's miraculous power to heal, but now a somewhat disreputable paradigm, demoted to horror movies—the narrative of *The Exorcist,* for example, wherein an innocent child is hideously colonized by evil.

There's always that aspect of violated normality. On the perfect morning of September 11, 2001, the bustling, complex normality of commercial Western civilization (all the computers up and running, airliners vectoring across borders, world trade clicking and humming, the great hive busy making honey), suddenly the airplanes went off their normal disciplined paths and smashed spectacularly into the hive itself. Normality revolted. Or rather, something turned normality (scheduled planes, bustling towers) against itself. Why? *Non serviam?* Lucifer's "I will not serve"? Some other principle of aggressive incompatibilities? Since then, in the world and time in which we live, evil has become, as it were, so fitfully predictable as to seem almost the new normality.

Each age and place has its own style of evil. Evil exploits available resources—turns them to parody and destruction. Evil is a wit among the witty, an imbecile among morons, an industrial program among the industrious, and an apocalypse in the hands of religious fanatics who have abandoned the smaller mortal human decencies for visions of righteous obliteration—an escape from time into the absolute.

Evil refines itself as technology proceeds, and as with nuclear fission, works on a disproportion between cause and effect (the tiny seed produces an apocalyptic blossom) that gives us part of our difficulty in thinking about evil; our moral thinking remains stubbornly Newtonian—the model of weight and counterweight acting proportionately is the basis of our idea of justice, for example, in which the punishment should fit the crime—even as the universe has long since passed on to new surprises and outrages of that sense of residual cosmic seemliness that we (slow learners from the Pleistocene, firing along at the speed of light) may have brought along with us into the twenty-first century.

The world's new dimension (computers, Internet, globalization, instantaneous communications, widely available instruments of mass destruction, porous international borders, ease of global travel, and so on) amounts to a new metaphysics that, by empowering individual zealots or agitated tribes with unappeasable grievances, makes the world unstable and dangerous in radically new ways, and, in doing so, transforms both the political and the personal dynamics of good and evil.

Whether or not there is "an axis of evil," there is distinctly a new ambience of evil—or of what we have to think of as evil, when human behavior crosses certain lines beyond which more civilized vocabulary refuses to follow. Violent religious extremism has reappeared as a world-historical force for the first time since the Enlightenment. Terrorism has become an active, globally mobile, flittingly visible evil. Nuclear war—a monster kept locked in siloes during the Cold War—has become a real possibility in the Middle East and the Indian subcontinent.

The nuances of projected evil have changed. We no longer fear a big bang of nuclear extinction, as we did in the U.S.-Soviet balance of terror, but rather, seem to discern, sooner rather than later, a future of survivable regional apocalypses. September 11, 2001, becomes in our minds a probably modest preview of the previously unthinkable. People have learned to expect such novel evils as dirty radiation bombs, or anthrax in the mail, or smallpox on an epidemic scale.

Evil, of course, is the sensationalist branch of theology. It is impossible to discuss evil, surely one of the two or three most significant and mysterious facts of human existence, while employing euphemism or other methods of veiling.

Are we mistaken in our unconscious assumption that life is essentially good and that evil is an anomaly? Maybe evil is not an anomaly but the rule. Maybe evil is the rule and good is a grace and a rarity. That has been the case from time to time in totalitarian societies, and in the most brutal subdivisions of totalitarianism—in Auschwitz or the Gulag, for example. More confusingly, it is frequently part of evil's sleight of hand to impersonate good, and even to make good and evil seem, by a sort of metaphysical magic, to be interchangeable. In an essay about Dostoevski's Grand Inquisitor, D. H. Lawrence wrote: "Think how difficult it is to know the difference between good and evil! Why sometimes it is evil to be good." It is evil, for example—one assumes he means—to impose brutal, Dickensian rectitudes upon innocent children; or evil, in Lawrence's scheme of things, to align oneself with "the terrible mad mistake that money is life." Notice, however, that Lawrence did not say that "sometimes it is good to be evil." In any case, there is always an interesting recreational perversity in the trick of arguing that black is white and white is black. Oscar Wilde's career as a wit was founded on this principle of metaphysical switching. As Richard Ellmann wrote in his biography: "[Wilde] was proposing that good and evil are not what they seem, that moral tags cannot cope with the complexity of behavior." Bernard Shaw's cosmopolitan hell in *Man and Superman* is preferable to his charmless and anodyne heaven.

2

HUMOR'S COUSIN

Evil and humor seem to come from the same neighborhood of the brain. What is their relationship?

They apparently play for different sides (at first glance, humor seems to belong to the benevolent side of things, which is not always true), but their games are similar, and so, abstractly, are some of their techniques—surprise, exaggeration, a way of coming up on you from the blind side.

Humor, like evil, is a mystery. It is as hard to say why something is funny as it is to be sure that something is evil, or to know where the evil came from. Humor and evil are unstable elements, with a flickering, trompe-l'oeil quality: Now you see it, now you don't. Both humor and evil manifest themselves in sudden, unexpected eruptions. Both leave you a little dazed and, in different ways, appreciative, so to speak: diverted.

The essence of evil, like the essence of humor, is elusive and indefinable.

What makes us laugh, what's funny—the sudden something that creates hilarious disorder of expectation—is, like evil, a saboteur. Both evil and humor are gratuitous. Both tend to be tricksters—impersonators, quick-change artists. Humor, like evil, may be a flash out of nowhere, and tends to dissolve current arrangements. Humor goes off like a bomb. Evil is a bomb. One causes laughter. One causes death.

If humor and evil are cousins, it is a relationship of inverse proportion: More evil means less humor. More humor means less evil.

Humor at its best may disarm evil. Evil at its worst may commit genocide. Humor is essentially humane; evil is, by definition, inhumane—humanity turned against itself. Humor can be cruel and heartless, but its ambitions are rarely ruthless or totalitarian, as evil's usually are. Humor can be wicked and destructive. I doubt that humor can be evil. In acts of evil, power imposes itself upon powerlessness. In humor, powerlessness fights back.

Evil has no sense of humor. Evil takes itself seriously. It hates to be laughed at. Evil is an abstraction of high prestige, an absolute that partakes of the great solemnities: It demands awe, and dark reverence, and submission. Evil likes the aesthetics of tragedy.

Humor, whose business is irreverence, works in comedy, farce. Evil and humor often steal one another's material, but adulterate it to suit their different purposes.

"Dr. Evil" in the Austin Powers movies is amusing precisely because he is not evil, but rather is a child's version of evil, a sweet send-up of the harmlessly world-menacing James Bond megalomaniacs who stroked Persian cats and wore Nehru suits. Evil as cartoon, as schtick.

Active evil—evil in the midst of committing genocide, for example—is not funny. Mel Brooks's movie *The Producers* turned the Third Reich into *Springtime for Hitler*, a hilarious Busby Berkeley spectacle thrice-removed (a Leni Riefenstahl Nazi extravaganza travestied within the Bialystok sham musical-meant-to-fail within the Mel Brooks production), but even with those three layers, the comedy succeeded only because Hitler's Germany had been conquered long ago. If Auschwitz were still in operation, *The Producers* would not be funny.

There are satanic jokes, I suppose. The original meaning of "sarcasm," from the same Greek root that gives us "sarcopha-gus" or "body-eater," is "a tearing of the body." But the cruelty always cancels out the humor, so what you are left with is the heartless being horrible to the helpless, and thinking it is funny if you take everyone by surprise. The late Roman emperors were good at this sort of thing: ordering someone to be killed in the middle of a dinner party, for example, and expecting the other guests to laugh. There was nothing funny about it—just the drama of power showing off, trying to be ingenious and unpre-dictable. In the same way, Stalin used to gather cronies and henchmen and nervously sweating fellow thugs for all-night dinner-and-drinking sessions; at dawn, for fun, one or two of the guests might be led away, in sodden terror, to be executed by the NKVD. No explanation—just the heavy whimsy of the Antichrist awarding a door prize at the end of his party. Power is a form of idiocy, and the powerful often feel disconsolate that people do not like them better, or appreciate them.

People attending tortures have been known to laugh uproari-ously. But no one has ever considered such behavior normal. In the anthropologist Colin Turnbull's famous 1972 book, *The Mountain People,* a study of a traumatically dislocated African tribe, the moral fabric had so deteriorated that the young consid-ered it a joke to push weak old people into the campfire, and adults snatched food from the mouths of their own children—all such depravities attended by merry laughter.

Laughter may be an unreliable signal of humor. In Vietnam, American soldiers were sometimes surprised to find villagers laughing in the midst of great carnage, surrounded by the corpses of their families. The Americans told themselves the villagers were laughing because they were still alive. I would have diagnosed hysteria—laughter as the discharge of terror. Hysterical laughter and hysterical weeping sometimes become interchangeable.

Evil represents, among other things, the failure of humor. Sometimes evil arises from savage frustration. The absence of humor creates a kind of moral vacuum, all of the human oxygen sucked out of it. Nature abhors a vacuum. Evil, the great negative, rushes in. Humor plays for humanity. Evil plays for inhumanity.

What was the Third Reich but an evil national mirthlessness? No people with a decent sense of humor would have tolerated Hitler and his grotesque crew and absurd racial theories for five minutes; the Germans backed Hitler & Co. for 12 years. The Reich's cities had to be reduced to rubble, and even to the very end, in the spring of 1945, the kommandants of death camps worked overtime to fulfill their quotas of extermination. By then, of course, what they were doing was frantically trying to destroy the evidence.

Perhaps it is a fallacy to think that either laughter or poetry has the power to change anything. During the 1850s, Walt Whitman entertained the conceit that a poem sufficiently grand and embracing and national, his *Leaves of Grass,* would be powerful enough to prevent the evil of the civil war that he saw coming. The war arrived, and, his poetry having failed, Whitman moved to Washington to nurse the wounded. W. H. Auden famously wrote that "poetry makes nothing happen." The same might be said of humor. Charlie Chaplin wonderfully satirized and ridiculed Hitler in his 1940 film *The Great Dictator.* But it did nothing to interrupt Hitler's progress. How many divisions did Charlie Chaplin have?

But it may be that laughter sometimes deflects evil, as garlic or the sign of the cross were once said to ward off vampires. Evil usually hates to be laughed at, and makes it a policy to suppress comedians who mock the regime. There is always the wistful thought that dictators could be driven from power if they could be shown to be ridiculous—with their pants down, sitting on the pot, something of that kind. The CIA once entertained the scheme of trying to sabotage Fidel Castro's charisma by covertly giving him depilatory powder to make his beard fall out.

Years ago, I set out to write an article for *Time* magazine asking the question whether there was one universal joke, told everywhere on the globe. I sent a query to all of *Time*'s bureaus around the world—Moscow, Beijing, Tokyo, Sydney, New Delhi, Jerusalem, Rome, Bonn, London, Paris, Rio, Buenos Aires, and so on. I asked the correspondents to tell me one or two jokes then current in their part of the world.

It turns out that there is a universal joke. It is what Americans refer to as the "Polish joke." Except of course that everywhere, the role of the dumb Poles in the "Polish joke" is enacted by some appropriate other group. The Flemings have Walloon jokes, for example. The English tell Irish jokes, and vice versa. The Hutu have Tutsi jokes and the Tutsi have Hutu jokes. The people in Tokyo have jokes about the people of Osaka. I was once on the tiny island of Grenada (133 square miles) and was told that people on one side of the island had a large stock of vicious jokes about people on the other side; and vice versa.

In the universal humor, as in the universal evil, you need the Other. The Other is the butt of your joke, or the butt of your evil.

3

A CURRENT
THROUGH THE WORLD

It seems odd that there remains doubt about "the existence" of evil, after the century of Stalin and Hitler and a half dozen thorough-going genocides has given such irrefutable testimony for the prosecution. What more proof is needed?

The unedifying human record goes back to Cain and Abel—a 50 percent murder rate that was not promising for the later descendants of Adam. But after the century of the Holocaust and the Lubyanka, of the Gulag and Treblinka, of the Somme and Armenia, of Ukraine, Pol Pot, Rwanda, Bosnia, and so on, a century in which tens of millions died unnatural deaths at the hands of bombs and gas and torture and bullets and monsters— after all of that, one would think that the world would emerge believing in almost nothing except evil.

What could be more certain than evil, given what we have seen? Why are we not immobilized by the sheer horror of our insight into human depravity? Why do we not see the devil in every unfamiliar face, hear him in every politician's voice?

Based on the evidence available everywhere in September, 1945, what future would you have predicted for the world? You would have momentarily felt triumph at the evils subdued, of course. But Nanking, Dachau, Auschwitz, Hiroshima, Nagasaki—none of these would have given a thoughtful person much hope that all would be well in years to come.

Why—upon crawling out of such wreckage, the still smoking evidence of the human will to destroy—would you not at least acknowledge the reality and power of evil? By its works, you know it. Behold its works. There it is.

Yet even in the midst of new evidence provided by eruptions later in the century, we began to treat evil as if it were an atavism, a hallucination, a superstition—a force not to be credited by civilized and educated people. The overused twelve-step word "denial" comes to mind: Evil was the elephant in the living room of the twentieth century. It's still there at the start of the twenty-first.

William James saw the essential thing as early as the beginning of the twentieth century. He understood evil with a clarity that reached beyond the unhelpful question of whether it "exists" in order to seek the meaning behind it.

In *The Varieties of Religious Experience,* he wrote:

> The evil facts . . . are a genuine portion of reality; and they may after all be the best key to life's significance, and possibly the only openers of our eyes to the deepest levels of truth. . . . The normal process of life contains moments as bad as any of those which insane melancholy is filled with, moments in which radical evil gets its innings and takes its solid turn. The lunatic's

visions of horror are all drawn from the material of daily fact. Our civilization is founded on the shambles, and every individual existence goes out in a lonely spasm of helpless agony.

WHAT IS EVIL LIKE? How does it behave? What are its qualities? What is its personality—if it has a personality? Lucifer has a personality. Hitler had a personality. Nero had a personality. Stalin had a personality. But perhaps evil does not, and is something else altogether—a germ, a virus, a bug? Or as Hannah Arendt said, a fungus?

Justice Potter Stewart's litmus test of pornography ("I know it when I see it") can be usefully applied to evil, although the test is sometimes unreliable: people may be shockingly slow to detect evil, whereas they generally recognize pornography instantly.

It is part of the nature of evil that it is inexplicable. It is felt rather than understood: "I know it when I see it." Better to say: I know it when I feel it. Evil registers itself upon the deepest, most primitively feeling areas of the brain, upon some obscure moral equivalent of our sense of smell. We tend to recognize evil through a primitive faculty of the senses, in the way (at the other extreme of the good-evil continuum) that a newborn baby smells its mother.

The sense of smell is often mentioned when people talk about identifying evil. Cardinal Newman warned of "the smell of evil." Petrarch thought of a sewer. Ranting against the papal court at Avignon in the fourteenth century, he declared: "This is a sewer to which all the filths of the universe come to be reunited. Here people despise God, they adore money, they trample underfoot both human laws and divine law. Everything here breathes falsehood: the air, the earth, the houses, and above all, the bedrooms."

There's a scene in a movie called *Khartoum,* made in 1966 and notable for grandly hammy performances by Charlton Heston, as the eccentrically messianic British General "Chinese" Gordon, and by Laurence Olivier, as the late nineteenth-century Sudanese religious demagogue known as the Mahdi. General Gordon rides, alone, into the desert wastes of Sudan to visit the Mahdi in his camp. The two men eye one another for a long moment.

The Mahdi speaks to Gordon: "Is it because you are an infidel that I feel myself to be in the presence of evil?"

Gordon replies: "I doubt it, Mohammed Ahmed. For you are not an infidel, and I too smell evil."

I imagine evil sometimes as a kind of gas, toxic and possibly undetectable, making its way through the world, slithering upon the currents of air.

Evil is a seepage across borders, across great distances. Herman Melville, in *Moby Dick,* wrote that a colt in rural Vermont, if it smells a fresh buffalo robe (the colt having no knowledge or experience of buffalo, which lived on the plains) will "start, snort, and with bursting eyes paw the ground in phrenzies of affright. Here thou beholdest even in a dumb brute the instinct of the knowledge of the demonism of the world."

I like the image of evil as a current that passes through the world, as it has, in one form or another, from the beginning, a sort of invisible electromagnetic flow through the globe, pole to pole. From time to time the evil force manifests itself in violent displays—moral hurricanes, earthquakes of pathology and slaughter. The force is more active and surprising than gravity, but like gravity it is mysterious and evident only in its consequences. It may be visible as an aura, or felt as a dark force field.

Classic science fiction imagines evil as a body-snatcher that empties out the human self and replaces it with a compliantly malevolent not-self—as an alien force that steals the soul, as Dracula's bite does: Evil brings on a falsifying transformation, the sudden substitution of a wicked shadow self, of Mr. Hyde. Evil is your horrid alternate suddenly emerging. Evil is the wicked twin, your negative, your Cain that kills the better self, or else your Smerdyakov half-brother, your evil bastard sibling Edmund, your Caliban.

One of the stranger and more fetching renderings of evil is Christina Rossetti's poem "Goblin Market," a sort of pre-Raphaelite allegory, written in energetic doggerel, in which "goblin men" advance like salacious greengrocers offering all manner of luscious fruits to the maids Laura and Lizzie. The little men tramp down the glen (to pick up Rossetti's rhythms) in a surreal parade that suggests somehow a troop of winsomely bobbing and variously hideous penises—

> *One had a cat's face*
> *one whisked a tail,*
> *One tramped at a rat's pace,*
> *One crawled like a snail,*
> *One like a wombat prowled obtuse and furry,*
> *One like a ratel tumbled hurry scurry.*

The girls hide from the goblin men.

> *"Lie close," Laura said,*
> *pricking up her golden head:*
> *"We must not look at goblin men,*
> *We must not buy their fruits.*
> *Who knows upon what soil they fed*
> *Their hungry, thirsty roots."*

One of the sisters, Laura, succumbs to the fruit of the goblin men, paying for it with one of her golden curls:

> *Then sucked their fruit globes fair or red:*
> *sweeter than honey from the rock,*
> *stronger than man-rejoicing wine. . .*

She sucked and sucked and sucked the more
fruits which that unknown orchard bore.

It is a strange, confusing story. Laura has yielded to some temptation of forbidden pleasure, sexual or otherwise; the first time has given her ineffable delight. But it is an experience never to be repeated, as if the evil of the fruits, like drugs or, one presumes, like the sacrifice of virginity to pleasure in the nineteenth century, replicates all the postlapsarian misery of Adam and Eve.

You know evil when you are in its presence. I think you do, anyway. You feel it as a vibration, a hum that seems to emanate almost from a disorder of the molecules. I felt the flow of a sick dark current once when I was led down the corridor of a cold prison in Sarajevo, and a metal door opened, and I was in the presence of a murderer named Herak. A friend tells me he gets the vibration when he talks to Claus von Bulow, as he must do from time to time on business.

On the other hand, Harry Truman was able to chat at Potsdam with Joseph Stalin, one of the monsters of the world, and sit next to him for hours (Truman had just learned, but did not reveal, that he himself had in his hands a new weapon of immense destructive capacity—a windfall of discretionary evil, the atom bomb); and come away confiding to his diary that Stalin was a "fellow I can work with, though tough as hell." Was Stalin thought to be somehow disinfected of his evil because he was an ally in a world war? That was the effect—a remarkably convenient and casual way to set aside something as important and basic as evil. But one does not inquire too deeply into an ally's domestic arrangements. American virtue could confront only one evil at a time; the evil enemy of my evil enemy is my friend for now. Our monster: "Uncle Joe."

In my magazine article I referred to evil in one or two traditional clichés as "a dark presence" or "dark force." An African-

American newspaper columnist complained that the metaphor was racist. But of course when you refer to the Prince of Darkness you refer not to race but to absence of light, the negation of divine light—of *la prima luce*, Dante's light of creation. And when you refer to the Prince of Darkness, you adduce an idea of evil in a medieval, monarchical world: you do not refer to the President of Darkness or the Prime Minister of Darkness—or the Director of Darkness, or (as might be appropriate for Adolf Eichmann) the Clerk of Darkness. Even in the twenty-first century, evil is anachronistically discussed in language appropriate a thousand years ago.

And has the theological context of long ago skewed an understanding of contemporary evil? Do such terms as *la prima luce* (as an atheist or agnostic would argue) heedlessly empower the idea of God, who, after all, does not enjoy universal diplomatic recognition? Is it possible that evil is a problem that is more intelligently addressed outside the religious context of God and Satan?

Perhaps the concept of evil is aesthetic rather than moral or philosophical or social. We call something or someone evil because of a kind of aesthetic perception—moral instinct exercised on the level of artistic instinct, of "taste" in both senses. Moral judgment implies a due process of reason. Judgments about evil often arise from instinctive revulsion; the judgment is made on some level of mind that is not entirely conscious and reasoning. We recognize evil sometimes without formulating an articulate case against it. This may, of course, be a dangerous business: that instinctive judgment may be entirely wrong—and may be manipulated by the leaders of lynch mobs and witch hunts.

The word "evil," in any case, may answer an aesthetic demand. That is, human beings, in contemplating certain horrors in the world (child murder, or some other wanton act or sadistic act, in which the only intention can be infliction of pain) rummage through the resources of language to find a word with sufficient darkness at its edges to express the mystery involved—and the underlying sense we have that something too glibly articulated does not do justice to the evil of the act. And therefore we need to say "evil," which is a label that we put on a door beyond which we do not go. Evil is the forbidden room in Bluebeard's castle. The word itself is a token of taboo, a warning nailed to the door. To use the word "evil" is to draw a line. The word "evil," I think, is necessary to the human community, because it indicates what we collectively will not tolerate.

But of course the trouble arises because there are many "human communities" and collectivities, and they very often do not agree about what they will and will not tolerate. Frequently, what one community will not tolerate is precisely . . . another community, which therefore gets deemed evil.

4

WHY DO THEY DO IT?

WHY DO PEOPLE DO EVIL?

- Because it gives them pleasure.
- Because it gives them power.
- Because they don't know any better.
- Because they are afraid of their victims.
- Because they think that the evil they are doing is righteous, or good, or necessary.
- Because they are indifferent to the suffering of others.
- Because they are too morally stupid to recognize the evil they are doing.
- Because they are forced to do it by people holding power over them.
- Because they are caught in a mob's frenzy.
- Because they feel a perverse itch to do harm and it occurs to them that they may do so.
- Because it is customary among their people, and not to do it would be a breach of community tradition or ceremony.

- Because it is an accident.
- Because they are habituated to it.
- Because they suffer from a compulsion.
- Because they themselves were treated evilly once.
- Because Satan makes them do it.

People who write about evil as if it were a phenomenon sub-ject to measurement and scientific inspection—which it is not—make distinctions between "natural evil" and "moral evil," between "hard evil" and "soft evil," between "strong evil" and "weak evil."

Natural evil, much like soft evil or weak evil, means earth-quakes, cancer, and other evils arising in the course of life.

Moral evil, or hard evil or strong evil, has human agency and presumably involves evil acts committed by human choice. The most profound, painful, and potentially humiliating question that human beings have to ask themselves about evil is whether moral evil exists. Do people really have a choice? Do people choose to do what they do, or are even manifestly evil acts (such as serial killing) predetermined—the wires of slaughter and atrocity and genocide, for example, manipulated by other forces? By heredity? By brain chemistry? By God?

If moral evil does not exist, how can society itself exist? Why have laws against murder if the murderer cannot help himself? No one has managed to reconcile divine determination and per-sonal responsibility—or brain-chemical determination with the idea of an option to say no. Maybe the dilemma is precise proof of the duality, rather than the unity or monism, of all life. Each thing has its shadow and contradiction. The universe, like the brain, is bicameral.

This would be Lao Tzu's thought as well: "When people see some things as beautiful, other things become ugly. When people see some things as good, other things become bad. Being and non-being create each other. Difficult and easy support each other. Long and short define each other. High and low depend on each other. Before and after follow each other." Each thing has its twin—matter and anti-matter, good and anti-good. Why do we trouble our minds by worrying about these things?

The evil that any society commits reflects the styles and techniques and social structures of that society. In any case, the medieval language of the Prince of Darkness needs to be considerably updated. Eventually, a democratic world will need a more democratic sense of evil—an understanding of the ordinariness and shallowness of evil. The idea of evil presided over by a Prince of Darkness is as archaic today as the concept of absolute monarchy. But democracy is a responsibility; and one of the key human responsibilities in the world now is to see what evil in this world is, and what it does, and to take responsibility for it.

But evil enjoys being discussed in heightened language, in the rhetoric of Milton, of Dr. Faustus. Evil has had a vivid and successful career in literature, dramatized in a diabolical presumption to the throne. The evil Claudius in *Hamlet* murders the king so that he may be king himself. Macbeth does the same thing. So, in their way, do the wicked daughters Goneril and Regan in *King Lear*. Iago brings down the majestic Othello. Evil is seen as a usurpation of rightful authority. Evil in this tradition may represent treachery and disloyalty, but it also evolved, especially through the romantic imagination, into a kind of defiant positive—the rebellion against authority, the Byronic gesture, for which human nature has a natural if sneaking, admiration.

When two snipers were terrorizing the Washington, D.C., area in the fall of 2002, at one point they left a Tarot card, "I am God," in an empty shell casing at the scene of one of their murders. The snipers were a study in the dynamics of doing a certain sort of evil: the gratuitousness of their predations, the secrecy, the terror, the (one gathers) satanic glee, the random quality of their shootings, the sense of power, the immense injustice of their inflictions, the people struck down indiscriminately, with no reason, no order, no rationale, all at the whim of the destroyer: Evil is an imitation of God—of God's inscrutable, peremptory, mysteriously smiting self. This, again, is the evil of a usurping pretender: the insurrection of the negative.

There is in part an immense freedom in such cutting loose— the exhilaration of giving oneself unconditional permission to obey whatever whim may stimulate the trigger finger.

Why, exactly? In Vietnam, Americans in helicopters some- times fired their .50 calibre machineguns at any peasant they saw in the paddies below. The freedom of evil is the freedom of what the military called a "free fire zone." During the terrible siege of Beirut in the 1980s, snipers would pick off pedestrians in an almost recreational way.

Evil is often happiest when it operates in the autonomy of the gratuitous—enjoys the ease of movement, prefers to be the mas- ter of its own motions. This is evil's idea of an aristocratic dis- cretion. Evil demands discretionary power. If evil operates under compulsion, it is not evil, but something else—an agent, a ser- vant: Just following orders. Evil, properly, is an exercise of malig- nant mastery.

Evil can do anything that it can imagine. Evil has a reasonably fertile imagination. It has expressed itself in ingenious ways. It learns new techniques and styles.

Does evil evolve? Does evil learn from its experience? Is it the case that evil evolves roughly as human beings evolve, *pari passu,* a dark parallel evolution? Evil keeps pace. New technology enables new evil. New bureaucratic techniques may help to organize a genocide. Developments in physics enable the incin- eration of cities. Evil is limited by its resources, or empowered.

Evil, an opportunist, lives as a parasite upon even the honest exertions of the mind. Germs have some of the same patterns of behavior, and tend to exult and riot in the same spirit when they achieve the freedom that is their pleasure and fulfillment.

If Aztec priests at the Temple of the Sun had plausible and pious reason to engage in human sacrifice, applying sharp flint knives to extract the living hearts from hundreds of thousands of victims—important work, after all, keeping the sun appeased with daily human blood—should the practice be arraigned as evil? If Pol Pot and the Khmer Rouge had an elaborate utopian rationale for the radical cultural discipline of their killing fields, does it make sense to impose a moral judgment? If understanding everything means forgiving everything, then the decent conscience has reason, as an act of moral obduracy, to say, I refuse to understand evil, I refuse to grant it the dispensation of comprehending analysis and sympathy. Evil makes its bed. Let it lie there.

I APPROACH THE MYSTERY of evil as a layman. I was born in the morning of the Age of Monsters, three weeks after Hitler marched into Poland in September 1939, in the immediate aftermath of Stalin's Great Terror of 1936 to 1938. September, 1939, began what became America's "Good War"—good because it was a worldwide struggle, obviously, against Evil, even if one ally (Stalin) embodied evil himself.

And what of the lingering terrible facts of August, 1945, when the forces of good ended the "Good War" by dropping two nuclear bombs, on Hiroshima and Nagasaki, thereby introducing an unprecedented new instrument of evil into the world?

5

THE HERMIT'S TALE

WHEN REAL EVIL PASSES BY, you may feel a little concussion of dark wind, a chill. It recedes, and leaves you with a clammy intuition, a sense of wonder that the famous thing has come so close, and that you have felt its breath.

Evil is always a story.

Here is a story of micro-evil—or maybe not even that: a near miss, an either-or, a fly-by of bats.

The hermit lived in a deer hunter's cinderblock cabin in the woods by the bend of our dirt road in upstate New York, half a mile from our farm, across from the old gravel pit—a dark shoe box of a cabin, windowless to the road.

The hermit drove a rusted, mustard-colored Plymouth, 25 years old, and kept two junked wrecks of similar make and model on cinderblocks in his front yard—a hillbilly squalor—so that he might cannibalize spare parts for the one car that still ran.

No one on our road ever spoke to the hermit, and he never spoke to us. Even an 80-year-old woman who has lived on a farm down the road for more than half a century had no idea of the man's name or where he came from or what he did for a living. Some said he had once been a schoolteacher, but had retired. A neighbor who passed by the cabin reported hearing classical music coming from a phonograph. Another said that the hermit sometimes played golf on the public course two towns away. He played alone.

The hermit drove by our house every morning at exactly seven. I recognized the sound of his passing engine, or rather, of his hoarse, perforated muffler. When I heard his car, I knew it was time to get up and make coffee. He drove at 40 miles an hour, the posted speed limit, and never took his foot off the gas, or slowed down or swerved if he approached someone walking on the road. He powered relentlessly by, as if his car were a train on tracks. Pedestrians stepped back and sucked in their breath like matadors. This seemed dangerous. We shook our heads in irritation.

As the hermit powered by, we would see his hard, impassive profile, like the head on a coin. He never turned, but looked dead straight ahead. His hair was iron gray, close-cropped, and spiky. His skin had an odd phosphorescent shine, a bit like the smooth, healed scar-skin of a burn victim. He might have been 50 or 60 years old.

My wife and I walked by his house sometimes, going up the road with our dog in the late afternoon, and might see him up on his roof replacing shingles, or repairing an electric line. He did not raise his head from his work as we passed.

On the road just past the hermit's house, our dog Fred would often shy, and dig in his heels and demand to go back, resisting the leash. We assumed that coyotes crossed the road just there, and that the dog picked up their scent. Or perhaps he caught the smell of one of the bears that had moved into the neighborhood. We had not actually seen the bears yet, but one of them not long before had wrecked our beehives to get the honey.

People were not exactly afraid of the hermit, but rather, curious. One winter day, after a heavy snowfall, we passed by, walking on the road, and were amazed to see the hermit lying on his back in the snow, making snow angels. He liked to lie in the snow. Once, my wife saw him sprawled in the drift beside his house, and thought he had died, and ran down toward him in some alarm, but then realized that he was luxuriating in the snow as a man might enjoy stretching out on the grass. My wife retreated, embarrassed.

One fall when the sugar maples were blazing red and orange, the hermit's comings and goings on the road became more frequent and more urgent. Every hour or two, or even every half hour, his car sped by our house, billowing dust. A tow truck came one morning and dragged away the two junked cars from in front of his house. We speculated that some happy change had come over the hermit's life. In place of the junkers in his yard, we saw a more respectable Plymouth, well painted and washed, but like the other cars, some 25 years old. I joked that the hermit had fallen in love, and was cleaning up his life.

All day, up and down the road, kicking up dust, the hermit sped by on mysterious, frantic errands.

Then he died. Someone walking by the cabin found him slumped dead at the wheel of the Plymouth that had been washed, and even waxed. He had rigged a hose from the exhaust pipe to the front vent window. The engine had run until the car was out of gas.

On the passenger seat the state police found medicine bottles from Eckerd's pharmacy in town—morphine, and pills that our neighbor, a nurse, identified as cancer medicines.

We gossiped about it along the road—a curio, a sad little mystery of a life. After several weeks, the police located the hermit's family, and one weekend some people who were apparently his relatives came by in a van, and threw open the cabin, and spent a day, with a matter-of-fact, detached, ungrieving air, clearing it out. They took away whatever was worth taking, and junked the rest. The cabin stood empty for a year. When we passed it walking on the road, we were obscurely relieved to know that the hermit was dead.

Then a young man from a nearby town—a handsome, competent, cheerful man who worked as a carpenter and contractor—bought the place. He planned to make the cabin a project, to transform it, and move from his house in town, and settle in the woods.

The young man set about gutting the house. When he tore up the floorboards, he made a discovery: arranged in secret compartments beneath the boards, he found dozens of little girl dolls—dolls of various styles and vintages, collected, it seemed, over many years.

Their doll dresses had been torn or cut below the waist. The genital areas—if dolls had genitals—were mutilated one way or another: gouged or scissored out or otherwise brutalized.

The young man took the dolls to the state police. The police had no records of unexplained disappearances of girls. They dismissed the matter with a shrug. Weirdness. No crime.

When I heard the story of the dolls—from our neighbor the nurse, as we were out on snowshoes in another part of the valley on a pristine day just after Christmas—I thought about the macabre possibilities of the gravel pit across the road from the hermit's cabin. It had been deeply excavated at one time; but the quality of the gravel was bad (too crumbly; the road surface that it made would hardly last through a decent season of rain) and the great pit had been steam-shoveled over, and now was grass and wildflower meadow again.

THIS STORY OF THE HERMIT and his secret dolls was an ugly speculation—but the man was now dead and gone, thank God, as the nurse said to me with a sharp, comprehending Presbyterian eye; still, the business under the floorboards seemed no less evil, no less real, I thought, inasmuch as evil moves around by hearsay and vapor.

I thought when I heard the story: That is what this kind of evil is like: fetid and secret and banal (the man seems familiar from the checkout counter—life imitating tabloids) and unmistakable, like the smell of something that has died in the wall.

But it occurred to me later that there might be a different reading of the story: that perhaps there was at least the possibility that the meaning might be the reverse of what it seemed—that it might be a story of evil resisted, with great struggle, at great cost, over a period of years.

The mutilated dolls were proof of a violent temptation. But the damage done—for all I know—was harmless: He does not seem to have yielded to his temptation to pass from the symbolic things he did to the dolls to doing actual harm to human beings. He was, in a horrible way, playing with dolls. But he did not, as kidnappers and rapists and murderers do with hideous frequency, touch little girls.

Do you recoil from this interpretation? Bear with it a moment.

Our hermit seems to have sentenced himself to some sort of death, not only when he killed himself with the car's exhaust, but years earlier, when he had sealed himself off in the woods from other human beings. Perhaps he became a hermit precisely in order to isolate himself from children, in order to reduce the danger that he might harm them. Perhaps the way he drove, firing along the road on an undeviating path, suggested fierce struggle and self-discipline in the face of the evil infecting his mind.

Perhaps it meant he kept himself to certain rigid rules—that he had a dangerous capacity for evil, and knew it, and kept the evil harmlessly symbolic and hidden beneath the floorboards.

He sacrificed dolls instead of little girls.

Perhaps the dolls were his ritual of *Apage Satanis!*—Get thee behind me, Satan: a reminder and a warning, to himself. Or an occasional yielding to homeopathic evil, simulating a ritual evil (upon the dolls) to forestall the necessity to commit the real thing, upon live people.

I do not know. Evil has many surprises, and often carries a double-bottomed suitcase. The dolls were the first surprise. Maybe the secret doll chambers beneath the floorboards con-cealed another layer of surprise, which might have disclosed the hidden life of a kind of desert monk, and—who knows?—of a saint? Perhaps he lay in the snow to take some purification, and perhaps the classical music and the snow angels represented an antidote, some better possibility asserting itself.

I'm going too far. I understand if you reject this interpreta-tion. I'm not sure that I believe it myself.

But it is important to have hope.

6

A CATASTROPHIC EDUCATION

THE PHILOSOPHER RICHARD J. BERNSTEIN has written: "It is not a rhetorical question to ask whether we can still believe in morality after Auschwitz. It is the most serious question to be asked." Emmanuel Levinas, in *The Paradox of Morality,* puts it this way: "The essential problem is: Can we speak of an absolute commandment after Auschwitz? Can we speak of morality after the failure of morality?"

I do not see why not.

Bernstein, following the thinking of Hannah Arendt and Levinas, suggests that

> the evil that burst forth in the Nazi period indicates a rupture with tradition, and reveals the inadequacy of traditional accounts of morals and ethics to deal with evil. [Arendt] declares: "We have witnessed the total collapse of all established moral standards in public and private life during the thir-

ties and forties. . . . Without much notice all this collapsed almost overnight and then it was as though morality suddenly stood revealed . . . as a set of mores, customs, and manners that could be exchanged for another set with hardly more trouble than it would take to change the table manners of an individual or a people."

After the failure of morality—Auschwitz was actually far more than that, it was the failure of decency, the abdication of humanity, and the triumph of a gray, frozen indifference that is the worst possibility of the heart—morality should become the central topic of conversation among civilized human beings, as it did become the intellectual and moral preoccupation of thinkers like Arendt.

After Auschwitz, it became infinitely more necessary to believe in morality, and to understand its fragility—to see the indispensability of morality, and the need to encourage it. Auschwitz was evil. Why should it annul the possibility of morality?

Would it not be more sensible to think that the example of Auschwitz would encourage societies to promote rules, laws, and moral awareness that would make a repetition of Auschwitz less likely?

Why not say that Auschwitz disabuses us of illusions about the depths to which even an advanced civilization may sink. Auschwitz is a landmark in the moral education of the world, and the world can no doubt profit from its contemplation.

There seems to me, in any case, to be something hysterical in the conclusion that nothing can be said in the face of Auschwitz, or that no morality is possible after Auschwitz. Auschwitz was a terrible lesson. It humbled the moral and cultural pretensions of civilizations that have been heir to the Enlightenment—a lesson in the possibilities of Endarkenment. Colonialism—look at the horrors committed by the Belgians in the Congo—was also a powerful lesson. So were Hiroshima and Nagasaki.

Evil is a learning experience. The Holocaust was a catastrophic education in the diabolical possibilities of advanced societies—and in the nature of evil itself.

Auschwitz was hell. So were the trenches of the Western Front. Trench warfare prefigured the fatal industrialism of the Nazi death camps: There cling to the gray, corpse-littered wastelands of World War I something of the same atmosphere: individual life stripped of meaning, dignity, all life and all death rendered purposeless, and reduced to absolute metaphysical insignificance.

Auschwitz—far from being a precipice from which morality tumbled into the abyss, never to be seen again—was the beginning of a profound and at the same time widespread popular preoccupation with public morality, with issues of war, prejudice, racism, and the relationships between people and the behavior of their governments. Elie Wiesel's book *Night* is known to most high school students in America, even though students today read few books. The terrible events of the twentieth century, tragically and dramatically compressed in Auschwitz, stimulated—indeed, created—an unprecedented popular public conscience in the West. This conscience, with its origins in the shock of the Holocaust, of Hiroshima, and the revealed horrors of the Stalin era, evolved through various issues and stages of indignation during the Cold War, nuclear proliferation, the end of colonialism, the Vietnam era, and has attained new levels of involvement and passion in the early twenty-first century in controversies surrounding terrorism, globalization, and American doctrines of strategic pre-emption.

What we have witnessed in the West after Auschwitz has been the democratization of morality and the sense of public responsibility for the actions of governments. Television and other instruments of the communications revolution (faxes, international telephones, computers, E-mail, and the Internet) in the second half of the twentieth century resulted in a radical contraction of the world. Marshall McLuhan predicted that television and the rest would produce a global village: Global City would be more like it—the world turned into a sprawling and dysfunctional megalopolis with rich neighborhoods and poor neighborhoods and terrible slums and, to date, no police force, no sanitation department, no department of environmental protection, and no fire department. But the McLuhanesque contraction of the world has at least produced the beginnings of a global conscience, which has evolved in parallel with the instruments of mass destruction and the ever nearer reconciliation of micro-evil and macro-evil.

At the same time, that emerging global conscience can often be a messy, fatuous, self-righteous thing—merely politically correct, maddeningly smug, and, in its turn, dangerously out of touch with the real possibilities of evil. It risks becoming a paradox, that insufferable thing, a conscience that is irresponsible.

7

THE AXIS OF WRONG

ANTHROPOLOGISTS HAVE FOUND THAT when they ask people to describe the most evil act they can imagine, different cultures may produce different answers. A Japanese, for example, may mention a corrupt politician, who thinks of himself rather than the community—a perfect reflection of self-effacement in Japanese social ethics.

When I have asked Americans and Europeans to tell me the most evil act that they could imagine anyone committing, they have almost always spoken of acts against children—torture, rape, murder. It would be difficult, in their reading, to surpass in evil a father who a few years ago set fire to his eight-year-old son—not killing him, but disfiguring him horribly. I will return at length to the subject of evil and children, as it is a dominant motif.

We do not have instruments to detect evil, as we have, say, Geiger counters to measure radiation. The only instrument we have is instinct, connected to moral sense. Instinct makes mistakes, it is true, and can do terrible damage when it is guilty of zealous misidentification, as, for example, once in Salem, Massachusetts.

But such mistakes and ensuing tragedies of persecution and fanaticism and prejudice and brute stupidity do not necessarily mean that evil does not exist—only that one must be more careful in the future. Serious mistakes, in any case, also occur in the other direction—in a failure to identify evil as evil soon enough, before it does its damage.

The Enlightenment thinks it is smarter than the Endarkenment; but often it is the other way around: The Enlightenment always overrates its own mastery, and therefore is compelled to play existential catchup because it has not sufficiently appreciated evil's genius for subterranean persistence and surprise, and for turning the most enlightened projects—the ruthless rationalism of utopian projects, for example—into murderous nightmares.

The essence of evil does not change; only its forms do. Edgar Allan Poe starts his story "Metzengerstein" with a melodramatic generalization that no one would dispute: "Horror and fatality have been stalking abroad in all ages." Gilles de Rai, the fifteenth-century marshall of France, general to Saint Joan of Arc, and witness to her miracles, became, a few years after that, one of history's most monstrous child-murderers—and as such, seems entirely contemporary, the sort of man who might be led shackled into a California courtroom to be charged, five centuries later, with the same crimes. Evil has a sense of continuity; history is an elevated tram passing late at night, and the yawn (or the stabbing) begun by a man in the first car may be completed by a man in the last (to borrow an image from Vladimir Nabokov).

It begins to seem that not to see evil, not to "believe in" evil, is the primitive view. If there are religious primitives at large in the world, it may be that the really dangerous lack of thought and lack of realism is to be lamented, and corrected, among those whose relative safety and wealth and privilege have tended to blind them to William James's evil facts, which eventually have a way of directing the privileged and civilized mind back around to the matter of evil.

Evil has come back into the world and has become such an insistent, overt fact—manifest in so many places in so many ghastly ways—that the question seems to be not whether it exists, but how to organize our thinking about the thing in the face of its confusing multiplicity.

It seems to me in any case that we are obliged to assume that evil does exist, since the manifestations are all around us. If we do not call them evil, perhaps we need to invent a new word.

What if, instead of evil, we said wrong? Right v. wrong. Good v. wrong. The world is filled with wrong, with what the dictionary describes as "not in accordance with law, morality, or with people's sense of fairness, justice, and what is acceptable behavior."

Is that a workable definition of evil? The word "wrong," like evil, has the versatility to be used both as an adjective and a noun. Wrong may be a little . . . secular. But that could be part of its charm—that people of diverse cultures and backgrounds could perhaps discuss wrongs a little more dispassionately than they discuss evils or, more to the point, evil.

A crucial difference between wrong and evil is that people are implicitly in charge of the universe in which rights and wrongs are discussed; people have systems of laws to right wrongs. But evil implies a different universe, controlled by extra-human forces. Wrong is a human offense that suggests reparation is possible and deserved. Wrong is not mysterious. Evil suggests a mysterious force that may be in business for itself and may exploit human agency as part of a larger cosmic conflict—between good and evil, between God and Satan.

Evil has the dark old majesty, and belongs to the realm of the sacred. "Wrong" is a utilitarian word employed in the profane transactions of human life. Evil goes to the origins of things.

Wrong applies to the process of the world. It is the difference between Captain Ahab and his first mate Starbuck—Ahab cosmically, melodramatically, obsessed by the white whale, and Starbuck simply interested in harvesting whales and getting the oil back home to Nantucket. Evil belongs to eternity. Wrong is a word that lives in time.

Wrong would be the better word for the language of international diplomacy, the less inflammatory term—since international relations are conducted within time. "Axis of wrong" does not engage absolute theological energies, the old *Gott mit uns*. You can argue against the word "wrong." There is no debating the word "evil"—it conjures up a primordial conflict whose terms are not negotiable now and whose outcome will be determined only at the End of Days.

Perhaps the solution lies in using "wrong" for certain situations and the word "satanic" for others. "Evil" is a somewhat smudged word that carries both senses. But if we separated out "wrong" and "satanic," and used them separately, according to the context, a useful clarity might be achieved.

If I said "satanic," it would signal that I really meant to suggest something with an origin in some supernatural malevolence. If the President of the United States referred to an "Axis of the Satanic," his meaning would be clearer than when he said "Axis of Evil." If he had to choose between, say, "Axis of Wrong" and "Axis of the Satanic," he would say neither. One would be too weak and the other would be too theologically specific. "Axis of the Satanic" would sound a little weird in any case. As rhetoric, "Axis of Evil" had just the right cloud of dark smoke around it.

It might seem useful, therefore, to decide to abolish the word "evil" from one's working vocabulary, as many in the West have done, as being a mischievous, inflaming idea, not useful now in human affairs, if it ever was. I see the point. No doubt "evil" should not be used much, if at all, in political or diplomatic discussions. The dynamic of such discourse is exaggeration, anyway—hyperbole and cartoon. "Evil" is a word that should be used sparingly, like "genius" or "masterpiece," because, among other things, it has the quality of *ne plus ultra:* Where do you go from there? Part of human responsibility in regard to evil is responsibility in the use of the word "evil," and some sense of perspective.

And yet the reality of the world is larger than politics or diplomacy, and the things of God and eternity do touch time and history—however mysteriously they do so. The occasion to use the word "evil" is as persistent as the temptation to evil itself. The spectacle of evil is before us, or in any case the spectacle of something so terrible that to use lesser words seems fatuous; the spectacle of something that it would be inadequate to call, merely, wrong. I would not be satisfied by a discussion that described Auschwitz as being "wrong." I would not think it sufficient to say that the rape and torture and murder of children is "wrong."

But is it right to call these deeds evil? Is it fitting to associate such acts with the absolute and eternal implications of the word evil? If not, why not? Are human beings merely to judge themselves and their moral behavior on the mechanical, utilitarian grounds implied by words like "right" and "wrong"? Is human life susceptible to the vocabularies of good and evil? Should it be?

Law courts cannot judge good and evil; they must deal with lawful and unlawful, right and wrong. But the fuller human imagination does not think merely like a lawyer or a policeman; it is also a poet and, it may be, a theologian. Its range of inquiry in any case is broader.

And, in any case, we have inherited this language, however atavistic and elusive, and these questions.

Is the idea of evil merely a formulation posed by an earlier stage of the human brain? Or is it possible that an intelligently elaborated concept of evil will be seen in the future as the mark of a higher civilization?

Who is evil? What is evil? Above all, how to handle competing evils that vector in, so to speak, multiculturally, and defy and confuse the judgment of independent moral systems, which have grown up over the centuries like autonomous feudal kingdoms? May evil be something different from what you thought?

Half a century ago, the anthropologist K. E. Read studied the Gahuku-Gama people of New Guinea; he concluded that they had no universal or abstract sense of reverence for humanity, but rather based their moral norms and rules of behavior entirely upon particular social ties, upon the specific links at a particular moment between particular people. Whatever—or whoever— fell outside that social relationship (the network of the known, the walls of the established city, so to speak—the working tribal machinery of custom and law and nuanced familiar practice) was the Other, and beyond the pale and protection of moral norms. Beyond the boundaries of the understood arrangements, good and evil had no particular meaning or relevance—no more meaning, in moral terms, than, say, the death of a chicken intended for the pot. Others are Strangers, and Strangers are Objects. Certain aborigines of Australia, it is said, thought it entirely permissible to kill a man if you encountered him while wandering in the Outback and he was not personally known to you; the jurisdiction of moral judgment stopped at the boundary of the known. Concepts of good and evil, right and wrong, did not apply to strangers.

But the globalization of communication, the abrupt technological shrinkage of the earth, means that the human race has acquired a magnificently agile forebrain that also catastrophically empowers its most primitive impulses (kill-the-infidel religious fanaticisms, for example). Abrupt globalization of the instruments of evil demands that the world arrive at global understandings of what conduct is to be regarded as evil and what conduct is, if not good, at least tolerable. You cannot run a global civilization under tribal rules. A moral indifference to strangers—the ancient human habit of relegating strangers to the realm outside the walls, where they are prey to wild beasts or to the casual omnivorous appetites of human nature—now may have fatal planetary consequences.

Human nature (in its aggressions, in its myopia and obtuseness) remains dangerously primitive. But the weapons at its disposal—nuclear or chemical-biological—now have global range and potentially apocalyptic force.

The Holocaust was a parable of terrible foreboding: The German people under Hitler's tutelage—like a tribe in New Guinea, but with industrial might, the complete material product-line of Western civilization's evolution at their fingertips—placed Europe's Jews outside the walls of humanity, outside the walls of German (that is, as the Germans thought, human) social relationships, and therefore made the Jews, stripped of the moral protection even of their humanity, subject to Eichmann's transports and—to speak with horrible precision—his pesticides.

The problem of evil in our time rises like a thick black gas from the gap between our destructive capacities, which now have instantaneous planetary reach, and our working social arrangements. The first thing to ask is this: Is there a global standard of evil? Can there be?

It helps to start by admitting that evil cannot be satisfactorily explained—and that perhaps it should not be explained, since explanation is a slippery slope that tends to tilt toward acceptance, by way of that immense inanity, the fallacy of *Tout comprendre, c'est tout pardonner.*

At the same time, evil can't be ignored, or dismissed. Evil is emerging with a new urgency; it has to be thought about in a new way.

The global development of our technology and weapons exceeds the speed of our moral development as a planet. The net result is planetary regression. We default to our basest instincts, and our ingenious toys speed the descent. Our very technological brilliance presents us with moral dilemmas that we lack the sophistication, the generosity, the wisdom to work our way through.

The story of evil in the world is so often a matter of hardware outperforming conscience: Can outruns Should. Or rather, Can outruns Should Not.

We grope our way in a new world.

The globalization of evil means not only evil-by-terrorism, with its nuclear and chemical-biological possibilities, but also evils visited on the planet's resources, whether depredations by populations in the poorest countries in the developing world, or by global corporations that have colonized the planet, and, over-all, by the earth-choking detritus of mass production and mass consumption.

8

SARAJEVO:
LEX TALIONIS

IN NOVEMBER OF 1992, I flew to the Balkans with Elie Wiesel to have a look at the war there. We checked into the Inter-Continental Hotel in Belgrade. I had barely set down my bag in the room when someone slipped a brown manila envelope under the door.

Inside were dozens of eight-by-ten glossy photographs of corpses. Decapitated corpses. Burned corpses lying in a blackened pile in a ditch. A Muslim (it said in the caption) holding a severed Serb head in each hand. Blood-smeared women and children corpses.

This was the Yugoslav press kit. Welcome to our neighborhood. Before you accuse us of committing atrocities against them, have a look at what they do to us.

Tu quoque. You too. No one is innocent.

Or if you wish: I am innocent because they are just as guilty as I. I have no choice. My evil is only a response to their evil. *Lex talionis,* the law of retaliation. Newton's Third Law of Motion. And therefore, by such physics, my evil is not evil, but rather, an excusable attempt to obtain justice.

Maybe my evil is just a reflex. Maybe it is merely rage—rage burning so hot that it achieves a sort of purity, refines itself to an annihilating abstraction.

The press kit included a Serb politician's speech that caught the spirit of things: "People must decide whether they choose to be the carcass or the vulture."

In the Balkans, I felt, as nowhere else I had ever been, the chronic, constant presence of evil. The landscape, the buildings, the streets, the weather, all were suffused with evil. The trees were full of crows.

In Belgrade our Serbian hosts led us to the Museum of Applied Art to see a photo exhibit designed to justify their ethnic cleansing and brutal destruction of Vukovar. In a glass case was a steel instrument that looked like a tuning fork, with prongs spaced three and a half inches apart. The Croat Ustache used to employ the device to gouge out Serb prisoners' eyes, both at once. Convenient. Applied art.

Dusko Zavisic, a young Serb photographer who had escaped from Sarajevo, told me that as a boy he was taken to visit the museum at the World War II Croatian concentration camp at Jasenovac. The pictures there of murdered Serbs were so horrifying that he could not eat for two days afterward. In the latest war of Serbs and Croats, the Croats destroyed that museum.

The year before my visit to Sarajevo, Zavisic had taken photographs of atrocities in Vukovar. He said that he was afraid for days to close his eyes because when he did, afterimages of mutilated bodies and smashed heads would jump into the foreground of his mind.

IN A SERBIAN TWILIGHT, they took us to see Slobodan
Milosevic in his presidential residence. He wore a brush cut that
looked like static electricity firing up from his pink skull. Milosevic settled complacently onto a sofa, with Elie on his right, and
cocked one leg onto a cushion, showing an expanse of hairless,
pale calf above his black sock.

"Truth is the first casualty of war!" Milosevic announced with
a flourish, and a subliminal wink, as if to say, "Ah, you are surprised I speak in your clichés?"

Lies must have their ceremonies. Milosevic said: "There is no
Serb aggression. . . . We are merely protecting ourselves."

This is the invariable formulation of evil. Evil portrays itself,
almost without exception, as injured innocence, fighting back.
(In *Mein Kampf*, Hitler portrayed innocent German girlhood corrupted by Jewish rapists; American racism contrived immense
outrage at predatory Negro sexuality—a hilariously perverse
interpretation of all the white blood and features that are visible
in the "African-American" population of the United States today,
mixtures that resulted almost entirely from white masters' sexual
predations upon their black slaves.)

On another day, the president's people staged a lunch. It
dragged on for hours, into the gloomy Balkan dusk. The bruised
voice across the banquet table from me belonged to an inter-
preter, off duty for the moment, a thin, brittle woman with black
circles under her eyes. She smoked cigarettes one after another,
down to the knuckle. She said she had not slept in days. Outrage
burst from her mouth in agitated spurts of smoke: How could the
world be so stupid? How could the media be so evil? How could
everyone treat the Serbs—the Serbs, of all people!—so unfairly?

The air tasted of heavy, acrid Eastern European woe. Beside
the woman, a Serbian political journalist, a dandy in houndstooth

jacket, wearing Jean-Paul Sartre glasses, nodded agreement and angrily flicked ashes onto the fish carcass on his plate.

I had wondered for months how, in the face of the world's condemnation and disgust, the Serbs could keep up a war conducted by rape, murder, and the starvation of whole cities. How did the Serbs keep on? How did they explain themselves to themselves?

They found a remarkable solution: They felt sorry for themselves. They marinated in self-pity; self-cherishing, they fairly caramelized themselves in sentimentality. They solved their formidable moral problem by declaring themselves the injured party. An artful if disgraceful display of jujitsu; this is a tactic one encounters in wife beaters and child abusers, who ingeniously manage to convince themselves, if not the authorities, that they were driven to it by the terrible behavior of their victims. The Belgrade television stations endlessly showed atrocity scenes, dramas displaying Serbs as victims, with grinning Muslim devils holding the severed heads of Serbs.

Mobs have an evil dynamic. An ethnic tribe, at its worst, is a supermob. A sense of narcissistic self-pity that is merely contemptible in an individual is transformed to heroism in the tribal context: a fierce, virtuous assertion of the group. What would be individual shame (even murder, even rape, even torture, even genocide) now becomes shamelessly virtuous and honorable. The weak and the vicious apply their worst qualities to the larger cause—and of course exploit it, as Milosevic, a hack of the old Communist regime, found his cynical path upward by engineering the crusade for Greater Serbia. Thus does self-pitying mediocrity become selfless heroism and, by this magic, righteous. Being a victim is the Rolls-Royce of self-justifications, a plenary indulgence.

FROM BELGRADE, we flew in a windowless United Nations cargo plane to Sarajevo. Coming in, the plane descended steeply, zigzagging, dodging anticipated fire from the hills around the town. On the ground, rosy-cheeked UN peacekeepers hurried us into flak jackets and blue helmets and put us into armored personnel carriers to ride through "sniper's alley," the exposed stretch of road between the airport and the city of Sarajevo.

The city had become a carcass. Fog, shot through with morning sun, rose from the ruins in a clinging, ragged aura. Fog seeped through shattered buildings. It puffed through the bullet holes in windows, like the Camel cigarette sign in Times Square long ago. The people of Sarajevo were starving and exhausted. Life went on, one way or another, in the ruins.

As for the vultures, they perched in the hills above the town— the Serbian snipers with slivovitz to numb their consciences and keep their trigger fingers loose. They would wipe their mouths with the backs of their hands (wool gloves with the trigger finger cut off) and settle down to aim ... and squeeze off shots at pedestrians through the clearing fog and intermittent radiance.

Serb artillerymen worked in slower, heavier rhythms, like stevedores, firing from the slopes on one side of the city. Muslim artillery, though vastly outgunned, shot from the other. Sometimes Serbs and Muslims threw shells at one another. Sometimes they dropped them into the town. The big shells arrived with a crisp, concussive WHUMP!

You heard the snipers' gunshots only at the shooting end—an irregular background noise from the hills: flat, hard pops. You looked up wildly at the slopes above and imagined the snipers squinting through cross hairs. You wondered what they might be able to see through the mist. You thought about the physics: The sound you heard had been taking its time, traveling a lot more slowly than the bullet itself. So that, of course, if you heard the shot, it could not kill you. Somehow this was not reassuring.

Our Renault sedan scurried across the Miljacka River on the little bridge where Gavrilo Princip assassinated the Archduke Ferdinand in 1914.

Along the streets, we caught the haggard, unslept faces of the besieged, a glimpse of their trudging, cringing body English. The shops were boarded up or covered with steel grates. The driver—improbably, a Russian, a hunching, agitated bear—pitched the Renault along, over-revving and popping the clutch, lurching around corners, accelerating through the open squares, until we arrived at the National Library, a splendid nineteenth-century Moorish building that had been hammered so often, so heavily, that it was now a gutted shell.

I visited Sarajevo as a journalist that late November. More than 17,000 people had been killed and 110,000 wounded in the city since the siege had begun the previous spring. But at that moment, lurching up to that blackened shell, what struck me was the fate of the library. To murder a library struck me as especially sinister and wanton—spiritual and intellectual insult piled on top of dire physical injury. Killing people, as the Serbs were killing now, was evil enough. It seemed, so to speak, an ordinary, customary evil—evil working its purposes one death at a time. What died with the library, however, was the treasure house—consolidated memory, the data bank of all its stories and accomplishments. If you annihilate such a concentrate of the past, the future becomes culturally homeless. The future becomes a refugee. Which was what the Serbs had in mind. Rape takes many forms.

Hitler burned books. When Pol Pot came to power in Cambodia, he ordained the annihilation of the country's intellectuals—anyone who spoke French, anyone who wore eyeglasses, anyone who knew anything. The Serbs desired the destruction of Sarajevo's library for the same reason. Knowledge is dangerous. Stories have power. The past has power. The key to understanding good and evil may be concealed in the dynamics of memory. Great good and great evil may proceed from the promptings of memory. We remember and interpret the past—turn the past into stories. And act on the stories.

Great evil is done to avenge past wrongs, in the manner of Newton's tit for tat—for every action there is an equal and opposite reaction. Are we speaking of evil, or of a kind of psychological mechanics?

I was traveling that day in Sarajevo with Abe Rosenthal of the *New York Times*. We talked to the Russian driver. Abe asked about electricity in the city. None for 17 days, the driver said. Do he and his wife fetch water in buckets from a central supply somewhere?

"My wife does not," the driver said. "She was killed by a shell 67 days ago." Silence. I could not see the driver's face. Abe muttered, "Sorry."

The driver hurtled on. I was moved by the precision of that "67." How long would the driver go on counting the days so exactly?

Elie Wiesel had arranged the trip for a few of us into parts of what used to be Yugoslavia. Elie, of course, preached the principle of Never Forget! But that principle uses "forget" as an intransitive verb. Never forget what? In Elie's case, the Holocaust, the fate of six million European Jews destroyed by Hitler's industrial genocide. Never forget the lesson of the evil that caused it—the revelation of a new dimension (bureaucratic, systematic, among other things) of the evil that human beings may visit upon one another.

How did the principle of Never Forget! apply itself now, to the Balkans, to the Serbs and the Bosnian Muslims?

What happens when each tribe—Serbs, Croatians, Muslims, Kosovars, and so on—lives by the principle of Never Forget!? What if no one ever forgets? Then we all eventually live in the cemetery, and tell stories about what it was like in the days before our universes of incompatible memory collided and made such terrible fission. What life is that? The Serbs never forget the Battle of Kosovo in 1389, when the Ottoman Turks under Sultan Murad I defeated the Serbs under Prince Lazar in their advance toward Vienna and began the 500 years' subjugation of Christian Serbia by the Muslim conquerors.

Remembering is indispensable. Evils arise from not remembering (those who do not learn from the past are condemned to repeat it, etc., etc.). But evils, terrible evils, also arise from not forgetting. Obsessive memory mandates revenge. Ralph Waldo Emerson, the least Balkan of men, formulated the American secular theology of forward spin. He might have been addressing the Balkans when he asked, "Why drag about this monstrous corpse of your memory?"

It had always seemed to me that evil is a wandering presence in the world, and that it alights—metastasizes—here and there, descending into the places where it finds conditions ripe: that, as Satan says in the opening scene of the Book of Job, it "travels up and down in the world, and goes here and there." Evil seemed to visit the Balkans more often than it did other places. The Balkans seemed predisposed to evil.

I have sometimes asked people whether they "believe in" evil—an odd way to put it, I suppose, as if the "belief" in evil arose from faith. Perhaps it does. In any case, the Balkans in that autumn felt to me as if they were suffused with evil, saturated. Drowned in evil.

Elie Wiesel has become an unusual figure in the world—winner of the Nobel Peace Prize, a moral celebrity, a prophet much loved by his following (which includes me) but who, I suppose, is heeded no more than most prophets. I and the rest of our small party were part of his entourage. We traveled under a kind of immunity, visiting all sides in the vicious fighting, passing across the lines from Serbs to Muslims, moving mostly in UN vehicles and wearing the UN's blue helmets, but enjoying, as we saw, a forbearance and grace that made us bulletproof. So we hoped.

We had come to inspect what seemed, at the time, to be the world's most urgent manifestation of evil—the Serbian national-ist drive to exterminate Bosnia's Muslims, or drive them into exile, and thereby secure Greater Serbia. It was an old-fashioned and familiar motif—what the Turks attempted with the Armeni-ans, for example.

Elie did not publicly use the word "evil" while we were in Bosnia. Evil is not a judicious or forbearing word; Elie wished, I think, to preserve, for the moment, the appearance of impartial-ity. He reported what he saw. He told a press conference that Sarajevo looked like "a ghost city, a tragedy formed into a city, like a city in Germany in 1945." He said: "I saw a cat that was a ruin of a cat. I saw a dog that was a ghost of a dog." He added: "I feel the time has come to weep."

I was not so sure it was time to weep. I revere Elie, but when he said that about weeping, I rolled my eyes. Bosnia filled me with anger and disgust. I was merely a visitor—a transient big-foot (with a flak jacket under my Brooks Brothers overcoat) inspecting the Bosnians' misery and grief.

But I thought: What purpose does it serve to "weep" in the presence of evil and vicious stupidity. "Weep" is a literary word. So is "tragedy." The words "weep" and "tragedy" gave the filthy business an undeserved moral elevation, I feared, and subtly aggrandized a stupid horror. I wondered if even the word "evil"—the 800-pound gorilla of our moral discussions—had an unfortunate transformative effect, turning the lowest, most rot-ten impulses of human behavior into something darkly grand and important, romantic.

The word "evil" tends to dramatize, to poeticize, the worst that is in human nature. The John Milton effect—Lucifer aggrandized, ennobled. Is it possible that evil is simply not very important—awful, horrible, unbearable, but not important? Perhaps evil should be thought of not merely as a metaphysical negative, an absence (as some theologians speak of evil as the absence of God), but as our filth—our garbage, pus, feces, our cancer and rot. Shit happens. Evil happens. Anyone thinking about evil finds himself thinking, preposterously, about Martin Luther's famous constipation, his preoccupation with the dynamics of the bowels, his theology of the toilet: Unbearable accumulated pressure finds release.

The self represents an unbearable predicament—imprisonment in mortal, perishable, suffering flesh, for one thing, proceeding at the speed of light toward inevitable death. Suffering demands patience. But patience has limits. The self, unless it finds affirmative expression in love, is hell. When hell erupts, its effluent is evil: the shit of the self. Evil is the filthy non-self that must be constantly expelled.

Martin Luther quoted a popular poem about a monk who is caught by the devil reading his prayers while defecating:

DEVIL: Monk on the latrine! You shouldn't be reading matins here!
MONK: I am purging my bowels
While worshipping almighty God.
You can have what goes down
While God gets what goes up.
In other words: "Get thee behind me, Satan."

In the presence of evil, you may feel fascination. But if you look closely at evil—the Bosnian kind, for example, or the Cambodian or Rwandan—your interest turns to revulsion. You want to resign from the race of devils that do such things.

What had happened in the Balkans was that sort of filth, was squalor and barbarism—the work of liars and cynics manipulating tribal prejudices, using atrocity propaganda and old blood feuds to accomplish "ethnic cleansing." The displacement of a million innocent civilians, turned into refugees, was not a consequence of the war, but precisely the purpose of the war. It had worked. As a tactic of that war, the Serbian soldiers gang-raped Muslim women. The rapes shredded the tribal and social fabric. If a Serb soldier refused to rape, he could be shot by his comrades. Rape bonded the men in atrocity. Some Serb men forced Muslim men to use their teeth to castrate their own sons, and the sons to castrate their fathers.

All this is known. The question is what it tells us. Anything?

In all of this blood feuding, are we in the presence of evil? In the highlands of Scotland in October of 1603—the highlands had a history of tribal rampage as bloody as that of the Balkans—60 widows of the slain Colquhouns from the Battle of Glenfruin against the MacGregors rode on white horses before the king at Stirling, each carrying a pike displaying the bloody shirt of her husband. Waving the bloody shirt is an ancient semaphore that signals the passage, from one generation to the next, of the obligation of revenge. They wave the bloody shirt in the Balkans in this way—grandmothers showing to grandsons the shirt in which their father died, and exacting a pledge to avenge the death. Is the generations-long bloodshed to be seen as evil, or as something else? A Darwinism of the highlands, the rough play of undomesticated genes? At what point do we consider that tribal feuding has crossed some moral line and become "genocidal"? If it's just a tribe being wiped out, is that merely the fierce sociobiology of the mountains? Is it "ethnic cleansing"? Why would not this tolerant, animal behaviorist's view apply to Hutu and Tutsi in Rwanda? Or to Serbs and Bosnian Muslims? What's the difference between Stewarts and Hamiltons slaughtering one another in the sixteenth century (at the same time that Hurons and Senecas, say, were doing the same thing in what would become upstate New York) and the Hutu and Tutsi hackings on such a terrifying scale in the 1990s? Is it the sheer body count of the Rwandan slaughter that makes it evil?

Do the victims of the Hutu-Tutsi feuding seem more real to us somehow, while the Scottish feuds, perhaps because of their sheer remoteness in time, seem victimless? Modern postwar humanitarianism posits a victim, an innocent victim. In recent years, Hutus have slaughtered Tutsis, and Tutsis have slaughtered Hutus, tit for tat, so that either everyone is a victim, or no one is. Two of the interesting questions that evil poses are these:

Are all victims innocent?   Plainly not. In the reciprocal slaughters of Hutu and Tutsi, there were often victims of one who had been, a little while before, murderers of the other, and murderers who would become victims. The same is true of Hindus and Muslims in India. The moral question is then whether one round of unspeakable killings somehow justifies the next round, conducted in the opposite direction. If so, moral indignation, witnessing endless exchanges of reciprocal evil, loses its sense of shock, and falls silent, or having seen too much blood, is transformed into mere disgust.

Does evil require a victim? Can evil exist without a victim? Would Nazism have been evil without its victims?   The evil consists in the deed, not in the mere potential for the deed. Evil fulfills itself in evil results—like Auschwitz. If there are no evil deeds, then evil unfulfilled remains only a sort of daydream of itself, a vicious fantasy.

Elie came to Bosnia, among other things, in order to try to make the killers ashamed of what they were doing. It is true that publicity sometimes disconcerts evil, and may even cause evil to alter its plans. Publicity invariably causes evil to lie. I once thought that the coming of electronic glasnost to the global village (to use two terms—glasnost and global village—that once seemed suffused with bright future, but now seem dangerous disappointments) would bring a reign of sunshine in which the germs would have trouble surviving. I was wrong. A saturation of news coverage does not seem to make evil recede. The germs can flourish in the light.

It is difficult to make evil ashamed of itself. I am not sure it can be done. Not with true shame, surely, which implies a remnant decency.

Evil is a hermit crab. It takes up residence in people. That specific evil may be conquered, by love, or by other enlightenments. And when that evil has been driven out, then it can be said that the people are capable of redemption. But evil, the hermit crab, moves on to find a new residence.

One day in Sarajevo, we put on bulletproof vests and blue helmets, and climbed into a UN armored personnel carrier, and crossed the lines from besieged to besiegers. We went into the hills above Sarajevo to see the Prince of Darkness.

Radovan Karadzic, the Serb nationalist war chief, was also a poet and, bizarrely enough, a psychiatrist: Renaissance Man—a sleek, fattish character in an expensive, double-breasted suit, with expressive bushy wigwag eyebrows and flamboyantly styled long gray-black hair flying out in wings above his ears. He looked like an Eastern European opera impresario, the dramatic sort of man who should wear a cape and smile at ballerinas over midnight suppers.

I tried to conjure up a psychiatric session with a head doctor who would lead his patients not out of murderous fantasies, but deeper into them. In the Balkans, the mind tends to slip into hallucination—which is of course one of the preferred mediums of evil.

We met Karadzic in a one-story modern building that looked like a suburban American grammar school. Coming up from the city, we had passed through one checkpoint after another. At one point, our caravan of UN vehicles halted upon the road for long minutes. Abe Rosenthal and I sat uncomfortably in the dark belly of the armor and waited. A French boy, a UN blue helmet sitting above us in the vehicle's turret, started to open the hatch to poke his head out for a look, but another blue helmet spoke to him sharply. It seemed that a couple of days before, another blue helmet along one of these roads had shown himself like that, and had been drilled through the face by a sniper.

Our driver talked on the radio, then reported to us that a vehicle ahead had hit a mine. No one hurt, vehicle disabled. We waited in silence for half an hour; then started cautiously forward.

Our caravan at last pulled up in front of the school. We stepped from the APC to be met by Karadzic's bodyguard of Serb fighters—unusually tall young men in combat gear, with hand grenades dangling from the chest-loops of their jackets and, in their belts, extraordinary menacing black-handled daggers—the blades a foot long—that had been fashioned to look like miniature replicas of the swords that Crusaders carried centuries before, blade and handle forming a fierce dark cross. I wondered if the men drew the daggers very often, or used them as a warning, merely, of their seriousness about killing.

The men had brutal, uncompromising faces, eyes angry, wild, and their skin reddened and hardened by cold and exposure. I saw that these were men who had indeed done some killing and would not hesitate to kill all of us. Their gaze was distantly appraising and obscurely disappointed. We represented the outer world that condemned them, that did not understand them, that reviled them. They were torn between a desire to justify themselves to us, and a yearning for more savage satisfactions.

The men—all of them above 6 feet 2 or 3—surrounded us and, looming above Elie, led us inside the school, to a classroom with a long formica table. There stood Karadzic with both arms raised in vaguely ecclesiastical welcome, like some saturnine bishop. Elie advanced to him coolly. We deployed ourselves around the formica table, and the praetorian guard arranged themselves to stand against all four walls, scowling and dripping grenades.

The room was cold. We did not remove our overcoats. A moment of silence. Wiesel and Karadzic sat side by side, like panelists. We would have a moral symposium.

The psychiatrist spoke guarded, anodyne words of welcome. We must understand the Bosnian Serb position, he said with an air of elaborate, injured innocence. One encountered that air among the Serbs—again, the strange self-pity, the atmosphere of indignant grievance, as if the world had gotten everything backwards.

Karadzic said, with disarming accuracy: "This is not an ideological war. This is just two close neighbors who hate each other." This seemed, for all the candor, a somewhat primitive line for a shrink to take. True, but unhelpful.

Elie asked, bluntly: "Why are you besieging Sarajevo?"

Karadzic said: "We are not besieging Sarajevo."

Oh.

Why did the Serbs destroy the National Library?

"We did not destroy the National Library. They did. You can see. It is ruined by fire from the ground floor up. We could not have done this. They removed their books and burned the building."

This line had the familiar low cunning of spin and hallucination. We are not killing them. They are committing suicide so that they can blame it on us. You see what devils we are up against!

We have already seen one motif of evil, that of revenge and counterrevenge: For every atrocity there must be an equal and opposite atrocity. A second motif is complete denial: We did not do it; they did.

This yields evil's third theme: Everyone is a victim, which means that everyone is justified in committing any act whatever. Grievances become interchangeable and the mechanics of Who-

Whom reversible. Rage and outrage reverberate through the mountain forests and down the generations.

Karadzic explained: "This war is a continuation of World War II—the same families, the same revenge."

Everyone agreed about that. After the war, Tito and the communists merely suppressed the region's blood hatreds. Tribal memory and the dynamics of revenge were put on hold for nearly 50 years. With the collapse of communism, all the terrible deeds committed during World War II (and World War I, for that matter) came streaming back, crying for vengeance.

NOW THE LAST LEAVES clung to the trees. It had rained, and the water caught in furrows in the fields held reflected sunlight—sweet sky visible through holes in the earth. We crossed the Bosna River and headed into the mountains. There was a sliver of new moon. It looked somehow covert, like an eyelid, watching.

It was full dark at the Manjaca camp. There the Serbs held more than 3,000 prisoners, mostly Bosnian Muslims, mostly fighters, we were told. We found one smirking kid who was a German; he joined the Croatian forces, he said, because he wanted an adventure that he could write a book about. The camp commander, Lieutenant Colonel Bozidar Popovic, was a barking, strutting martinet who wielded a mini-Mag lite as if it were a swagger stick. His voice never dropped from a shout. He bellowed: "I am a humanist!"

An enormous milking barn, unheated, dark except for a few short-wicked oil lanterns, smudged night-lights. The hundreds of prisoners slept close together, in orderly right-angle ranks. They had straw mats and blankets, though how many blankets was a point of argument—the colonel claiming five per man, which seemed extravagant, the prisoners saying fewer. They kept their possessions in cardboard boxes that they hung from the railings that the dairy farmers had used to hold the cows as they were milked. The barn smelled of cows—an effect both disturbing and wholesome, a smell from childhood.

We interviewed prisoners, alone, out of hearing of their jailers. The men were cautious, accusing little; why should they trust us? When we are finished, Popovic burst in, wagging his finger: "I can disprove all of their lies. They say they are innocent. But did they tell you about the lists of Serbian women that they wanted to put into harems?"

I suppose that if I have ever been in the presence of someone I considered to be evil, it was the afternoon in Sarajevo when we came to the Muslim prison—a cold, gray former factory, and there, in a dark cell down a dark corridor, encountered Herak.

He was tall and very thin, about 20 years old, or 21, with a small flat head that was triangular, pointed at the chin; his face resembled a spade. It was his eyes that shocked me—not dead, exactly, but deathly, and dully lit by an enameled malevolence. He had about him a low, buzzing energy.

Elie questioned the man for a little while. He did not deny the crimes with which he had been charged—raping and murdering some 17 Muslim women. He said his captain had ordered him to do it. The claim was half-credible; Serbian officers sometimes ordered their men to commit atrocities. But I doubted that the captain ordered him to do it 17 times. That much zealotry suggested that evil in the boy had become autonomous.

At a distance of some years now, the vividly malignant impression that Herak made upon me has dimmed slightly; I find myself wondering if I do right to call him evil. Was it a merely subjective impression? What else could it be? The memory of that day now has a quality of sleight of hand.

9

THE RIFLEMAN'S
DILEMMA

At a political luncheon in Washington in the fall of 2001, I sat across the table from a distinguished academic—an elderly man, with a florid face and thick white curly hair. He was nattily dressed in a three-piece navy suit, and looked cherubic, younger than his years. From what he told me about his service in World War II, I calculated he must now be 77 or 78. His voice was distinctive. He spoke with hoarse, concussive force. We were talking about war, and the necessities of war. The events of September 11 were on everyone's mind.

The old academic fingered his fork, turning it slowly between thumb and forefinger. Out of the blue, he told me the following story:

"I was a rifleman toward the end of the war, and my squad was moving out in advance of the American lines—in a no-man's-land. We came to a small river, and we captured eight Germans there. They were little more than kids, 16 or 17 years old.

"We had a dilemma. We were very far from our lines. We couldn't take them prisoner and bring them back to our own people. The country was too dangerous, and we had our assignment. And we could not let them go."

The academic paused and looked at me steadily for a moment, to allow me to absorb the situation.

"What did you do?" I asked.

I had a premonition.

"We made them turn their backs and face the river. Then we went down the row and shot each one of them in the back of the head. . . ."

I worked to absorb that.

"Funny," the academic said, chuckling in a sad way. "They were so obedient. Germans! They just stood there in the line and waited their turn to be shot!"

I was silent. I thought for a moment.

The academic continued to twirl his fork slowly. His eye, bloodshot with age, was entirely steady and matter-of-fact. Not defensive. He raised his eyebrows and looked at me searchingly, to see what I would make of the story.

His attitude said: These were the necessities of war.

It said: In the same circumstances, I would do it again.

I asked: "Do you ever think of it now?"

"Oh, sometimes."

"Does it bother you?"

"Not really. We had seen so much. Our friends had died, we'd seen them blown up, dying in all sorts of horrible ways. This was something we had to do, and we did it."

Well. I tried to imagine alternatives the Americans might have had. Let's think: Tie the Germans up? Take their weapons, strip them naked, and tie them up?

Find a farmhouse basement, strip and tie and gag the prisoners, out of sight, and leave them? I scrambled back and forth among possibilities and soon ran out of real ideas and slid for an instant into legalistic fantasies, trying to evade the simple necessity.

Gruesome hypotheses: Cut their tongues out so they couldn't report the Americans to other Germans? Put their eyes out? Worse and worse. I was on the slippery slope myself, trying in a speculative way to find an escape from the inevitable, long ago. The dilemma felt claustrophobic. A simple enough trap, with no exit except a terrible one.

Checkmate, I supposed.

Even if I had thought of something, I would not have presumed to tell the academic what he might have done in order to spare the German boys. I was not sure he wanted to spare them. Hard to reach back through the layers of so many years to try to discern the state of mind, in the confusion of war, between the lines, of the young man whom this old man had once been. Why, after all, would he have wished to spare the young German soldiers? If they had lived, they would have rejoined the army that had already killed so many of his American comrades. Why turn them loose to do that?

What humane principle in the young American's mind could have superseded the simple battle logic of kill-them-before-they-kill-you—a logic compounded of common sense, anger, fear, adrenaline, and the impulse for revenge? The Geneva Convention did not enter his mind. The only alternative to shooting the prisoners would have been to take a chance and let them go (even if tied up and gagged).

But in war's binary them-or-us, you do not operate as an individual. You are part of an army; that army is at life-or-death risk, and you cannot make narcissistically virtuous decisions (like releasing dangerous prisoners in no-man's-land).

After the attacks of September 11, I had written an essay for a special issue of *Time* magazine. The headline on my piece was written by an editor; it said, "THE CASE FOR RAGE AND

RETRIBUTION," which made me sound a little more blazingly irrational than I wished. The case that I made in the article (written on the afternoon and evening of September 11, when my blood was boiling) rested on a foundation of logic not unlike the academic's thinking on the day he shot the German boys beside the river. What I meant, beneath my anger, was that the people who attacked the United States that day must be stopped. Period. Because if they were not stopped, they would do it again and again—next time, probably, with far greater loss of life. The essential point was neither revenge nor rage, but something more practical—prevention, survival. That's the logic that drove the academic to kill his prisoners.

When my students read "The Case for Rage and Retribution," they were respectful but, I could see, horrified. Their professor was crazy.

It was the beginning of the semester, and the students, who were so young as to have no collective public memory more apocalyptic than that of the Challenger blowing up in blue cloudless sky over Florida when they were little children, had been raised in an America that owed its moral atmospherics to an odd intersection of sensationalism and *Sesame Street*. Television taught them to think like Big Bird, with goofy, saccharine good will, but also to suspect, in their hearts, that in the real world Oscar the Grouch might turn into O. J. Simpson.

They had been taught that murderous fierceness is always wrong, and horrifying. What case could there be for rage?

The key to the children lay in their parents. Their parents had been instructed by Vietnam, which taught lessons different from those of World War II. World War II had been a crusade against incarnate evil—and even the German adolescents beside the river could be seen to deserve killing because they were little satellite devils of the great Satan, Hitler. The perception of evil always has something to do with the optics of the moment. We drive at night on a winding road, and see only as far as our head-lights. Or else we are blinded by oncoming lights.

World War II showed Americans the face of evil (Hitler) and the consequences of evil (Auschwitz). What did Vietnam have to tell the American conscience about evil? Not the evil of Others, but the evils of Us—American evil. Something about My Lai. Something with a little girl running naked down a road, away from American napalm, which had burned off her clothes and much of her skin.

The media forms collective memories and moralizes them: Eddie Adams's photograph of Colonel Loan pressing a snub-nosed revolver against the head of a young Viet Cong and blow-ing his brains out in downtown Saigon during the Tet offensive becomes a primal icon. The lessons that Vietnam had to teach centered around the principle of American evil—the evil of great power, conscienceless, arrogant, misapplied.

But all of that sixties business belonged to the generation of my students' parents. The sweet, stricken faces that looked out at me in the classroom in the days after September 11 reflected their softer history in the nineteen-eighties and nineties, prosperous and peaceful on the whole, and governed by guidelines of political cor-rectness. They emerged from a somewhat anodyne and feminized place that had been, to some extent, scrubbed of masculine aggressions (or rather, of any hint of admiration for masculine aggression, which became the ideological taboo of the bien-pensant). Evil had displayed itself to them in the media, not as an overwhelming, enveloping world trend (incarnate in warrior-monsters like Hitler and Mussolini and Tojo), but rather, case by case, as news and entertainment, a democratized tabloid confla-tion—serial killings, Columbine, and distant eruptions of tinhorn terrorism. Evil in their generation had become consumer goods.

Global trends, AIDS and drugs and pollution, for example—all environmental "evils"—proclaimed a world that, while fallen, was at the same time prosperous, at least for my first-world students. Therefore, the evils had about them an ambiguous and even guilty quality, almost as if they were not so much evils as the price that must be paid for so much well-being.

It was for fundamentalists—whether American Christian or Middle Eastern Muslim—to interpret the damages of Progress as moral corruptions, as the harvest of evil.

The America in which I was born tended to think well of itself in a moral sense—to think of itself as Good in the world. The students I faced in class after September 11, 2001, were, in their way, more realistic than I had been at their age. Their Vietnam-generation parents had told them so much about America's evil that some of them surprised me with their readiness to think the attacks of September 11 were America's fault. We came from different worlds that had entirely different moral arrangements.

At a faculty-student reception on September 13, while the ruins of the Trade Center still burned in New York and the digging searchers had hope that some of those caught in the titanic collapses might still be alive, a freshman told me: "This whole thing is media hype, you know."

The boy had a soft wisp of beard and his shirt hung out of khaki trousers, and his sneakers were untied: He was going for an Einstein-at-Princeton look, mommy's little darling as distracted genius.

I did not reply, but looked back at the boy with what he must have seen as the fossilized impassivity of a creature from the Jurassic. Behind my mask of inscrutability, I wondered if the boy had given much thought to the subject of evil—and, if he had, how it had seemed to him. What mask it wore.

The little Einstein with the wisp of beard was just the same age, I figured, as the academic had been when he and other American kids, but from a very different age, had lined up the Germans, also the same age, and shot them on the riverbank.

Evil is sometimes a matter of generational perspective. That does not mean that evil itself changes; only that it is seen, or not seen, in different lights.

Around me and the academic at that lunch, the other guests, mostly politicians, chattered on. I ate my lamb in silence. I was back to mutely parsing the story that the academic had told me. I wondered, for example, whether my lunch companion would have killed the Germans if he had been alone to make the decision.

That is, what he would have done if he had not been influenced by the group—by the cohesion of men acting in such concert that the collective may be relieved of blame, and even of the rule of conscience, in a way that the individual would never be.

Suppose that my young American had had to make the decision entirely on his own? I did not ask him to speculate about that. If alone, would he have devised some other plan? Would he, alone, have had the brutality, or the courage, to shoot all eight boys—one, two, three, four, five, six, seven, eight—just like that? A group, acting together, is morally absorptive. It shares the burden of such deeds. It deflects individual guilt.

Alone, a man might be more scrupulous.

On the other hand, he might be far less scrupulous, seeing that there was no one to witness his act, or to report him, or to blame him.

Perhaps, acting alone, he would have shot them even more quickly, in a burst of automatic fire, because surely the line of eight Germans would not have patiently awaited their turn to die if only one American was strolling down the line to shoot each, seriatim, in the back of the skull? They would have turned and mobbed him before he got to prisoner number two.

The academic would have been 18 or 19 at the time he stood by the river in France shooting Germans in the back of the head—boys executing boys. But he seemed to insist that if he had to make the decision again, more than half a century later, he would do the same thing. The intervening years had not, it seemed, changed his mind.

What would you—what would I—have done with the German prisoners? Shot them? Let them go? Tied them up?

The Catholic catechism says that when a child reaches seven, he comes to the "age of reason"—is old enough to understand right and wrong, and therefore, old enough to be capable of committing sin.

But there is childish "sin" and adult sin, the real thing. Seven is old enough to know that you did wrong when you disobeyed your mother. In adolescence, the conscience passes from innocent ignorance to responsible knowledge. Is eighteen old enough to know whether it is right or wrong to kill eight German teenaged enemy soldiers in cold blood beside a river in France? And was it, indeed, wrong?

If it was wrong, was it also evil? If I, as a much older man, have trouble deciding these questions, how much more difficult for an 18-year-old to make the actual life-or-death decision in circumstances of great danger and anger and fear.

On the other hand, age and time fall under the general theory of relativity—are plastic and individual, compressed or attenuated by such factors as experience, violence of emotion, intensity of life. By the fall of 1944, my lunch companion had surely been much older than 18, having seen so much battle and death. Surely a zone of his conscience had descended by this time into his reptilian brain, where murderous behavior is a reflex. Some burnt-out part of his 18-year-old mind must have been nearly 80 years of age, even then—as old as a man can get, if the wear and tear of violent experience determine age. He may have been older at the age of 18, in 1944, than he was when I spoke to him at our academic lunch 59 or 60 years later.

How did the incident shape the man's life in the years after it occurred?

It had been a good life, it would seem. My new friend had inherited money from his mother, and had been generous with his inheritance, donating much of it to education and the arts, and to do good works no one would ever know of. He studied, did research, and taught thousands of students just the same age as the adolescents whom he had shot in the head that day. He cultivated thousands of young minds, and filled them with what knowledge he had to pass on.

Surely those young minds count for something against the eight young minds that he had put a bullet through? Life sometimes achieves compensating graces, and destructive necessity in one season may, in time, refine itself to a creative result—in the way that a forest fire replenishes and fertilizes the soil and produces, eventually, a greener and healthier forest.

If that is true, do we assume that what we call evil represents only a natural phase, the downstroke of a dialectic? If so, then the evilness of evil is surely compromised, and—like the misanthrope who shows up with a goose on Christmas morning— shown to be, in the end, a devil with a heart of gold. Or anyway, a salutary function in the scheme of things.

And is that compensatory replenishment a universal principle? If so, can it even be said that the Holocaust was, in the end, a salutary forest fire that brought new, healthy growth (Israel?) and that Auschwitz was therefore, somehow, worth it?

The academic's story haunts me a little. When I think of what happened on the riverbank, I do not sense the overwhelming immediate presence of evil (it was a tiny event, after all, in the time of Auschwitz and the gulag, in a war that killed over 60 million and ended in mushroom clouds over Hiroshima and Nagasaki). But the business by the river, which took eight adolescent lives and cannot have lasted more than 15 or 20 minutes from capture to execution, is, in a strange way, even more unsettling, in the sense that it does not represent frank, full-frontal evil but rather, a teasing proximity of evil—eight sharp little cracks of evil inferred: a glimpse of the devil.

The scene by the river represented to me a cameo of tragedy. The American boys thought they had no choice but to do evil. Perhaps they were right. Evil forced itself upon them, and they did evil because they could not think of what else to do. Murder *faute de mieux*. Evil is quite often like that. Sometimes evil is simply a failure of imagination. Sometimes it is a triumph of the imagination.

Later, I tried to compare the academic's tale to the My Lai massacre. That day in 1969, an American infantry company led by Captain Ernest Medina and Lieutenant William Calley walked into a Vietnamese village they called "Pinkville," thought to be heavily Viet Cong—where, several days before, the company had taken terrible casualties. Medina's and Calley's men were combat-exhausted and very angry, and they perpetrated a day-long massacre (they even took a break for lunch) in which they slaughtered hundreds of the village's men, women, and children.

The academic and his comrades had also been enraged by the casualties they had taken and the brutality they had seen. They killed captured soldiers, in no-man's-land. They thought they had no choice. They did not kill, it seems, out of revenge: They had a plausible *raison de guerre*. Calley's men had a choice. They killed men, women, and children in what was said to be an enemy village. They might have secured the village and removed the men by helicopter to be interrogated elsewhere.

But I think I was wrong to set the academic's story beside the My Lai story, as if one event could be weighed against the other. Evil is not a comparative idea. You cannot say that one evil is "more evil" than another evil. Evil is evil. Evil, inserted into a spectrum of relative horrors, ceases, in some subversive way, to be evil. You cannot compare acts of evil, and, in fact, must not, for comparison results in confusion and falsification. Each act of evil is *sui generis,* and has evil's quiddity, the mark of Cain.

That may be why we need the word "evil"—the idea of evil. I do not think our minds can function morally—and they must try to function morally if we are to avoid capitulating to evil—without having the idea available to us. We need to write the word "evil" on our moral charts in the way that medieval cartographers wrote, in uncharted mid-ocean regions, "HERE BE MONSTERS."

The modern mind is confused by the idea of evil in part because, when so many acts of evil are on display in the media, individual evil may lose its distinctiveness, the force of its special horror. The imagination cannot entertain so many disturbing, horrific dramas simultaneously—cannot process and judge them. In the presence of a relentless pageantry of hideous behavior, something in the moral imagination shuts down, or acquiesces, or else denies that all of this gaudily squalid awfulness should be described as evil at all. We absorb more horrors than our systems can tolerate. We overdose on horrors; eventually, inevitably, horrors begin to cease horrifying us. The moral system, and with it the capacity for outrage, shuts down.

We become immune to evil—indifferent. Indifference is evil ripened to fulfillment. A conscience hardens itself to the sight of cruelty, of suffering, of violent death. When indifference at last settles in, evil comes into its own. It has conquered, and gone into business for itself. It flourishes. Evil thrives upon indifference—moral negligence, a stupor of uncaring.

You confront another problem when politics—a form of caring, to be sure—overrides primary instincts of decency and common sense. Think about this story: A Cambodian named Youk Chhang says that in 1977, under the rule of Pol Pot, his oldest sister found herself accused of stealing rice from the collective kitchen.

"Despite her repeated denials, the Khmer Rouge cadre refused to believe her, and to prove his allegation, he took a knife and cut open her stomach. My sister's stomach was empty, and she died."

What do we say about such an act?

That it is evil? It certainly savors of evil. It has an indelible simple horror—a vivid gratuitousness—that we associate with acts of evil. Each act of evil is supposed to be unique.

What happens when we reflect that the world is full of such acts? Certainly even worse things, more shocking and wanton acts of evil, occurred in Cambodia in those years—and happened in Bosnia, in Rwanda, in Iraq, in Auschwitz, in Ukraine during Stalin's terror-famine, in Armenia during the Turks' genocidal house-cleaning.

While Pol Pot prospered and murdered in Cambodia, certain leftist ideologues in the West defended his regime against criticism that they said was "anticommunist propaganda." Their ideology had suffocated their better human instincts—a pattern that, in fact, came to define America from the sixties on, a pattern of politics overruling common sense in the new battles of identity politics and cultural war.

Similarly, in 1932, the *New York Times*'s Moscow correspondent, Walter Duranty, was awarded the Pulitzer Prize for foreign reporting. Duranty's award-winning dispatches sang the praises of Stalin's regime and echoed Lincoln Steffens's line ("I have been over into the future, and it works!") at precisely the time when Stalin, as a matter of official Soviet policy, was starving to death more than 10 million Ukrainian kulaks who had resisted collectivization.

Lenin appreciated the work of people he called "useful idiots," like Duranty and Steffens. Is the smug, thoughtless, incurious behavior of such uncomprehending cheerleaders of evil to be deemed evil itself? I think it has the taint—although of course such misguided enthusiasm usually arises from a good-hearted and even dreamy desire to believe. Utopian projects frequently turn out to be evil and totalitarian (Pol Pot's "Democratic Kampuchea," starting idealistically at the Year Zero, for example); those who fall in with utopian enterprises that turn evil must be judged to be at least accessories to the crime.

Power aspires to fulfill itself, in the same way that a loaded weapon craves to be fired. If you can do it, you probably, eventually, will do it. The rule applies especially to power in the hands of the inexperienced, the weak, the stupid, the immature.

The Khmer Rouge cadre who cut open the woman's stomach to prove she had stolen rice did so because of a fatal convergence in his mind of political rationale (stealing rice was a crime against the regime, the People), empowerment (he held the authority, and the knife), and sheer stupidity (he was probably an overindoctrinated country boy who knew almost nothing except the year-zero cant of the political overlords).

It's often a country boy. Some of the worst atrocities of war are committed by young peasants transplanted far from home, removed from the familiar contexts of their lives, and given orders that they find impossible to evaluate from a moral point of view. Willing bumpkins are drawn into acts of evil that they cannot comprehend. It is possible that Herak was such a man. Was he therefore a victim himself?

The effect is visible not only in third-world bumpkins; in Vietnam, young first-world soldiers, far removed from the contexts of home and armed with deadly, expensive weapons, found themselves endowed with Caligula's power in a nation of peasants that was both prostrate before their superior arms and also terribly dangerous to them. That contradiction sometimes maddened the Americans. They sometimes committed evil acts, as at My Lai.

Do you judge that what my lunch companion did, that day in 1944, was evil?

You probably do not.

Why not?

Because war always transpires somewhere in the neighborhood of evil, which lies next door to the zone of righteousness (war almost always involves righteousness, on either side). And in its context (surely the war against Hitler was a "just war"), individual acts, such as this one, are to be called, at worst, "necessary evils"? Or "unavoidable evils"? Or "inevitable evils"?

This is the "shit-happens" defense. Once at a morning story conference at *Time* magazine in New York, the writers and editors discussed the story of a man who, the day before, had walked into a grammar school in Dunblane, Scotland, and opened fire upon the children with an automatic weapon. He killed 15 of them. Evil often has something to do with violence against children.

The writers and editors shook their heads for a time over the story, and, as storytellers, began searching almost unconsciously for a story line, a way of interpreting the attack. Finally, a pock-mocked deputy chief of correspondents ended the discussion by saying, "Shit happens."

Meaning, "evil happens." "Shit happens" is how the department of journalism explains some of these things.

Returning to the riverbank in France, you would, I guess, ask yourself: Was the individual adolescent American soldier responsible for whatever evil was committed there? Or was the war itself responsible?

Or does the "shit-happens" metaphysic take us out into more nebulous realms? Is evil an autonomous something in the world, part of the weather, part of the magnetic flow and physics of the world, as mysterious in its way as gravity?

Maybe evil has nothing to do with individual conscience, or with the vicious programs of dictators, or even with the impersonal agendas of conscienceless sociobiology.

Maybe evil is in business for itself.

I do not for a moment think that my academic's behavior beside the river—killing eight young German soldiers because he could not figure out what else to do with them that day—compares, in any sense, to what was done at Auschwitz or Treblinka, or in Pol Pot's Cambodia.

And yet the vibration of evil was there beside the river, was it not? I raked my fork lightly over a mound of mashed potatoes on my plate, making ordered furrows in the contours. My academic shrugged, as if to say: A man understands such things. Life is brutal and proceeds sometimes toward good ends through brutal or even evil means, and those dead German boys needed to die that day so that we could get on to the Rhine, and across it, and on to Berlin, in order to advance the day, still months in the future, in the spring of 1945, when Hitler would die in his bunker amid the rubble of his incontestably evil project.

The academic's friendly, bloodshot eyes implied a warning to me: Do not confuse yourself about this. The warning meant: War is brutal. We were fighting evil—or in any case we were kids fighting for our own lives—and we did our best. We were bringing down Hitler. That was the main thing. Do not confuse yourself about an incident on a riverbank.

IO

JEAN VALJEAN
AT WENDY'S

Let me arrange the academic's dilemma beside a second story.

At eleven o'clock one night in late May of the year 2000, two men walked into Wendy's fast-food restaurant in Flushing, Queens, New York.

The men, named John Taylor and Craig Godineaux, waited until the last customers had left. Then Taylor, who had once worked at the restaurant, went downstairs to the manager's office and announced a robbery. The manager, at gunpoint, summoned the restaurant's six workers downstairs. Taylor and Godineaux tied them all up, sealed their mouths with duct tape, and placed plastic bags over their heads.

Then the robbers marched all seven into a walk-in refrigerator and there, shot them one by one in the back of the head.

Taylor and Godineaux left the Wendy's with $2,400.

Five of the workers died—each one killed, if you do the arithmetic, for less than $500. One of the two wounded survivors worked himself free of his bonds after Taylor and Godineaux had left. He made it to a telephone and called 911.

The police had no trouble picking up Godineaux and Taylor, and identifying them as the killers. They had left behind ample evidence (including the restaurant's surveillance videotape) and, of course, two wounded witnesses.

It's part of evil's mystique that it is supposed to be efficacious. But if the Wendy's job was evil, it was evil in a particularly slovenly and ineffective form. Little cash gained in a notably imperfect crime.

The young American soldiers' execution of eight equally young German prisoners in no-man's-land had about it a vibration of evil. What would you say about the Wendy's executions?

If the executions in 1944 represented (forgive me) trivial riverside carnage (eight little uninnocent deaths in the midst of tens of millions killed in the context of Hitler, Auschwitz, and the Third Reich), what do we make of the thing that Taylor and Godineaux did in Wendy's basement refrigerator?

An element of the savagely gratuitous influences one's attitude, first of all. What do we make of the shit that does not have to happen? The American soldiers "had to" execute their prisoners. Taylor and Godineaux did not have to rob Wendy's. Once they were embarked on doing so, they presumably did not have to (try to) execute all witnesses, did they?

Do we come to evil, impure and simple, when we see that the deed flunks the test of human necessity? In Camus's novel *The Stranger,* the hero, or anti-hero, Meursault, murders an Arab on the beach not out of any necessity but out of a certain sun-dazed confusion that Camus—otherwise so intelligent morally—managed to turn into a sort of existentialist Gallic anti-bourgeois gesture of meaning-through-meaninglessness. The murder in *The Stranger* remains a disgusting piece of literary business: Camus defended it, and any number of young readers absorbed from that book the quintessentially immoral idea that one's subjective mood—whim—was all that one needed to justify murder. This is the it-seemed-a-good-idea-at-the-time defense—infantile and indefensible. The King brothers in Florida who beat their father to death were Meursault's American cousins.

Most of the people commenting on the Wendy's murders returned a verdict of evil. New York's Mayor Rudy Giuliani and others suggested the death penalty. John Taylor was indeed sentenced to death in January 2003, and Godineaux, ineligible for the death penalty because he is mentally retarded, received five life sentences.

One of the litmus tests of evil is whether or not it is gratuitous, whether or not it could be avoided. The Wendy's murderers had a problem: If they did not kill everyone, there would be witnesses. Their incompetence rendered their solution to the problem inoperative (they failed to kill everyone, and failed to disable the video cameras).

But if the American soldier was placed in his dilemma by a just war, the Wendy's killers deliberately chose an evil means (mass murder) in order to accomplish what would have been otherwise a merely immoral and illegal act (armed robbery).

A writer on the World Socialist website performed a moral autopsy, finding that the Wendy's murders were neither gratuitous nor evil, in a larger ideological context, but rather reflected the poverty, injustice, and frustration of American society at the end of the supposedly affluent Clinton nineties. The World Socialists' man contemplated Taylor and Godineaux and beheld, he thought, Jean Valjean. Giuliani's and other responses, the socialist said, "are symptomatic of the present political climate, in which the genuine causes of all social problems are studiously ignored in favor of demagogic efforts to divert popular concern into calls for more police, prisons and state-sponsored killing."

Here is the moral mirror-work that yields relativism. An evil act (whether it is murdering eight German prisoners or killing five restaurant workers in cold blood) can be sanitized by context. A just war against Hitler exonerates the young American. An unjust society's poverty (supposedly) clears the Wendy's killers, or mitigates their guilt. Society is responsible, not the individual criminals. An act that is apparently evil in may become un-evil when you change the lens and look at the larger picture.

Writing of the Wendy's murders, the World Socialist analyst claims: "The conditions which lead to this toxic combination of rage, desperation, and futility bordering on self-destruction must be considered."

How is it possible to excuse the young American soldiers' execution of the Germans on the riverbank—claiming that the evil deed was justified by the larger context of the war against Hitler—while condemning the Wendy's murders, whose larger context might be argued to be an unjust society?

You must decide what contexts you find to be sufficiently persuasive to make moral relativism acceptable. The wartime imperative of advancing ruthlessly against Hitler seemed to me a persuasively exonerating context. The idea that Taylor and Godineaux executed their victims at Wendy's because America is an economically unjust society seemed to me 1) patently untrue on the most literal level; and 2) a misguided ideological effort to explain away acts that originated not in the injustices of a social system but elsewhere—in viciousness and stupidity and indifference to life: that is to say, in an evil impulse. It maligns human decency, and slanders poor people, to suggest that being poor makes people evil. The evidence argues somewhat in the opposite direction. Wealth seems to produce an enormous amount of evil in the world. If poverty sometimes does lead to desperation that in turn leads to antisocial viciousness, to robberies and murders, it is also true that poverty may bring out in people qualities of generosity and kindness and human solidarity that are much harder to find among the rich. To claim that poverty makes people vicious is on occasion true; but the argument also unwittingly partakes of the smug, even venal, mentality that regards material wealth as virtuous and the want of it as immoral.

In the Wendy's murders, in any event, there were deviations from the Jean Valjean model. Taylor was 36 years old, the father of four children, and had worked for 14 years as an assistant manager of a MacDonald's in Manhattan. He lived in Lefrak City, the large middle-class apartment complex in Queens. At the time of the Wendy's slaughter, both Taylor and Godineaux (himself 30 and the father of a five-year-old girl) held jobs at a clothing store.

Out of this un-revolutionary material, the socialist hopes to construct something like a justification for the murders—or in any case, the argument that "what is revealed [in the killings] is the extreme brutalization of human relations in the midst of what is officially described as a golden age of wealth. The great majority of New York City's population is simply not involved in the unprecedented explosion of wealth and its ostentatious public display."

This line of argument dominates moral attitudes far beyond the relatively small orbit of World Socialists. What causes "the extreme brutalization of human relations"? Donald Trump's vulgarity? Or people who walk their victims into stand-up refrigerators and shoot them in the back of the head?

The question is not merely political, but goes to the heart of the question of evil, and to the heart of the nature of culture.

In any case, it is condescension to suggest that the poor—or in the Wendy's case, the working class—are not just as capable of committing evil as the wealthy. And if you were to eliminate social injustices, you would not eliminate evil among the affluent. The Leopold-Loeb case, the Columbine shootings, Ted Kaczynski's mail murders—these and thousands of other examples argue that evil afflicts and infects all social classes.

Evil is not an abstraction. It is always a story. It proliferates in systems of stories—lies and truth interwoven, myths, cultures.

II

VISIGOTHS IN THE BRAIN

ONE PRIMAL STORY—Hitler and the Third Reich were the exemplary tale of evil in the twentieth century—presides over variations. One deed of evil sets the standard by which other works of evil are to be judged. We use the word "evil" as an absolute, yet inevitably we compare evils with one another. It was a peculiarity of the exemplary evil of the Holocaust, for example, its monstrous originality, as it were, that other evils have suffered in comparison—have weirdly seemed to be less evil. Stalin's long reign of terror killed more people than Hitler's, and arguably caused as much evil mayhem in the world (though these things are never measurable and it is a kind of metaphysical error to compare evils). But Hitler's evil deeds became the dominant horror of the twentieth century; Stalin's offenses never quite achieved Hitler's stature of historic awfulness.

Evil does not become evil until it becomes a story. Until then, it is a tree that falls, inarticulately, in the forest, an event of cosmic indifference. Evil does not exist until made flesh in, say, Hitler's story, or Stalin's, or Pol Pot's, or Rwanda's story, or

Charles Manson's, or O. J. Simpson's, or Timothy McVeigh's, or Osama bin Laden's. It is drama, motion, act—an emission of dark light and lurid color from some activated malevolence. Evil strives to incarnate itself, in ugly emulation of divinity. Diabology emerges as reflection, as satire, of theology. Neither good nor evil means much in the human scheme of things until it is made flesh.

And so with the globalization of storytelling technologies— satellites, Internet, planetary television, videophone reports from the remotest villages and battlefields—the stories of evil, and therefore the character of evil itself, have been altered. As a sociologist might say, evil globalizes, routinizes, and normalizes itself, through technology.

If Hitler's evil genius organized inchoate German anti-Semitism into a systematic bureaucracy of genocide, Osama bin Laden saw that terrorism could wire up global technology and publicity to achieve horrific global amplifications. The human race has advanced, if that is the word, from a banality of evil to a normality of evil. The media, through global technology, routinely bring exemplary acts of evil into homes around the world.

Evil plays with mirrors in order to confuse the mind and erase distinctions between itself and good. Evil is a hall of mirrors— distorting mirrors, hallucinatory and holographic. Which is why evil is elusive, difficult to think about. Evil abhors clarity, except in flashes of pseudo-revelation—a sudden sensational injection into the center of the brain, the image unmediated by thought or understanding. The injections are made through the optic nerve, and in our time (this is the difference) are administered most often electronically.

How many times have people around the world—not only on television screens in the developed world but also on TVs set up in third-world villages, in cafes, in rude huts—witnessed the primal deed of the large airplane looping round to smash briskly into the second tower of the World Trade Center in a sudden bloom of flame? How many times seen the towers collapse into themselves with apocalyptic up-plumings of smoke and dust? Sermons in slow-motion dream images, tirades to the eyes, visual mantras. Over and over and over: How the mighty have fallen. Ka-boom.

Evil thus globalized need not be experienced first-hand. You need not have been standing in the streets of lower Manhattan on the morning of September 11, 2001, with a direct line of sight to the World Trade Center. For the vast majority of the world, the evil was not experienced directly, but rather electronically, symbolically—through that combination of remoteness and vivid intimacy that is the metaphysic of world television. The evil comes into the world's brain through those shared, shattering, and shattered images. Consider the power of those who are capable of administering such injections to the world-brain. Evil aspires to such power; and he who is able, suddenly and simultaneously, to inject such images as those of September 11 into the very centers of hundreds of millions of minds all over the world is working hard at Caligula's dream.

Of course, different parts of the world's brain processed the images in different ways. In some places, the spectacle was greeted with joy, admiration, satisfaction, a thrill of vindication, even a sense of ecstasy. The evil deed, though globally broadcast, passed through transforming moral optics of culture, history, religion, and emerged in some minds as a good. The cultural lens inverted the sight of people dying.

How can it happen that the sight of airplanes killing thousands of people—surely an evil act if judged in laboratory conditions, free of prejudices of history and culture and grievance—may be greeted with delight by decent men and women?

The question is primitive in its naiveté. The sight of people dying has always amused other people. How much more amuse-

ment do they feel when spectacular deaths also seem to settle a
score, to satisfy justice, and vindicate the righteous? Where is the
evil if those deaths are God's work? Can God do evil? Permit it,
yes: That is the demon that lives in the knot of theodicy. But
cause evil?

All stories carry cultural cargoes. Stories often carry a flag and
behave accordingly. If you watch Gillo Pontecorvo's film *The Battle of Algiers,* you may sympathize with Algerian women dis-
patched to plant their bombs, until you see a little French boy
licking his ice cream in one of the restaurants that will, in a
moment, be blown to bits. Which is, emphatically, not to say that
evil is relative, for that is a fatuous evasion. Only to say that evil
is complicated—that it is a shape-shifter with, shall we say, a
genius for moral simultaneity: A brilliant actor, evil may play several parts at once—hero, villain, wizard, ingenue. That evil may
have its political plausibilities and worthy adherents does not
make it relative, in the flaccid, who-is-to-judge-who-is-to-say
sense that "one man's terrorist is another's freedom fighter."

No: Mere politics is inadequate to comprehend evil.

Mohammed Atta left a suicide note that made it clear he
believed what he was about to do was not evil, but good—a
righteous and purifying act of martyrdom.

Compare Atta's premeditated act of fiery religious fanaticism
with the deeds of spontaneous heroism and self-sacrifice that
Atta's violence precipitated. People in the burning towers reflex-
ively helped others, shepherded the disabled down stairwells,
lifted burn victims onto their shoulders and carried them down,
calmed people and organized them to get out of the building
safely. Firefighters, police, and emergency medical workers did
their jobs, at the risk of their own lives—and many of them died,
trapped in the towers when they collapsed.

What do you conclude from the comparison of Atta's religiously induced, preprogrammed martyrdom with the sponta-

neous heroism and martyrdom of Atta's victims? What does the juxtaposition tell you about the dynamics of good and evil?

Is religion evil? Is the spontaneous human reflex good?

People are good? Religions are evil?

Or are good and evil in the world a simple-minded two-stroke engine: Evil induces good, good invites evil?

Good invites evil, we know that much. Evil is parasitic, and lives off good. Evil takes nourishment by ingesting good, as Satan sought to ingest Job who was perfect and upright and feared God and eschewed evil.

With the Enlightenment two or three centuries ago, evil was increasingly exiled to the realm of the exotic, the glamorous, the alien—the luridly supernatural, the unreasonable, the irrational and superstitious zones beyond the reach of science. Now, science and technology have made evil once again quotidian, familiar.

New forms of evil raise new moral questions. Who is to blame for them? Are they natural evils—that is, acts of God and therefore his responsibility, or acts of the blind universe and therefore no one's? Or are they moral acts, acts that men and women must answer for?

Padrica Caine Hill, former bank teller, Washington, D.C., mother and wife, dresses her three children one morning, makes breakfast for them, smokes some crack cocaine and lets the kids watch cartoons. Then with a clothesline, she strangles eight-year-old Kristine and four-year-old Eric Jr. She tries to strangle two-year-old Kennifer, but leaves the girl still breathing softly on the floor. When the police come, Padrica Hill says she loves her children. Why did she kill them? "I don't know," she answers in apparently genuine bewilderment. "I hadn't planned on it."

Who or what is responsible? The woman herself? She did smoke the crack, but presumably the effect she anticipated was a euphoric high, not the death of her children. The drug arrived like Visigoths in her brain and destroyed the civilization there, including the most powerful of human instincts, her mother love. The crack itself? The dealer who sold the crack? The others in the trade—kingpins and mules who brought the cocaine up from South America in condoms they had swallowed? The peasants in Colombia who grew the coca plants in the first place?

Or everyone? Moral evil descends from the upland settlements of conscious individual human will to the swamps of the involuntary id. Moral evil becomes very nearly irresponsible. Where conscious human will remains in working order, judgment and shame and blame attend the evil act. Where mere involuntary compulsion is at work (the pressures of psychosis, say, or of unhappy childhood, or cultural precedent—as with, for example, Aztec sacrifices or Iroquois tortures), why, then, we confront, not moral evil but, so to speak, an act of nature—a natural cause-and-effect. Auden also wrote:

I and the world know
what every schoolboy learns:
those to whom evil is done
do evil in return.

12

THE AXE IN SPACE

IN A DREAM brought on by fever, Ivan Karamazov meets a devil. He is a figure of shabby gentility, sinister in a casual, sleazy sort of way—a sporty Beelzebub, dressed in clothes that were fashionable a few years earlier, but no longer.

Ivan's devil has something of the raffishness of the Satan in the Book of Job. Unlike the Satan in Job, Ivan's devil seems a little stupid. Oddly—for a devil on a mission—he dithers, and sounds more preoccupied with himself than with souls he might corrupt. He shudders, and complains to Ivan about how cold it was in outer space, from which he has lately come, clad only in an evening suit and open waistcoat.

The devil makes small talk. He speaks of the game of village girls who persuade an unsuspecting child to lick a frosted axe, to which, of course, her tongue sticks.

The devil wonders idly: "What would become of an axe in space?"

He conjectures: It would orbit there, "and the astronomers would calculate the rising and setting of the axe."

Dostoevski's stupid nineteenth-century devil is suddenly a rocket scientist, with the prescience to envision an axe launched into earth orbit 100 years before Soviet and American satellites began to fly off the earth and circle round it.

I like the image of evil as an axe in space. It catches the spirit of the thing. Evil is capable of surprising tricks: Pandora's jack-in-the-box. It floats outside the laws of gravity, performing stunts of flashy telekinesis. An axe in space, in any case, has more metaphysical flair than the usual banalities of the paranormal—pictures falling mysteriously off the wall or tables banging up and down.

I once met a KGB agent who reminded me of Ivan's devil. He did not seem evil, did not strike me as a bone-crusher from the basement of the Lyubianca, the Moscow torture house where his predecessors worked under Stalin. My KGB man seemed merely comic—a cartoon, some Soviet counterpart of Maxwell Smart, a clown of glasnost. He was a short, stocky character, dressed in a loud, hound's tooth jacket with a bright red tie that he wore in an obnoxious Windsor knot. His face, a big, tough trapezoid, was goggled in thick-framed, square-windowed glasses. He would flash a wide smile from time to time—a dazzle of piano keys, a mirthless harmonica. But the smile would as quickly vanish, dissolved into an expression of squinting shrewdness—a stupid man's notion of how to present cosmopolitan skepticism. He looked like a very stupid version of Nelson Rockefeller.

We met for lunch at a place on Forty-fourth Street in New York City. The man, named Davidov, was a "cultural attaché" in the Soviet Embassy in Washington, and had done some favors for Strobe Talbot, a Soviet expert and friend of mine who at that time was the Washington bureau chief of *Time* magazine. Davidov's superiors in Moscow had ordered him to talk to American journalists about public opinion in the United States, and Davidov, calling in a favor from Strobe, flew up to New York to have lunch with me.

We settled in for lunch. Davidov began by calling for a double vodka on the rocks and a dish of vanilla ice cream. Odd, I thought. Davidov squinted at me like a prosecutor and began a blowsy, hilariously ill-informed lecture on American public opinion.

When he finished his ice cream, he flagged the waiter and ordered a steak, "Bloody!" Bored by his own analysis of the American mood, he changed the subject. He told me that one of the things he liked about being stationed in America with diplomatic status was the fact he could take an entire suitcase full of *Playboy* magazines back to Moscow.

This time the harmonica he flashed had a salacious warmth about it. He wagged his eyebrows in a semaphore of lust.

Davidov finished his inverted lunch by ordering a shrimp cocktail. (Was this supposed to be like walking backwards in the snow, to throw trackers off the trail?) In those days, one could still smoke in New York restaurants. Davidov extracted a Dunhill cigarette, lit it, and held it, Russian style, between his thumb and forefinger, with the palm of his hand against his mouth. His squint amid billowing cigarette smoke narrowed to twin slits of dreamy contentment.

The evil empire debauched, I thought: A stock Russian devil of former days, transformed into a buffoon. I could not know, of course, whether Davidov had participated in any of the evils for which his employers were famous. He came out of the Stalinist apparatus of Yagoda and Yezhov and Beria, the monsters of the Soviet nineteen thirties and forties, but his clownishness seemed to originate in Gogol.

IT'S INTERESTING TO THINK about the relationship between stupidity and evil. A neglected dimension of evil is its stupidity. As Oscar Wilde put it, "There is no sin except stupidity." (Stupidity has its fascination: in the words of Jean Cocteau, "Stupidity is always amazing, no matter how often you encounter it.") Toward the end of World War I, when labor unions threatened strikes in England, Minister of Munitions Winston Churchill sternly blamed "evil and subterranean influences," meaning, he said, "pacifism, defeatism, and Bolshevism." Of course, the real evils of World War I, which slaughtered an entire generation of Europe's young men, were obdurate military stupidity, the lethal effectiveness of newly industrialized war, and a monstrous official indifference to the value of human life.

Theology has neglected the low end of evil—its buffoonery. Stupidity—evil's idiot half-brother and occasionally comic sidekick—no doubt seems beneath serious notice as a player in the universe. Theology makes the error of projecting its own earnest and well-educated intelligence, its own quest for design, upon the subject under inspection.

But there seems no reason to suppose that the supernatural cannot be stupid; sometimes that is the only explanation. That God Himself might be stupid from time to time, or inattentive, seems an insufficiently examined hypothesis.

Reverence is stuck with the ungainly puzzle of theodicy. Irreverence, on the other hand, proposes possibilities:

- God is dead.
- God is absent—he has retracted himself to some other part of the universe.
- God is himself at least partly evil, and reflects that facet of his nature in the evil so pervasively evident in his creation: By his works shall ye know Him. Yahweh's wrathful violence in the Old Testament, as Mircea Eliade has written, "sometimes proves to be so irrational that it has been possible to refer to his 'demonism.'" The British writer J. R. Ackerley once wrote to a friend: "I am halfway through Genesis, and quite appalled by the disgraceful behavior of all the characters involved, including God."

- God partakes of human fallibility, and struggles as we all do to overcome the stupidities of the world that, as it happens, he created. In this attractive possibility, God and man make their way forward together through the evils of the world. God, in this reading, is not all-powerful in the sense we have traditionally thought, but rather participates along with us in the dynamic of creation, the tumultuous articulation of the universe.
- There is no God.

If you assume the possibility of cosmic stupidity, of titanic pratfalls, of black holes of brainlessness and corruption (the Greeks made such assumptions about the gods all the time), then a lot of the universe, previously inexplicable, falls into place.

Theology, of course, claims first option on the subject of evil—good and evil being light and shadow where the absolutes dwell. Philosophy—agnostic, speculative: theology in mufti—has second claim. Atheism, of course, clears the decks. In an atheist universe, why should not evil be the province of medicine, politics, psychiatry, social science, and so on? But atheism suffers a gag reflex when confronted with the word "evil." The term has such a medieval aura clinging to it that the essentially atheist mentality of, say, psychiatry or sociology repudiates the term as an atavism. The clinical mindset closes the door upon evil—in effect denies that it exists—and then seeks to explain the immense presence of evil in the world (not calling it evil) by giving it anodyne technical names. This is unwise, for it encourages the delusions of specialists: They are apt to forget a critical thing: the universality of evil, and the implications of that universality.

William James said: "Evil is a disease." But not a specialized disease, like diabetes or Alzheimer's, or, for that matter, Dutch Elm. James should have omitted the indefinite article: Evil is disease. That is one way of thinking of it—a virus, a blight with a life of its own.

A central question about evil, universal or not, is whether it is profound or shallow. Hannah Arendt stated the case for the shallow end. In her letter to Gershom Scholem in July, 1963—in the midst of controversy over *Eichmann in Jerusalem*—she described evil as a fungus.

"You are completely right," she told Scholem, who was disgusted by the Eichmann book, "that I have changed my mind and now no longer speak of radical evil. . . . The fact is that today I think that evil in every instance is only extreme, never radical: it has no depth, and therefore has nothing demonic about it. Evil can lay waste the entire world, like a fungus, growing rampant on the surface."

Arendt meant that evil is not demonic, but demotic—and dangerous precisely because it is not extraordinary. She was right about the shallowness of much evil—and about the surprising, terrifying ease with which people (in Nazi Germany, in Cambodia, in Rwanda, in Bosnia, and many other places) are persuaded to commit acts of cruelty, torture, and murder. The most terrifying fact of human nature is that people commit evil (or permit evil) not because of some impressive grandeur of Luciferian defiance, but instead for reasons arising from everyday stupidity, inattention, convenience, cowardice, peer pressure, momentary entertainment, or idiot ideology. All over the world, you encounter the fungoid brainlessness of evil—the leering, recreational malice, the dull gleam in the eyes, the air of almost surprised delight that a previously forbidden viciousness may now be indulged in, casually, at whim. I think of the Serbian snipers in the hills above Sarajevo, peering through sniperscopes, their trigger fingers lubricated by the slivovitz (potent plum brandy) that they drank all day from canteens. They would put the crosshairs on a housewife darting through the streets far below, carrying a bag of groceries to her famished family—and shoot her (remember to exhale, hold breath, then squeeze) because they could, because they had the power to do so, because they relished that electrical thrill of cause-and-effect when something so slight as the pressure of the forefinger would dispatch an invisible vector of death across such a distance and instantaneously cause that woman and her groceries, far away, to crumple.

But I do not see why the fungus quality of evil, the lack of depth, means, as Arendt says, that evil "has nothing demonic about it." It depends on what you mean by "demonic." Might we not conclude simply that stupidity and shallowness and, as Arendt would have it, banality, are among the many modes in which evil works and manifests itself? We have a folklore of the evil genius, why not add the folklore of the evil moron, or the evil bureaucrat, or the evil religious zealot, and see that in the house of evil (to give it the sort of blasphemous gloss that evil delights in—a travesty of gospel), there are many mansions?

Even if Dostoevski's devil was as stupid as agent Davidov, he did propose interesting theology: Evil is an axe in space. It orbits the world.

The globe-circling axe suggests evil's public dimension—not the eye of God watching from the heavens, but something else up there: an omniscient and well-honed malevolence. By sleight of hand, God is supplanted in space by a flying axe.

The devil, an instinctive storyteller who thrives on anecdote (story being a conjuration), tells us further that in its private work, evil might amuse itself by making cold metal stick painfully to the tongue of a trusting child. For an instant, you see in the eyes of the village girls an ignition of devilish glee.

The image of the devil's axe seems poetically true. It addresses the mind on the level of art, appeals in a way that other approaches do not. I doubt that such disciplines as theology, philosophy, politics, or science—for all their institutionalized intellectual apparatus—deal very well with the subject of evil.

On the other hand, Susan Neiman, a philosopher and author of *Evil in Modern Thought,* is brilliant on the subject. But late in her book she goes to the great moral detective Dostoevski to make a point, as if to confirm that it is through poetry, or drama, or journalism—in any case through stories—that you come closest to the mystery of evil, the *mysterium iniquitatis,* to use Augustine's handsome phrase. Ivan Karamazov, after describing cases of tortured children, declares: "I understand nothing. And I don't want to understand anything now."

Neiman remarks: "Dostoevski underlined the idea that evil is not just one more mystery. It is so central to our lives that if reason stumbles there, it must give way to faith. If you cannot understand why children are tortured, nothing else you understand really matters."

The historian Jeffrey Burton Russell asks: "What kind of God is this? Any decent religion must face the question squarely, and no answer is credible that cannot be given in the presence of dying children."

But my dogged pessimism speaks up from the back of the hall: Since when does anyone have a right in this world to demand an explanation—demand it of whom?—for whatever awful things happen, including even the torture of children?

And if no answer is forthcoming, what right do we have to go into a philosophical pout and to declare that, lacking a satisfactory explanation in this matter of tortured children, we will abandon our effort to understand anything? The world is not like that. Faith and fatalism pull in the same direction. We do not understand because a lot of things in the world are very hard to understand, but we keep trying anyway. We do not have the privilege of throwing up our hands.

There may be many reasons why children are tortured. Some wicked people enjoy doing it; and they find that children are weak and vulnerable. Evil is usually an exercise of power; power inflicts itself upon the less powerful. So the torture of children may, among other things, simply reflect the moral food chain of power: Big fish devour little fish.

But that is too mechanical—too sociobiological. The torture of children is quintessentially evil not only because of the powerlessness of children, but because of their innocence, their blamelessness. The evil becomes in some cases more exquisite for the torturers precisely because of the gratuitous malice—the delectable inexplicability, the metaphysical effrontery—of the act. Evil seems to take exotic pleasure in transgressions targeted to be exquisitely offensive to the decencies of the realm.

We can make such easily noticed points. But what strange sense of entitlement leads us to think we deserve a larger and more cosmic explanation? Children are tortured because that is the way the world is—the way, alas, that human nature is: capable of vicious acts, even against the innocent, or especially against the innocent. Perhaps only a child or a childish mind would characterize this quotidian capacity for evil as "mysterious," since "mysterious" implies a frustrated effort to penetrate a universe that we, for some reason, expect to be rational.

Theodicy, which seeks vainly to explain how God can be all-powerful and all-good at the same time that so much evil exists in the world, is a wistful Zeno's Paradox. Anxious to preserve God's reputation for benevolence in the face of evidence to the contrary, theodicy is a pseudo-rational conundrum of three irrationals slapped together: God's purported all-goodness, His omnipotence (which goes with the definition of God), and the immense rogue elephant in the room, evil. Two of the propositions can be put together without logic trouble. But to fit all three persuasively into the same conceptual frame is a task to which moral logic is not equal. You must take refuge either in poetry or in faith. Or in the daily business of life as it is lived—in thick-skinned stoicism, in resignation, in momentary satisfactions of work and love.

I am not sure how many people, when they look at manifestations of evil at the beginning of the twenty-first century, turn to the Book of Job to understand it. What is the Book of Job, magnificent and cracked, maddeningly unsatisfying, except a quarrel between those two modes of dealing with evil—faith and poetry, that is, between, on the one hand, the almost animal submission that is signaled by the phrase "fear of the Lord," that immense surrender; and, on the other hand, the wonder of diverse creation: "Hast thou entered into the treasures of the snow, or has thou seen the treasures of the hail? . . . Out of whose womb came the ice? And the hoary frost of heaven, who hath gendered it?" The poet in the Book of Job struggles with the prophet. The prophet offers submission and self-abnegation before the inscrutabilities of God. But the poet offers a Lucretian abundance of nature, precious and articulated and refined: "Surely there is a vein for the silver, and a place for gold where they find it./ Iron is taken out of the earth, and brass is molten out of the stone./ He setteth an end to darkness, and searcheth out all perfection: the stones of darkness, and the shadow of death."

Faith is the mind with its eyes fiercely closed. Poetry is the mind with its eyes open. Each is a different form of transcendence.

In any case, the lesson then is useful now: It's a mistake to think you are entitled to an explanation.

Evil is a famously elusive subject. Evil is black magic; magic is a performance art. Evil is something that we do not so much understand as feel. Evil by definition defies understanding. If we understood it, we could not quite call it evil, for understanding implies that something is manageable, correctable. Evil prowls at the margins of our rationality—in the shadows, inside the tree-line, like wolves.

We are either Ahab or Starbuck. Starbuck is practical and businesslike and does not consider it his business to understand evil. He accepts it as a condition of things. Ahab, of course, pursues the elusive thing obsessively. Moby Dick kills both of the men in the end, and sinks the ship.

If you begin a consideration of evil by thinking about stupidity, you may throw evil off a little: Enter by the side door. A frontal approach, as by political analysis, for example, cannot do much better than theology in penetrating to the heart of evil, I think, even though it keeps trying, even though politics is a classic form that evil takes, and even though George W. Bush's "axis of evil" and Osama bin Laden's terrorism and rogue entrepreneurial nuclear warlordship around the world have given international political wickedness more global publicity and pertinence than it had had since Hitler and Stalin, in the days of the terrible giants—or, as Camus called it in his notebook in 1939, "the reign of beasts."

Strangely, evil seems to resist earnest, deliberate thought. The ink disappears from the page. Evil shimmers out of the mind. It beetles off. It ducks into a cloak of inexplicability, and vanishes.

I once asked Sir Brian Urquhart, the longtime Under-Secretary General of the United Nations, if he had ever known anyone who was evil. There was a long pause, before he said, "I don't think so."

He told me the story of how, at the end of World War II, he led a team of British commandos who were streaking across Germany ahead of the Allied lines, in hopes of capturing the German rocket scientists before the Soviets got to them. Entirely by accident, Urquhart's team happened upon the Nazi concentration camp at Dachau. The German kommandant greeted Urquhart and his men courteously, and, with an air of embarrassment that was weirdly mixed with proprietary pride, he showed them around, as if he were a summer camp director leading a tour on parents' weekend: "And this is the dining hall . . ."

But was the man evil? Urquhart, talking about it many years later, said, almost regretfully, "No."

Not the least struggle with evil is to preserve simultaneously in our own minds—and still retain the ability to function—the otherwise maddening paradox of evil and not-evil dodging in and out of one another, playing peek-a-boo. The kommandant becomes a summer camp director. Karamazov's devil's playful little girls trick another to lick the frozen axe.

It takes a stronger mind than Job's, or ours, I think, to understand evil, and we are left with the Book of Job's definition of wisdom—"fear of the Lord." Interesting phrase.

13

WHAT HAVE CHILDREN
TO DO WITH IT?

IN THE SUMMER OF 2002, the billionaire British newspaper owner David Thomson paid 49.5 million pounds for Rubens's *Massacre of the Innocents*. The price made it the world's most expensive work of art to date.

The Massacre of the Innocents is a large tableau, the size of a small movie theater screen, depicting Roman soldiers knee-deep in butchered babies as they carry out Herod's order to slaughter all newborn boys in order to forestall any child becoming the Messiah.

It is not a very good painting; the previous owner, an unidentified Austrian woman, had so disliked it that she permanently lent it to an Austrian monastery, where it had been hanging in a dark hallway since 1923. The purchase by Thomson—conspicuous consumption of a rarefied kind, high-style art patronage—represented more broadly a convergence of twenty-first-century themes, a bundling that is almost too perfect: 1) the whimsical squandering of great wealth in order to purchase 2) a gaudy work of soft-core pornographic violence, a rather cheesy sample of a brand-name Master that depicts 3) the wholesale suffering of children—suffering inflicted so that 4) hope of salvation—for children are, after all, the future—will die in Herod's pre-emptive bloodbath.

The transaction at Sotheby's in London succinctly brought together the age's signature motifs of evil and tastelessness, which so often turn out to be silent partners, or co-conspirators. Herod calls out, across the centuries and across a landscape of baby corpses, to Mammon, and they make a deal for *The Guinness Book of Records*.

EVIL IS THE BAD when it goes over the top and achieves the status of the inexplicable. Atrocities against children are impossible to understand.

Ivan Karamazov speaks of a Russian nobleman who had his hounds tear an eight-year-old boy to pieces in front of the boy's mother because he threw a stone at one of the dogs. Karamazov asks the bitter question that is at the heart of the mystery of evil: "What have children to do with it, tell me, please?"

Indeed. Why does evil have an affinity for children? Simply because children are weaker than adults, and more vulnerable? More than that, evil seems to be offended by the innocence of children, by the promise of children, and takes prime satisfaction in ruining it. There's a metaphysical effrontery in harming children that evil finds irresistible.

The world in the early twenty-first century is in many ways a catastrophe for children, which means, of course, that the future itself arrives already damaged.

Children are a litmus paper for the detection of evil. There may be dispute about whether an act of gratuitous cruelty by adults against adults is evil—maybe there is even a reason for it, if there is ever a reason for evil, and maybe they somehow even deserved it, as people say the affluent polluting oil-guzzling West deserves, in the way of rough justice, the terrorist attacks made upon it in behalf of the have-nots; the violence of adults against adults may sometimes be thought of as peers of equal power setting upon one another, so that there might be some rough quality of a fair fight. In any case, adults, having had some trajectory of life, are closer to the destination of death, the inescapable evil—supposing for a moment that death is an evil—and so there is less pain of the sense of opportunities annulled: But evil done to children by definition cancels all prospective good things, most importantly the love and hope with which we invest children, and the forward trajectory of genes.

In violence against children, adults assert an evil disparity of power. How can there be acceptable reason for deliberately inflicting pain upon children? How can that cruelty be other than evil?

THERE ARE A THOUSAND STYLES OF EVIL.

In Sierra Leone, soldiers on both sides in the years-long civil war cut off the arms, hands, or feet of civilians, including children and even babies.

An eight-year-old girl, whose right hand was chopped off in Northern Province in 1998, told her story to investigators from Amnesty International: "The rebels came to Kabala. When they came to our house they forced us to go outside. They said they were going to kill all of us, and one of them ordered another rebel to go and get a machete. They pushed me to the ground and then cut off my hand. They called my mother and they cut off her hand, too. Nine other people had their hands cut off. They told us to go to President Tejan Kabbah and ask for new hands. The others were all killed. I don't know how many . . . "

What is the meaning of such acts, such scenes? How does one, as academics say, interrogate such deeds? How, for that matter, would you interrogate the men who did them? The only question to ask would be, Why?

What would "the rebels" answer?

The all-is-permitted Leninist among "the rebels"—the professor of violence, the jungle Fanon—might speak in this way: "It is necessary to instill fear in the population in order to demoralize it and undermine support for the regime. Such barbarous atrocities, deliberately inflicted upon children, transgress all ordinary decencies and bring the civilian consciousness into a zone of the forbidden where everything is possible and nothing is safe: This is the essence of terror, and terror is an indispensable political instrument in unstable conflicts of this kind. Besides, every amputated hand is one less hand to be raised against us when we leave."

Would such a discourse persuade you to revoke the accusation of evil?

Would you respond by saying, "Yes, I see what are you are saying. I do not agree with the methods of course—what civilized person could? But there's unquestionably a certain ruthless political sense in what you say. Terror against civilian populations is an effective military tool. And atrocities against children—like the systematic rape of women and girls, especially in a traditional society—may accomplish devastating results. I can also see the brutal and permanent efficacy of severing limbs—hands, arms, feet—so that the stumps of these children become, as it were, eloquent living witnesses to the consequences of opposing you, of getting on the wrong side. Ugly, doctor, but very clever."

But if you moved around the rebels' jungle camp and interviewed some of the men who did the chopping—some of them no more than boys themselves—and if you asked them, why, what would they say?

Much would depend on when you asked them, and in what context.

If you ask the question at an international tribunal hearing war crimes cases, you will get a different answer from the one you will hear just afterward, in the jungle camp. If you are another rebel asking a comrade why he did the chopping, you will get a different answer from the one he will give to an American journalist, or to a doctor from Médecins sans Frontières.

What would be the true answer?

Would the chopper say, "I did it because the Leader ordered me to do it"? One certainly would hear that repeatedly at the war crimes tribunal.

Would the chopper say, "I did it because I have been dehumanized by this long, bloody war, by the cycle of retaliation, by the sight of my own comrades mutilated and disemboweled"?

Would he say, "War is a state of insanity, in which horrible deeds that would be condemned and punished in a decent atmosphere of peacetime are not only permissible but expected, encouraged, effective, and inevitable. Out in this bush there is no Geneva Convention. You—white Europeans and Americans—take this hand-chopping to be yet more evidence of the heart of darkness, which is funny because the Belgians in King Leopold's Congo routinely chopped off native workers' hands and feet for the slightest infraction of the work rules."

If you were present at the scene itself, when the atrocities were committed, would you see in the soldiers' faces, in their eyes, the dull filthy light of pleasure in what they were doing?

Would any of the soldiers answer the question "Why?" by saying, "because it was fun"?

Would any of them say, "Because it was evil"?

Would he answer it by pushing you to the ground, and chopping off your own hand?

And when he saw the look on your astonished face as you held the stump and looked at your suddenly alien hand, an object on the ground, would he laugh?

And what would you say to the professor of violence then, about whether what had just happened was, or was not, evil?

There is always a professor of violence—realist, zealot, ideologue, the sort of speechmaking activist intellectual you find in Malraux, or Al Qaeda, always out of the middle class, a doctor or engineer or some such—who lays it down that evil is the price of change. The professor usually has a taste for especially dramatic and ostentatious evil, even a curious longing, almost a nostalgia, to put his intelligence to work commandeering brute horror, as if this violent mating of brains and bestiality would surely bring forth a better world, utopia.

And so as a moral matter, how do you judge the chopping of the children's hands? Intellectuals, alas, have an immense tolerance for—even an attraction to—evil if they see it as part of a means to a socially and intellectually satisfying end. Even the knowledge of Stalin's monstrous crimes or of the murderous idiocies of Mao's "cultural revolution" has not shattered the paradigm or caused intellectuals on the left to reflect or to abandon their wistful longing for world-changing, revolutionary savagery. If the locomotive of history severs children's hands, so what? It's the price of getting the train through.

Or is it evil? Or is it both—that is, a necessary evil?

True enough, some workaday evils are necessary; yet the concept of the necessary evil can become sinister and hilarious, evilly hilarious. Who judges the "necessity," after all? All of history's monsters—except for certain overprivileged Romans like Nero and Caligula, who favored a style of psychotic whim—have set their evils in motion on the premise of absolute necessity. Pol Pot had an elaborate rationale of social-cultural necessity when, in the declared Year Zero, he drove all the people out of Phnom Penh in 1975 and began the Cambodians' auto-genocide. Hitler posited all kinds of necessities to build the Thousand-Year Reich. Mao had fancy necessities. You cannot make an omelette without breaking a few eggs—a favorite Pentagon locution in the early years of the American war in Vietnam. The breakage is the necessary evil, the price of doing business.

But all of those cases and many more have demonstrated that the habit of evil, once established, dissolves all ideals or social designs, and absorbs their corrupted residue into its violent, vicious self. Evil is an addiction—as power is, as killing is. What you see in the rebels of Sierra Leone, or in the Serbian killers and rapists in Bosnia, is a cause gone feral and rancid. The overwhelming impression that these men—or occasionally, women—make is one of a strange and original form of stupidity (moral, social, intellectual), of stupidity carried into a new dimension: stupidity with a political portfolio, but essentially the stupidity of wild dogs.

So the professors of violence, the theoreticians, *les hommes engagés,* preside over armies of brutal morons—a fitting configuration that honors the professors' desires to annul all bourgeois autonomies and decencies (which might lead toward a democratic process that slights or ignores intellectuals) and to have at their command armies of slaves willing to do anything to implement the will of their Idea. In that configuration, the professors attempt the age-old intellectual's dream of alchemy—in this case, the effort to turn evil (orgies of hand-chopping etc.) into perfection: into social paradise. Alchemy has only a record of perfect failure. I know of no instance in which the professors' alchemy has delivered on its promises.

The most terrifying possibility is that these assaults have no meaning at all. Evil aspires to a state of perfect meaningless-ness—a mockery of meaning.

In the presence of the children's severed hands, what settles over the spirit, after shock and disgust have passed, is a vast weariness and emotional depression. The inexhaustible inven-tory of evil in the world exacts a toll—even upon a bystanding world hooked up by satellite to witness its works—that may lead the best people to consider suicide and the worst of us to be cal-lous and indifferent, and, if presented with certain opportunities or necessities, possibly evil ourselves, or passively complicit. The experience of evil may destroy the good, or turn them evil; in rarer cases it inspires people to resist evil, and to try to abolish it from the world.

THE MILITARY HISTORIAN John Keegan has admitted that when he came to write about the Battle of the Somme on July 1, 1916, an appalling slaughter in which some 60,000 British troops were killed or wounded in a single day's fighting, he felt "an awful lethargy" falling upon him, his typewriter keys—he wrote this before he got a computer—"tapping leadenly on the paper to drive the lines of print, like the waves of a Kitchener battalion failing to take its objective, more and more slowly toward the foot of the page."

Keegan is drawn to the admittedly "unhistorical" analogy made by another writer, Robert Kee: "The trenches were the concentration camps of the First World War." Writes Keegan, in *The Face of Battle:* "There is something Treblinka-like about almost all accounts of July 1st, about those long docile lines of young men, shoddily uniformed, heavily burdened, numbered about their necks, plodding forward across a featureless landscape to their own extermination inside the barbed wire. Accounts of the Somme produce in readers and audiences much the same range of emotions as do descriptions of the running of Auschwitz—guilty fascination, horror, disgust, pity, and anger."

The transcendently pointless slaughter of the Somme—and of the First World War altogether—was a mass production, industrialized murder, as Auschwitz and Treblinka were industrialized genocide. The immensely "productive" machine guns were indeed machines. If the Nazi death camps suggested a bureaucratic evil, the conscienceless and virtually oblivious meat-grinding of the Somme belongs, like the endless African civil wars—in Sierra Leone, Angola, Congo, Sudan, and elsewhere—to the history of the stupidity of evil. The developed industrial world of Western Europe and the undeveloped world of Africa meet on a common ground of brainless internecine slaughter, and the contemplation of both leave one with a sense of exhausted disgust.

Was the Battle of the Somme evil? Surely it can be said that all war is evil unless it is fought to oppose evil. Ulysses Grant, who in some ways invented industrial slaughter with his meat-grinder tactics toward the end of the American Civil War, fought in the just cause of a war against the evil of slavery. The combatants in World War I certainly worked themselves up to the notion that the conflict had to do with the conflict of good and evil, though the case on all sides was massively unconvincing. The war, with its terrible, civilization-destroying slaughter, taught a lesson in the ways that great evil may come into the world flying flags of higher national purpose and self-sacrifice *("dulce et decorum est pro patria mori")*. It showed how civilian populations can be coerced and seduced into crusades for the alleged political and moral

good, and swept along in waves of selfless fervor that may cul-
minate in the senseless evil of mass death. World War I was a vis-
itation of evil that took away an entire generation of Western
Europe's men.

Was it evil? Or was it simply history, which is not subject to
such massive moral taxonomies? The Battle of the Somme and
the First World War are surely susceptible to the same moral
process that we apply to Auschwitz. Of all human activities, war
is surely close to the most evil in its results; the question to be
asked, always, is whether it is a necessary evil (as the war against
Hitler was) or, so to speak, a just evil—to adapt Augustine's Just
War theory. To say that an evil is necessary is to say it is just—at
least to the extent that your notion of necessity coincides with
your sense of justice.

One primary lesson of such scenes (Sierra Leone, the Somme)
is that there is probably no such thing as progress. . . . Or, rather,
that whatever progress we have made, in some parts of the
world, in scholarship and understanding and manners, or in neu-
rosurgery and cardiology and electronics and aviation and micro-
biology and all of that, is accompanied at all times by the hideous
tendencies of the evil that we share this journey and planet with.

I think of stories in central and west Africa about baskets of
hands for sale in markets—hands being judged, among people
with an appetite for this, to be the tastiest part of the human
body. The amputation of hands and feet in Sierra Leone has barbaric equivalents and variations in the Balkans and in Chechnya
and Latin America and elsewhere. It is dispiriting to arrive at last
in the twenty-first century, a new millennium, and to understand
how little human beings have to congratulate themselves about,
how little they have to show for the struggles that got them here.

Progress may take many forms. But unless there is progress
against evil, then all other forms of progress are fragile and pro-

visional. They may in an instant (as in Nazi Germany, for example) be annulled. No country in Europe, except Britain, had a better education system than Germany at the onset of the Hitler era. The struggling, painstaking enlightenment of centuries was swept away in a few years. All civilization—all thought, all decency, all rationality—lives under the volcano.

What do we think of a kind of spontaneous, "natural" evil found among the young? I do not mean the weird evil you sometimes see in children, a creepiness of the kind that might, in time, mature into Columbine. I am speaking of a healthier kind of evil, if there is such a thing—an aggressive, exuberant malice of the kind one sees in boys delighting in wicked tricks played on animals or on other children. This is the sort of viciousness that folklore refers to in the cliché that "children can be so cruel."

Perhaps evil (if it is evil) among the young is divided between this exuberantly aggressive malice and the creepier kind. The first kind often makes a victim of the second kind, and may even cause the evil of the second kind. The conflict between the two kinds of evil may be tribal—distinct tribes of the young at one another's throats, as at Columbine, where two who felt themselves to be outcasts, mocked by the jocks of the school's establishment, plotted apocalyptic revenge.

I call one form of evil "exuberant," as if to exonerate it, to suggest an innocence of youth in the midst of wickedness, as if such an evil were a rite of passage. But of course it is often evil enough. And in fact, evil sometimes is exactly that—a process by which the innocence of children accommodates itself to the world and to its crueler business. Evil becomes a way of growing up. At lesser levels of brutality, however—that is, far short of murder—there's an aspect here of the homeopathic—the idea that introducing a touch of evil into a child's life, perhaps at the moment the child is on the threshold of adulthood, serves to immunize the child from becoming evil. Groups of boys commit acts of cruelty in order to solidify themselves as a group and to test the reliability of each individual. How else but by confronting evil in oneself—that is, by doing evil—can the boys become men, equipped to do what a man is supposed to do: to confront an evil world? Acts of adolescent cruelty become, in effect, a sacrifice: They sacrifice their own innocence. The evil acts of initiation that they commit become a kind of violent birthing.

If this rite of passage is omitted, something in the person remains childish.

14

THE TRIUMPH OF
GONERIL AND REGAN

Anyone who has lived in the corporate world that the baby boomers now control recognizes the difference between that world and the corporate atmosphere created by the boomers' parents, the so-called Greatest Generation. The difference between the boomers and their parents is in a sense the difference between wars—between their experiences of the varieties of evil.

The boomers' parents fought the Good War—World War II, against the forces of evil as represented by Hitler, Mussolini, and Tojo. The boomers, on the other hand, fought the Evil War—Vietnam. Or else refused to fight it, depending on their luck in the draft lottery, their skill at dodging by manipulating student deferments (as Bill Clinton and millions of others did), their idealism in emigrating to Canada, or their privilege in being able to afford money to bribe a psychiatrist or other doctor to certify them as unequipped to carry weapons and fight.

The division of that generation between those who fought and those who did not left a state of moral confusion about which side held the higher ground. One of the few virtues of evil is the candor of which it is capable from time to time: Evil looks and feels like evil. But when you have an entire generation of Americans—the children of those who were certain about their own good cause against the forces of evil—split on something as basic as whether their own country is asking them to do evil in an evil war, that moral uncertainty does permanent damage: It may produce ill-formed or incomplete characters. Or by contrast, it may serve the (sometimes) useful purpose of encouraging skepticism about applying absolute vocabularies of good and evil to a business as dangerous and treacherous as war. Yet without the battle cries of good and evil—which, by the way, are sometimes entirely accurate descriptions of the forces in play (see Hitler)—how can a people mobilize themselves and rise to the occasion?

There is something perverse in saying that 1) evil is a rite of passage, and 2) the draft resisters of the baby-boom generation, by refusing to participate in what they regarded as an immoral war, an evil war, thereby violated some sociobiological imperative and, in doing so, bypassed the rite of passage and thus weakened the muscle tone of the tribe and brought on a manipulative, narcissistic, Clintonian culture. Some generations do not have a foreign war to turn the males into men. Does that mean they do not become men? And how does the idea of war as a traditional male rite of passage emerge from the era of the new military, when women go through the trials of war as well? But life is sometimes perverse. There was a part of the boomers' narcissism that nested itself in a culture of uneasy self-satisfaction and self-righteousness, and came to feel as self-satisfied as Goneril and Regan did.

The sentimental West—under the management of the meliorists, who believed in health and non-smoking and helmet laws and the improvability of everything—hoped not only to preserve the innocence of childhood, but to turn childhood's innocence—its open-hearted tolerance—into the model for the adult world as well.

The baby-boom generation was raised to think that adults (Johnson, Nixon, the militarists) were the problem, and that youth was the solution. The children know best, the children will lead us. They thought to banish evil by force of will and common sense. One of their first measures—one of those unwritten ordinances that circulate as attitude and have the authority of law—was to send the concept of evil into a kind of exile, in somewhat the way that Goneril and Regan banished King Lear's knights, and then, in effect, banished the king their father himself. The king, the old majesty, was unmanageable. Evil, which also seemed to belong to the old, dangerously irrational adult order, was also unmanageable.

Perhaps evil was essentially male? Evil arose from a masculine world in which ungoverned masculine aggressions tore loose from their moorings and broke things and killed innocent people. Banish the king's knights—noisy drunks with too many weapons lying around. Banish the demented king. Banish the male.

Can it be that evil is a zero-sum game? That each generation is allotted its quota of evil, and must express it—discharge it—in any way it can? Is it possible that the baby boomers who did not go to Vietnam and fight in the evil war instead found other ways to discharge their allotment of wickedness? The generation who advertised themselves at the time—some still do—as the most idealistic and liberated and peace-loving ever born into American life proved, in the fullness of time, to be as vicious and money-grubbing and generally immoral as any previous generation. The boomers' claims to special virtue always seemed an unwitting echo of the claims of American exceptionalism; the boomers were jingoistic as a generation, and smug about their own manifest destiny.

What did they do for rites of passage? They disobeyed the law—smoked illegal drugs, for example. They overturned the order of authority in America. They committed forms of regicide and parricide. All of this, however, they accomplished more or less bloodlessly. It was the authorities, at Kent State, for example, who shed the preponderance of blood against the dissenters. That the National Guardsmen who fired the bullets at Kent State were mostly of the same generation as the people they were shooting illustrated the moral confusion of the split in the generation.

Dante sent those who were disloyal to the state to the lowest circle of his hell, where they were embedded for all eternity in ice. Much of the baby-boom generation appealed to a higher morality and made disloyalty to the state and its leaders a mark of virtue. In American history, Benedict Arnold is the generic name for traitor. The baby-boom generation rearranged the categories of good and evil in such a way that treasonous and semi-treasonous behavior—cheering for the enemy, subverting the American government—became the sign of idealism, and the distinctive mark of the generation, which defined itself as a tribe in opposition to all established authorities.

Each side of the generation found its rites of passages—and on either side, they were extreme. If one side fought authority in America, uniformed representatives of the other side found themselves committing bloody rite-of-passage violence in Vietnam.

There the American boys were not merely setting fire to cats or braining frogs, but rather were blowing up a country in the name of saving it.

War as rite of passage involves the initiate in an intensely focused, violent drama, in which his role may be that of active aggressor or passive victim of aggression. Or the two roles may be fused in the heat of action.

The moral meaning of the rite of passage very much depends on whether the soldier is preponderantly a victim or an aggressor—and, of course, in what cause he is fighting. It is a curiosity of World War I that the troops on both sides could be thought of, quite clearly, as victims: The aggressor was the superordinate imbecility of the war itself, and of the elders who so presided over the vast industrial meat-grinder of the Western Front. The Germans emerged from the war, of course, regarding themselves as victims, not so much of the metaphysical idiocy of the war itself but of betrayal by their leaders in capitulation. Hitler— gassed, the survivor of an incredibly long and dangerous career as a battlefield courier—had the indignant psychology of a victim: The conviction in the post-traumatic victim's mind of violated innocence and indignation may one of the most fertile preconditions of future evil. Regarding oneself as an innocent victim betrayed prepares the way for justifying virtually any act of retaliation. Hitler, seeing himself and Germany, the fatherland, as victims, was able to focus the blame upon Communists and above all upon Jews, as alien elements contaminating—victimizing—the unguarded German nation. And from that conviction of blameless victimness, of course, great historical evil followed. In Serbia, Milosevic and Karadzic gave off that air of wounded innocence.

In Vietnam, the young Americans in their rite of passage were victims indeed; they suffered terrible damage not only in their bodies (so many limbs lost, so many amputees returned, men who might otherwise have died but were saved by the efficiency and skill of medevacs and military medicine) but also in mind—suffering post-traumatic stress syndrome (as shell shock

came to be called), or addicted to the potent drugs they found
everywhere in Vietnam. For various reasons—most notably the
unpopularity of the war, the hatred of it at home—the killing
that they did over there was unsanctioned and unclean, and so
the rite of passage, far from ending in the emergence of the former boy as an ideal man, widely praised as war hero and ready
to assume his adult role of leadership in the nation's life, termi-
nated instead in anger, psychological conflict; when the soldiers
came back from their rite of passage, the country spit at them,
often enough. They would arrive back in San Francisco, the dirt
of I Corps still under their fingernails, and they would change as
quickly as they could to civilian clothing; and some remembered
that as they came across the Golden Gate Bridge, hippies threw
bags of human excrement at them and called them "baby
killers." One veteran whom I knew returned from Vietnam and
made his way to Las Vegas, where he lived in the city dump, in a
hut made out of cardboard, for nearly a year. That was his way
of welcoming himself home and presumably of estimating his
own worth as hero. Another veteran I knew slept with his rifle.
He and many other men returning from the War to "the World"
had evil dreams.

All wars leave their combat veterans more or less troubled.
Combat is a terrible shock to the nervous system and the moral
system—a horror and, every now and then, a guilty joy, something that veterans are reluctant to acknowledge. They have a way
of admitting it to one another sometimes on the seventh or
eighth beer during a reunion.

For all of that, the young Americans in Vietnam could plausi-
bly claim no victimness. They were too powerful; in World War
II, the Americans had been desperately and evenly matched—in
the beginning, overmatched—by powerful enemies with evil
designs. And so the Americans comfortably saw themselves in
the role of virtue beleaguered and at last triumphant—a highly

satisfying moral drama, if you happen to be on the winning side. But the dramaturgy of Vietnam was such that the Americans could never claim that quality that is indispensable to the Americans as they see themselves on the world stage: Innocence.

In the early stages of the war, American soldiers tended to entertain many of the martial fantasies that their fathers' generation had bequeathed them from World War II. In his scalding book *Born on the Fourth of July,* Ron Kovic, who took a bullet through the spine in Vietnam and returned home paralyzed from the chest down, remembered that he and his peers from gung-ho working-class America went off to Southeast Asia with John Wayne and Audie Murphy movies unreeling in their minds. John Wayneism—a muscular, competent manliness, utterly American and most convincing in a Western, frontier context where the strong individual might be autonomous and virtuous, imposing his own code in a lawless, dangerous territory—is attractive and morally permissible only in a righteous framework; otherwise, of course, it is mere bullying and oppression. Possibly the worst movie John Wayne ever made was *The Green Berets,* about Vietnam—a wincingly false effort to transport the American esprit of World War II to the dirty little war of the sixties.

The hardest possibility Americans have to confront about themselves is always the thought that they may be evil. That is the thing they find most difficult to face. If there comes a moment when John Wayne is evil, for example, the implications for Americans are intolerable; an entire edifice of American self-myth begins to disintegrate.

Americans are struggling now with the possibility that their country may be evil—or, to be more practical, that their country may be doing evil in the world. The death, in Americans' own minds, of the certainty of American exceptionalism opens the possibility of American evil and is itself a part of the whole revival of the idea of evil in the world: Bush speaks of the axis of evil, and there bounces back the countertheme of American evil, indeed of Bush's evil.

Americans since the 1960s have been struggling with the possibility that their country, which they had been accustomed to regarding as the world's paragon, the last best hope, the *summum bonum,* the richest and the best and most virtuous, might be the reverse of everything it had proclaimed itself to be.

America, the oldest functioning democracy in the world, is also a very unstable element in the sense that the nation is an idea that keeps changing, a gene pool that keeps changing—a self-conception always on the move. Being an idea rather than a fixed national entity defined by language and cuisine and long-established culture and custom—like Japan, say, or France or Sweden—the United States tends to be abnormally sensitive about its moral self-image. Americans need to feel virtuous. If they do not, they may even think of themselves of evil.

The disparity between visions of America as all-good and America as all-evil—a moral disjunction begun in the sixties, during Vietnam and the civil rights movement—has gone global, and lends a curious, dangerous totalism to discussions of world affairs now. It is difficult to discuss the most powerful nation in the world, the American hyperpower, in dispassionate terms, with nuance. Great power in another makes others angry. If America is an empire—not colonial in the old sense, but nonetheless a world force projecting its power everywhere in the globe—what exactly are its responsibilities, and what are its rights?

Does having the power to do ultimate evil—and America's nuclear arsenal could pretty much destroy the world—automatically make America evil, by some malignant capillary effect? It certainly helps to define America that way in the eyes of much of the world.

And yet relative weakness is also feckless—carping, whinging, morally irresponsible. What do these others want of America? That it be less rich? Less powerful? If it were so, what then? If America withdrew from the world and effaced itself, what other powers would rush into the vacuum? And with what effect? If America is an evil presence in the world, then presumably the withdrawal of that evil presence would be a net gain for good. Do America's enemies really believe that? The experience of history argues that a worse power would supplant America; and the constriction of the world makes the danger, post-America, far worse. What country, cast into the role of hyperpower, would not be evil—far more evil than the United States? Can any sane human being wish to see the Islamic *sharia* given imperial dominion? Would anyone wish the Chinese to succeed to the American dominance? The Russians? If not those nations, then who? The Germans? Not one of those prospects could possibly be satisfactory as a replacement for the Americans.

Those who consider America to be evil might think for a moment, if they can, of America's relative virtues. It is after all an enormous ingathering of the tribes of the world—more diverse than any other nation on earth. It has an admirable constitution and political stability. It is a functioning democracy—the elite of democracies.

15

TU QUOQUE

I STARTED TO THINK about evil by making an informal survey. I asked friends, or people at dinner parties: "Do you know anyone who is evil?"

The question, without preliminary, seemed strange—a line that would cause people to edge away from you at a bar.

I reframed the question slightly: "Have you ever known anyone whom you considered to be evil?"

That dampened the strangeness of the question only a little. Finally, I learned to start by explaining, "I am writing a book . . . "

Most people would stare into the middle distance for a moment, as if startled by the idea of knowing someone evil, of thinking of evil in such familiar terms.

Then they would reply, judiciously, as if disappointed by their own answer: "Noooooo. . . ."

They seemed to imply that the idea of a person being evil was not quite real, that evil had an element of charade, a shimmer of entertainment about it, as if to say, evil is a show, not an actual fact in the serious world. And beyond that, their tone suggested, what we call evil usually has some other explanation.

I saw their minds beginning to form the political thought that one person's evil, of course, is another's heroism, that an act of bloody terrorism, for example, if seen from the perspective of its authors, might be an act of patriotic resistance, and that therefore it was perhaps not helpful to use the term evil. A tolerant and civilized reading.

On the other hand, evil often has a rationale. Dressing up evil in an explanation—ethnic, psychiatric, political, sociobiological, medical, chemical—does not necessarily make it not evil: It may just be . . . evil in costume.

In the West, the sense of evil is vivid, anecdotal, and discontinuous—just as the experience of the larger world, through television and other electronic media, is vivid, anecdotal, and discontinuous. Evil comes to us in a ragged montage of news—evil tidings, mad autocrats, bomb blasts, kidnaps, the evidence found in basements and shallow graves.

But it is important to keep one's mind straight about it: Evil claiming to act in some righteous cause, or on behalf of some identity, remains evil, usually more so, since the virtuous cause itself may function as evil's turbo-charge, its intensifier, and make it more uncompromisingly evil. The righteous exterminator has a clear conscience. That is one of evil's secrets. A person with a clear conscience may do the worst of the worst. Ideology or religion has licensed his evil—endorsed it with authority and context and inspiration and the promise of a better world. And if the evildoer conceives himself to be a victim, that is an even more powerful dispensation: For if you are yourself a victim, then anything you do in retaliation is not evil but justice. To the victim, all things are permitted.

Many progressives in the early twenty-first century, witnessing another civilizational-religious confrontation between Islam and the West, have adopted this annulment by relative perspectives: This is diversity's *tu quoque,* which supposedly neutralizes an accusation even of something as absolute as evil. The *tu quoque,* so civilized, is, if you hold it to a different light, also a kind of schoolyard fallacy (one child says, "You're evil!"—the other says, "So are you!" and therefore the accusations cancel each other out) that nonetheless has proved successful in defanging cultural differences, the thought being that if we recognize that we all merely think that the Other is evil, then we come face to face with our own (correctable) intolerance.

The contradictions of cultural diversity as a rule merely cancel each other out. The fact that you have your way, and I have my way, means that neither way has moral force or authority. The result is a world in which there is no such thing as good or evil, but merely difference of perspective; and so, by moral and cultural default, what is left is the free market of the bright, commercial id.

A world defined by neither good nor evil but merely by a sort of gregarious multicultural difference of perspective is an admirable ideal, but also a potentially dangerous fantasy, a neverland. Indiscriminate tolerance is dangerous if it disables the ability to recognize real evil when it shows itself. "Judgmental" becomes one of the dirty words in the prelapsarian world as seen, for example, from *Sesame Street.* The world, so small, so diverse, so multi-ethnic, will be delivered from evil by an open-minded, innocent, good-humored curiosity—the child's purity of heart. This is a utopian vision of human nature—it dreams of training up a new generation of children by excising all the cancers of hatred and prejudice that contaminate the fallen world.

If only. It is difficult to sustain a child's faith in such a world when the same television screen where *Sesame Street* went about its business, a moment ago, now shows the World Trade Center collapsing. . . . Or erupts with other evil tidings of bomb blasts and dead children. Of little girls stolen from their beds in the middle of the night, and later found dead in the bushes. Of children drowned by their mother in the bathtub. Or of those sweet-looking men—Muhammad and Malvo, men with radiant faces, trusting and trustworthy, it would seem, if you judged by the photographs that the television kept showing, pictures that looked as if they were taken at a birthday party, or some other *Sesame Street* occasion—shooting down people at random from the back of their Chevrolet Caprice, their Batmobile. The child's world had grown cartoonishly surreal.

Globalization tends to strip the world of its inhibitions. The common denominator of the planet is human nature. And contrary to *Sesame Street,* the news about human nature is not all good.

INFORMAL LISTS OF THE all-time most evil people in history tend to be weighted in favor of public monsters, macro-murderers: Torquemada, Vlad the Impaler, Hitler, Eichmann, Pol Pot, Mao Tse-tung, Idi Amin, Stalin, Genghis Khan, Ceaucescu. Micro-murderers such as H. H. Holmes, a nineteenth-century London serial killer, and Gilles de Rai are included as spectacular curiosities, as items of entertainingly horrifying gossip.

Those old enough to remember World War II tend to think of the Nazis and the Holocaust as the baseline of evil. The twentieth century witnessed so many eruptions of evil that they formed a virtual continuum—the Armenian genocide; the apocalyptic famine that Stalin imposed upon the Ukrainians in 1930–1931, killing some ten million of them; Stalin's Great Terror of 1936–1938 (Stalin was no doubt responsible for more death than Hitler, if one reckons evil by numbers); the Pol Pot genocide in Cambodia; the Rwandan slaughters; various horrors in the Balkans. An archipelago of genocide.

In most people's minds, the least ambiguous case seemed to be that of Hitler. About him one would hear little argument. Hitler became evil's icon, its *ne plus ultra*. (Stalin's evil was harder for Americans to see, since he was after all a wartime ally—against Hitler—and, in those photographs at Yalta, was seated like an equal partner-in-virtue with Franklin Roosevelt, the American all-daddy, and indomitable Winston Churchill, lion and resister of evil. How morally confusing those graphics were: Stalin, enemy of our enemy, Hitler, was our friend, but was also an astonishingly evil man; but to judge Stalin as evil at that point would be to judge ourselves to be in some degree evil by association, and so Americans half-consciously wrote down Uncle Joe as at worst a necessary evil and, at best, a champion of anti-fascism, about whom nasty whispers might be heard from time to time in an imperfect world).

But the case against Hitler was pure and unambiguous. Indeed, it seems impossible today to talk about Hitler and his systematic effort to exterminate the Jews of Europe without unapologetic recourse to the idea of evil.

Occasionally, in an effort to locate true evil, uncomplicated by relativism, the people I questioned would look to the past, before the concept had been exiled, and would convict Hitler of evil, no question, and would add, with a gravity that seemed hilarious, as if they were scrupulously answering cross-examination under oath: "But of course, I didn't know him." The unstated thought being, presumably, that "If I had known Hitler, it is possible I might reconsider my view, and even take into account mitigating circumstances." Hitler's unhappy childhood, perhaps, or the deranging effects of mustard gas and his long service in the trenches during World War I.

That brought up another fascinatingly universal fallacy regarding evil—that if you get to know someone personally, the chances are you will see something good in him and discover your common humanity: You will find it difficult, in any case, to apply such a scathing word as "evil" to the personable guy with whom you have spent the weekend at, say, Berchtesgaden. There are in existence sweet pictures of Hitler up there in the piney mountains, nuzzling his German shepherd Schatzi, clearly a love relationship. Can Schatzi have been so wrong? If Hitler was good enough for Schatzi, then how could he be all bad? Evil often has a sense of public relations and photo opportunities: People do not expect evil is be nice, or familiar.

This is another awakening: People who do evil are often quite charming.

When the evidence is in—the mutilated bodies—those who knew the mutilator, back before the crimes were discovered, will tell a reporter incredulously: "But he was such a nice man."

Dr. Jekyll was an admirable figure. Who knew about Mr. Hyde? There is a Ted Bundy charm effect that is part of evil's sleight of hand. If the evil person occupies a position of power, it often happens that people of lesser power are flattered—and relieved—to find themselves treated kindly, warmly, humanly, by the great man. If you hear terrible things about him, and then he treats you well, you come away saying what people almost always say, "What a fine man! People have him all wrong!" Nikita Khrushchev's biographer, the political scientist William Taubman, has described the young Khrushchev's star-struck complicity in some of Stalin's crimes during the thirties. That period, one of the blackest in Russian history, represented Khrushchev's personal golden age, the time when he rose from petty party functionary to being a kind of personal pet of the *vozhd*, the great leader. As Taubman writes, "[Khrushchev's] complicity in great crimes was rooted in more than belief in the cause, or hope for advancement, or fear of prison or death. It was tied to nothing less than his own sense of self-worth, to his growing feeling of dignity, to the invigorating, intoxicating conviction that Stalin, a man he came almost to worship, admired him in return."

And so in January 1937, during one of Stalin's show trials, Khrushchev told an audience of some 200,000 Muscovites in

Red Square: "The stench of carrion rises from the vile, base Trotskyite degenerates. . . . Stalin is our banner! Stalin is our will! Stalin is our victory!" As Taubman notes, Khrushchev "assisted in the arrest and liquidation of his own colleagues and friends." He could not or would not prevent even his closest and most trusted associates from being arrested and shot. Khrushchev, who eventually began the Soviet Union's process of de-Stalinization, only partially acknowledged his part in the evil of the thirties. He wrote in his memoirs: "We were convinced then that Stalin could not be mistaken."

WHEN WILLIAM F. BUCKLEY, JR., was a young man, he knew Joe McCarthy well, and collaborated, with his (Buckley's) brother-in-law, on a book defending him.

I asked Buckley one Sunday afternoon nearly a half a century later, whether he had ever known anyone whom he considered to be evil.

Buckley did not hesitate. He said, as if the case were self-evident: "Well, Gore Vidal."

He looked at me. I could see that he was serious.

I have not had the opportunity to ask Gore Vidal if he considered William F. Buckley, Jr., to be evil. Long ago in the sixties, Buckley and Vidal confronted one another, like Chinese Gordon and the Mahdi, in a television studio where they were doing live commentary on the 1968 Democratic convention.

Vidal called Buckley a "Nazi." Buckley called Vidal a "fag." Both of them smelled evil. Which is not to say that both of them were wrong. Almost everyone reading this would say—the house dividing along political/cultural lines—that one of the men was wrong and the other was right.

You see the problem in our time: the matter of evil has seemed to pass from the theater of the theological, which deals in absolutes, to the theater of the political, which deals in opinions. Politicians use the word "evil" in an attempt to make their political opinions seem larger—absolute.

The Buckley-Vidal exchange was a trivial piece of celebrity theater, of course, and yet it dramatized the problem: How can such a thing as evil exist when it is merely a question of political opinion and—who knows?—even merely of different lifestyles?

EVIL CHARACTERS (Iago, Claudius, Claggert, Simon Legree, for example) flourish in literature, which isolates and heightens traits of character and creates personalities to embody abstractions. John Milton gave evil indelible form as Lucifer. But people in actual life rarely present themselves with such abstract moral clarity.

Instead of asking people if they had known anyone who was evil, I should perhaps have asked them, "Is this an evil world?"

The answer of course depends on which world you inhabit. Just after the turn of the millennium, by one count, there were 27 armed conflicts going on around the world; 1.2 billion people were living on less than a dollar a day; 2.4 billion had no access to basic sanitation. AIDS was devastating Africa and parts of Asia. This raises questions: Does poverty equal evil? Does war equal evil?

The contexts of poverty and war engender acts of evil as naturally as a master's systematic cruelty produces a vicious dog. Journalists and humanitarian workers who go from one war to another (from Bosnia to Rwanda to Chechnya to Angola to Afghanistan to the West Bank and Israel—the long march, the millennium's stations of the cross) see acts of wanton atrocity so ingenious, so gratuitous, so stupendously heartless, that it seems as if a trap door has opened at the bottom of human nature, and ordinary people have fallen through it, into an abyss. In his book *A Bed for the Night,* the author David Rieff notes:

One of the most important things that has happened over the course of the past fifty years is that the world has increasingly become divided into three parts. There is the small, underpopulated commonwealth of peace and plenty that is North America, most of Europe, and Japan; there is the part made up of Latin America, the former Soviet Union, China and India, in which wealth and poverty coexist and where the future is unclear; and finally, above all in sub-Saharan Africa and an area stretching from Algeria to Pakistan, there is a vast, teeming dystopia of war and want whose future no decent and properly informed person should be able to contemplate without sadness, outrage, and fear.

The answer to my question "Is this an evil world?" depends not only upon which world you inhabit, but upon which world you have understood, and come to fear. Since September 11, 2001, there has been a convergence of the worlds: Teeming dystopias visit fire and death upon the lands of peace and plenty. Religious fanaticism makes war across borders.

"Evil" is, of course, the word we use when we are horrified and fearful: But we must relearn the truth that our horror and our fear do not make the word evil inaccurate. On the contrary. Horror and fear may be entirely rational. If evil does not cause horror and fear, then some part of your humanity has died. Language keeps pace, and transcribes what it witnesses. We know evil by its works. It defines itself. Good is what ought to be; evil is what ought not to be. Do not trouble yourself overmuch about the definition of evil.

Evil is almost always a manifestation of power; the global, democratic accessibility of the instruments of destruction makes every man a king. Micro and macro have met before: Stalin and Hitler were mutilators of dolls on the grandest scale. Ted Kaczynski, the Unabomber, another forest hermit, was a prophet of things to come; his death toll (three) was minuscule compared to that of September 11, and that of September 11 no doubt will be remembered as insignificant compared to the destruction that will be possible when the globalization and democratization of the instruments of mass murder realize their full potential.

I have used the word "evil" to describe both the hermit's impulses (not different, in intention, from Jack the Ripper's mutilating compulsions) and the designs of ambitious terrorists equipped with weapons of mass destruction (chemical, biological, nuclear). It's difficult to talk about such dangerous and preoccupying matters without using the word "evil."

16

THE RATTLESNAKE
IN THE MAILBOX

EVIL TRIES TO BE COMPLICATED. Its methods are complicated—working by indirections and opposites, by mirror-effects and sleight of hand. If you want to see evil clearly, the thing to do is to keep it simple. Which means to look at it with a humane and steady gaze capable of penetrating to the essential. But to achieve clarity without dogmatism or bigotry, to find simplicity without simplism, is one of the toughest jobs of the moral intelligence. And of course it becomes infinitely harder in a globalized, mobile, highly diverse world. The word "evil," it may be, originated in homogeneous tribal contexts; it is a word that implies, even demands, consensus. The roots of the word in Old English *(yvel)* suggest "exceeding due measure" or "overstepping proper limits." What happens to the idea of evil in a commercially interlocking but morally and culturally fragmented world?

Does evil have the same meaning in the new dimension, in the newly globalized world, that it had in the old? Is the word "evil" still useful? Or should we find some other term to help us think about it?

For evil is an absolute, and if, in our age, absolutism is the enemy and the great danger—absolutism is the terrible energy of zealots—then do we not require a more civilizing and discriminating term?

Or is it the case that any lesser, weaker word would be a fatuous, dangerous compromise and an evasion of the truth of human nature and the way of the world? "Evil" is the word we use when we come to the limit of humane comprehension. But we sometimes suspect that it is the core of our true selves. Nathaniel Hawthorne's Everyman, Young Goodman Brown, goes to a satanic meeting in a dark wood, and the devil declares, "Evil is the nature of mankind. Welcome again, my children, to the communion of your race."

Every age, it may be, gets the evil that is appropriate to it.

If there is a new dimension in the world, is there a new evil? I would say that evil, an old and familiar force in the world, manifests itself in new, potentially apocalyptic ways, because of the ease with which tribal grievance or individual psychosis (or both) may go public—go global, even—and cause mass death and destroy the institutions of civilized society (civil liberties, freedom, tolerance).

What is new are the newly instantaneous and global consequences of the old dynamics of evil, which has always been a drama of power, abuse, grievance, retaliation. In this new dimension, it will not do to dismiss the idea of evil in the old way, by saying it is relative—that one man's evil terrorist is another man's martyr/patriot, or that mass murderers are not evil at all but probably were themselves abused as children.

The old way of dismissing the idea of evil involved an unconscious misreading of Terence's famous line, the very slogan of cosmopolitan tolerance: Nothing human is foreign to me.

The embrace of this welcome to all human oddity and quid-dity suggests, from another age, Walt Whitman, or, from our own age, an Eden of unshockable comparative sociology and psy-chology in which one hundred flowers, some of them admittedly poisonous, may bloom, but in none of which you will not detect any trace of evil.

There is not a little smugness in the dismissal of the idea of evil. The dismissers, saying nothing human is foreign to me, sug-gest (smugly) that those who believe in evil, and use terms like evil or evildoers are, in fact, primitives who mean to say, nothing foreign is human to me.

But the misreading, the fallacy, consists in this: Evil is entirely human. Not only have enlightenment and progress not expunged evil from the world, but, as we see, the products of enlightenment and progress—the worldwide web, nuclear energy, global communications, porous and tolerant democracy itself—have empowered evil to the point that it now threatens everything. The globalization of evil corrupts the future—threatens, indeed, to annul it—and sets in motion a new world characterized by the chronic anxiety of imminent surprise, an expectation that evil (the uncontrollable bad, jack-in-the-box destroyer) waits on the other side of the next tick of the clock. The apocalyptic expectation destroys not only peace of mind but the linear stability of all life and expectation, so that what exists on this side of the tick (my life, my home, my job, my hope, my plans for supper) can no longer be expected to be there on the other side of the tick. A blinding flash may intervene. There is a rattlesnake in the mailbox. There is anthrax in the envelope, and smallpox in the air. We will come to live in a maelstrom of con-tingency, a chaos that cannot be managed.

Will we hesitate to describe that world as evil?

The rich and safe are privileged to dismiss the idea of evil. Their insulation from evil effects persuades them that evil is a chimaera of the primitive. The servants and the know-nothings believe in evil.

But when the insulation grows thin—when cushioning political and economic power decline, or physical safety is no longer certain—and when this happens on a global scale, then the question of evil, the problem of evil, returns, as fresh and disturbing as when it sauntered into the first chapter of the Book of Job.

Evil re-enters history. A vibration of that violent re-entry passed through the Roman Catholic Church not long ago with the exposure of sexually abusive priests. Some floodboards of the church were taken up, and in the secret compartments revealed there were fetid secrets more evil than those of the hermit in his hunter's cabin.

Sexual crimes against the most innocent lambs in the flock are a catastrophe for the authority and moral geometry of the Church. Faith ascends on a vertical axis, to God. The vertical is supported by a horizontal axis—by trust, which is the everyday, stabilizing dynamic of a living church. If trust dissolves into doubt and disgust, if God's representatives on earth (keepers of faith and morals, interpreters of God's will on matters such as marriage, divorce, birth control, abortion, homosexuality, capital punishment, and social justice) turn out to be, many of them, child molesters and protectors of child molesters, then who will ever see such men at their priestly work—consecrating the body and blood of Christ, or whispering through the grill in the dusk of the confessional—without suspicion and unbidden loathing?

The little dog Toto takes the curtain in his teeth, tugs it aside, and gives the world a glimpse of the Wizard of Oz. The wizard turns out to be a pretty seedy character. So with the priests. To claim supernatural powers, and then to be caught in sordid acts—sexually abusing children or, even worse, shielding the abusers, so that they remain free to go on doing what they were doing—is not only a moral problem. It is a near-fatal professional error.

In the collapse of Enron and other corporations just after the millennium, one saw analogous institutional collapse and a similar shock to faith—not religious faith this time, but financial, social, and cultural faiths. Financial markets after all operate on faith that often enough proves to be fairly skittish and primitive. Markets are not rational, but, on the contrary, superstitious and almost infantile in their inclination to panic. A collapse of faith in the markets, if radical enough, and global, opens a trapdoor upon yet another dimension of chaos, wherein unarguably evil characters will emerge—"evildoers" indeed—and do terrible harm in the world.

In the meantime, Americans and others in the West absorb a relentless background noise of sensationalized individual dramas of micro-evil—adults murdering children (a housewife drowns her five children in Houston, for example), of children murdering adults (the King brothers beat their father to death with a baseball bat). Or they witness the micro- to macro-spectacle of the Washington, D.C., snipers, a bizarre Batman and Robin team who shot 14 people at random over a period of five weeks, firing a Bushmaster rifle from a slot in the trunk of their Batmobile, a shabby Chevrolet Caprice, and almost immobilizing an enormous metropolitan area, and costing the taxpayers millions in expenses for police and other law enforcement.

In all of this, saturation media coverage trivializes—routinizes, banalizes—evil at an astonishing rate. An abundance of horrifying, sensational cases and their media exploitation adds to a growing American sense of excess and self-disgust, the feeling of a soap opera in which everything is allowed and nothing is quite forbidden, and the culture itself is on the prowl, searching for new forbidden zones to transgress.

17

PERMISSIBLE EVIL

THE ANCIENT LAWS OF IRELAND made a distinction between "necessary murder" (which was either unpremeditated or done in self-defense or to exact revenge) and "unnecessary murder" (done for motives of gain). Beyond what has become the familiar idea of necessary evil lies the landscape of permissible evil—which has become the world's functioning workaday policy of evil, the framework within which we operate as a practical matter.

Permissible evil has the sanction of custom and experience. It is the human compromise with a force otherwise too corrupting, too radioactive, too horrifying, for ordinary life to tolerate. Permissible evil accommodates hypocrisy and, in doing so, domesticates evil. Permissible evil is the evil we can live with. It allows us to escape from the intimidating absolute that the word "evil," used alone, implies.

To kill is evil, we agree—the pithiest and least ambiguous of Commandments. But killing under certain circumstances—lots of circumstances, really—falls under the heading of permissible evil. In a "just" war, for example. (Nations and people do not parse too closely the Augustinian conditions of a just war when it is their own behavior that is under discussion; as a rule they simply consider that if they are waging war, it is for the moment anyway to be regarded as just. Rarely do warmakers think of their crusade as unjust.)

Or in the administration of capital punishment. Even when capital punishment cannot be demonstrated to be necessary (after all, the murderer could easily be imprisoned for the rest of his life if the idea is to keep him from killing again), there seems to be a superseding view, among the majority of Americans, for example, that executing the killer is, if not necessary, then permissible and for various reasons, not only satisfying but also socially wholesome, in a rough kind of way. Killing is evil, but by the Newtonian logic of proportionate action and reaction, putting the murderer to death seems to be fitting, seems (to our inner folkloric calculations of right and wrong) to be just, and therefore permissible. But these calculations are not made *sub specie aeternitatis,* but rather on a sliding scale of changeable social conditions and moods. A society that would accept public hanging as part of the normal course of criminal justice may, in a generation or two, come to think the practice barbaric.

The policy—the attitude—of permissible evil is human nature as it behaves in the flow of history. Permissible evil might as easily be called adaptable evil.

So, for example, the retributive function of justice, exercised in the name of outraged society, overrides the prohibition against killing, even though that prohibition comes with nothing less than the warrant of Sinai.

So, war makes evil permissible. So, at its worst, does religion, which, like war, has its rationales of righteousness and grants itself moral indulgences. So does cultural and social and political fashion (which may countenance capital punishment, as it once did for the evil of slavery).

If evil becomes "permissible," is it still . . . evil?

Perhaps, though it is no longer recognizable as such: Permissibility, like necessity, launders evil. The evil of killing is transformed by war—unless one loses the war, of course, in which case, the killers may be charged with war crimes: that is, killing reverts to the status quo ante, and becomes evil again, for purposes of the prosecuting victor.

It is presumably evil to incinerate a city filled with innocent civilians—as the allies in World War II incinerated Hiroshima and Nagasaki, Tokyo and Dresden and Hamburg.

But these evil incinerations became permissible in the context of the war: the evils of Hitlerism and Japanese militarism served to neutralize sharp moral judgments of the evils done in retaliation and served to silence (almost to silence) bad conscience later.

Acts of immense evil, like the deliberate incineration of a city and the murder of tens of thousands of innocent civilians, may lose the character of evil when those acts are compared with the evil acts of the enemy, which in the case of the Nazis and the Japanese in World War II were, arguably, considerably more atrocious (Auschwitz, for example, or the rape of Nanking) and in any case were at the moral disadvantage of having been committed first. The aggressor commits evil; the victim's retaliation represents justice.

What is the law then? That the atrocious act committed in retaliation for great evil is permissible and therefore, somehow, not evil? If you initiate the evil, you are evil; but if you reply to evil with more evil, then that retaliation is not evil, but something else?

What if the atrocious retaliation was not necessary? What if it was merely . . . understandable? Gratifying? What if it was useful in some secondary way, as psychological warfare, for example—

harsh punishment inflicted to break the enemy's morale (as, say, Sherman's devastating march across Georgia in 1864 was designed to crush the Confederate will to go on fighting)?

Americans have historically granted themselves a considerable range of permissible evil. Slavery was for generations after the Declaration of Independence ("that all men are created equal, that they are endowed by their Creator with certain unalienable Rights . . . ") judged to be a permissible evil. The displacement and (in the case of many tribes, such as the Comanche) the extermination of the Indians fell somewhere in the zone of the American conscience between necessary evil and permissible evil.

For several generations after World War II, enormously overindulgent consumption and the spoliation of environment by the waste of a throwaway culture have been thought of as permissible evils—permissible because of the virtue of America in rescuing the world from evildoers in World War II and because of the nation's self-conception as a beacon of liberty and refuge for immigrants fleeing evil regimes. Postwar Americans, remembering bitterly the Great Depression of their youth, built an exuberantly wasteful consumer society upon the older American premise of endless space and resources—an industrial version of the nineteenth-century expansion that wiped out the buffalo and deforested the upper midwest. The old premise arose from the essential American promise of God's providence and the implicit inexhaustibility of the continent, the free lunch, the vast buffet.

The American acceptance of permissible evil arises from the nation's immensely flattering conception of itself. Who is to blame a country of such virtue—divinely sponsored from its very origins—for certain inconsistencies and imperfections? Riverboat pilots on the Mississippi know that the great flowing force of the central channel creates, along the banks, swirling countercurrents that actually push upstream: So it is with the flowing force of American history: Slavery and those other negatives are like the minor eddies and counterflows of the mighty, virtuous story.

Who "permits" permissible evil? In a nation sponsored by God, permissible evil means that no less an authority than God Himself permits it to be done—just as in the world at large, God who is all-good and all-powerful permits evil to occur, creating, in that apparent contradiction, the conundrum of theodicy.

George W. Bush's rationale for the invasion of Iraq in 2003 rested crucially on the argument that it was a necessary evil. Critics of the invasion felt that, on the contrary, it fell within the morally suspect American zone of merely permissible evil—permissible meaning that the Americans gave themselves permission for it, drawing upon their immense resources of divine approval, the trust fund that God gave them when they started out.

What makes "permissible evil" such a useful, such an indispensable idea is the wondrous flexibility and range of "permissibility."

"Evil" is a powerful, absolute word. "Permissible" brings evil into a comfort zone, so to speak. To say "permissible evil" is like saying "atoms for peace" or "nuclear power plant." The terrifying absolute of "nuclear" is harnessed to daily use.

And permissibility generally means that you permit yourself to do something that you have grave moral doubts about—doubts that, in the course of calculating advantage and disadvantage, you have overcome. Permissibility opens a working space, a sort of twilight, between the absolute dark of evil and the moral clarity of unambiguous day.

Permissible evil means something we can live with—even if, perhaps, the other guy cannot.

The most difficult judgments we must make in the world are not so often between good and evil (those are pretty clear) as between permissible evil and impermissible evil.

We have no trouble deciding that Auschwitz was, to say the least, impermissible evil.

But what of Hiroshima?

Who judges whether Hiroshima was permissible or impermissible? Harry Truman? American troops in August 1945 steaming toward Japan for what promised to be a fight to the death for the home islands? The Japanese schoolgirl I talked to many years later, in the 1980s, who was collecting roof tiles that morning with her schoolmates and suddenly saw the entire world catch fire and turn to radiant ash and the river of corpses? What does God say about Hiroshima?

The usual Hiroshima argument turns on the question of whether the Japanese were on the point of surrendering anyway: Was the bomb necessary in order to stop the war immediately?

But suppose that it could be proved with certainty that the Japanese would not have surrendered for many months—could be proved that taking the home islands by invasion would have cost the lives of, say, 700,000 American troops and of millions of Japanese. If that kind of anticipated carnage could be proved with certainty, would that have made the use of the atom bomb permissible?

And if so, does that mean that the calculation of permissibility is a matter of the arithmetic of corpses? Does one simply add up the anticipated casualties from atomic bomb blasts at Hiroshima and Nagasaki and compare them to anticipated casualties from an invasion of the home islands, and opt for the lower figure?

That kind of brutal arithmetic—necessarily imprecise, since who can count corpses beforehand, or see very far into the cloud of violent contingency that is war?—dramatizes the calculation of permissible evil.

This calculation implies, of course, a decent respect for the opinions of mankind—or for the opinions of God. Or for the opinions of history.

Something in our conscience—a sense of shame, perhaps—seeks to protect us from human nature, which is ruthlessly self-interested and self-absorbed, and does not ask anxious questions about possible enemy casualties. Human nature, at war and armed with nuclear weapons, working at its own survival and persuaded (as a sort of charming but unnecessary bonus) that it is in the right, achieves an annihilating focus.

Evil is so often an act of power: We assume that the greatest potential for evil in the world lies with the most powerful, working on the Caligula paradigm: "Remember that I can do anything to anyone."

Yet when we look at nuclear weapons in the new dimension of the world—in the context of globalized proliferation—a different dynamic presents itself: the annihilating possibilities of weakness.

The Cold War superpowers, America and the Soviet Union, achieved over the decades a self-policing equilibrium of power: mutual assured destruction, as it was called, a metaphysically loathsome state of affairs that, as it happened, worked out: two nuclear negatives producing the positive of peace.

But when weak, even desperate, states like North Korea acquire nuclear weapons, it is essentially to alter the framework of one's thinking—to forget for a moment the evils of great power and to consider instead the dangers and the evils that arise from weakness—or rather, from weakness that is narrowly empowered. Beware the angry impoverished man who suddenly can express himself through this one deadly, all-promising thing, the evil djinn. Nuclear weapons level the playing field as nothing else. They make the poor little man a god, with God's discretion to destroy, massively.

Weakness can be just as evil as power—sometimes more so. All power corrupts, and absolute power corrupts absolutely. But weakness corrupts too; weakness has its own style of evil.

And when weakness acquires nuclear weapons, it has none of the self-restraints, the superego, that is, at best, found in great power. Weakness is a victim, and the victim always judges himself to be justified in anything he may do by way of self-defense or retaliation. The psychology of the victim in an age of globalized nuclear arms has become one of the greatest dangers in history.

18

TAKING RESPONSIBILITY FOR THE REGIME

ARE PEOPLE RESPONSIBLE for their own evil regimes—for their own governments and the evil that they do?

No one would say that the Dunblane children were responsible for the evil that killed them. They had not the knowledge or the power to prevent it; they were entirely victims. But evil is in some sense a continuum: At one end is the entirely powerful victim, and at the other there is complete complicity—there is Pétain, and Vichy, just barely on the victim side of the who-whom of evil.

Were Iraqis responsible for Saddam Hussein's government?

Were the Germans responsible for Hitler and the Nazis?

Democracy means responsibility. The voters who install a government in power become responsible for it, do they not? In 1933, the German voters brought Hitler into power, and then he used legal machinery to obtain emergency powers and to abrogate the democratic process by which he had come to office.

Presumably, that let the Germans off the hook. They now became, themselves, victims of a ruthless dictatorship.

Except that the German people by and large acquiesced in what Hitler was doing, accepted it, approved of it, embraced it. They delighted in his accomplishments for Germany—the restoration of the German economy and German national pride after the terrible humiliation of the loss of the Great War and the impositions of the Versailles Treaty. They profited by his policies and endorsed them. They knew the thuggishness and anti-Semitism of the regime, and they either endorsed it or turned a blind eye to it.

Who is responsible for evil? Some external power, satanic, malignant? The person who does the evil act? The people who enable the evildoer? Those who are indifferent to evil?

Responsibility is a somewhat neglected idea. A consumer society, now gone global, operates on the premise of what might be called discretionary passivity, on a massive scale.

Billions are spent upon trying to induce consumers to buy, say, a Ford instead of a Honda. The mass audience, inundated for generations by such gaudy appeals, acquires a sense of passivity and entitlement: The consumer need not act, exactly, but rather merely obeys a whim of choice—a Heineken instead of a Lowenbrau or a Kirin or a Budweiser. Consumers in the developed world acquire a sense of passive comfort and entitlement that subtly disables the sense of responsibility; everything is brought to the consumer packaged neatly, the meat under the clingwrap, and very very far from its original source. A sense of responsibility—even the context of responsibility—atrophies.

Political acts of evil by definition implicate others—sometimes whole nations. The degree of responsibility involved must be calibrated—imprecisely—by degrees of power, knowledge, and intention.

What do people know about the evil? (What did the Germans know about the Nazi death camps?) What power do they have to change it? (Could the Germans have stopped Hitler? When?) Have they chosen this evil? Have they acquiesced in it once they knew of its existence? Are they themselves complicit in the evil if they know about it and yet decline to act against it? Are they obliged to act against evil even at the risk of their own lives and fortunes? At the risk of their families' lives?

How do we judge an artful and instinctively willful ignorance? How to judge the degree of complicit evil of those who sus-pect—and this is how it usually happens—something evil is afoot, and who, by subtle reflex, by a distinct early warning per-sonal radar, sidestep the knowledge of it, avert their gaze, and distance themselves from the immediate circumstances that might require them to act? They sense trouble coming, and they step around the corner. They absolve themselves by absenting themselves—their absence means, they sense, that they escape the gravitational field of responsibility.

Among other things, this raises complex questions about the United States and its responsibilities as the world's sole super-power. What is the American people's guilt if the American gov-ernment intervenes wrongly, immorally, even evilly, in some other part of the world? On the other hand, what is the Ameri-can people's guilt if their government fails to act? Were the U.S. government and the American people complicit in the evil acts of genocide committed in Rwanda in 1994 because the Clinton administration refused to act?

Realpolitik does not like the word "evil," for it imposes dis-orderly imperatives and a standard of absolute morals that is dif-ficult to sustain in the fallen real world. National interests must override absolute moral interests. Only God can remove evil from the world, presumably—or he could if he wished to do so—and until that ultimate intervention, politicians and nations must find ways. Genocide is an absolute word—a howl of a word—signifying an evil that transcends mere national interest and demands intervention to stop it. But nations, even the most idealistic, very rarely step in to stop genocide They quibble about whether the evil at hand really "rises to the level"—as they put it—of true genocide. In her book *A Problem from Hell: America in the Age of Genocide,* Samantha Power painstakingly reviews the performance of the world's powers in the face of the genocides of the twentieth century, starting with Turkey in 1915–1916 and going through Rwanda. In every case, Power found, the United States and others who might have stopped genocide declined to intervene, or only acted after it was too late. At its worst, bureaucracy tends to resist moral action-and at its very worst, as with Eichmann, it remorselessly implements evil by paperwork.

It is curious to contemplate the different ways in which we judge the complicity of Germans in the acts of the Nazi regime as compared with the involvement of the people of the Soviet Union in the evil crimes of Stalin.

History tends to consider that the people in the Soviet Union were the victims of Stalin, whereas the people of Germany (the non-Jews) were judged to be the accomplices of Hitler.

This is surely slightly odd. Stalin maintained his absolute power for so many years (17 more than Hitler) through the most ruthless corruption of his own people, turning them into a vast army of informers and government stooges. So strangely thorough was his moral contamination of the people that during the Moscow show trials, defendants willingly embraced charges against them that they, and everyone else, knew to be entirely false. Parents informed against children, and children against parents. Everyone was victim of the evil, and almost everyone was stained by it.

The great Nazi crime was its program of industrial genocide, aimed at the extermination of Europe's Jews. The Holocaust seemed indisputably evil, whereas, without the Holocaust, Hitler's other ambitions—to conquer Western Europe and subsume it into a Thousand-Year Reich—might have fallen into the same moral category as Napoleon's or Alexander's campaigns: megalomaniac, immensely destructive, to be sure, and horrifying in detail, yet somehow not absolutely and entirely evil. Both Napoleon and Alexander committed many evil acts, but the sum of their bloody careers is mitigated in historical memory by their mystique of personal glory and by various cultural positives. Napoleon, for example, committed widespread slaughters and atrocities when he came to Egypt, but his strange expedition there also resulted in immense accomplishments of scholarship, including the deciphering of the Rosetta Stone. Would Hitler, if he had not pursued the Final Solution, have been remembered in the same category—a destructive conqueror, but not altogether a Satanic figure?

Stalin committed genocide against his own people—against virtually all classes and ethnic categories of his own people—scientists, artists, military people, professionals, peasants: a highly democratic program of persecution and extermination. Somehow the fact that Stalin's victims came from every avenue of Soviet life serves to exonerate the Soviet people of his evil; whereas the way that the Nazis, with the tacit acquiescence or even active participation of gentile Germans, targeted the Jews for systematic liquidation, serves to indict the Germans as a nation for complicity in Hitler's evil.

At the same time, a lingering sympathy among Western intellectuals for the project of Soviet Communism, which had such powerful prestige in the thirties, before Stalin's crimes became known, has encouraged a somewhat softer judgment of the evils of Soviet totalitarianism. The Nazi system itself was judged to be evil, along with Hitler. But while Stalin's evil is difficult to dispute, the Soviet system itself has often been half-exonerated, the beneficiary of a nostalgic idealism that many intellectuals in the West have been reluctant to repudiate as evil. Out of residual sentiment, they avert their gaze.

19

OFFICE MALIGNITIES

NOT LONG AGO, in the art history department of an Ivy
League university, there worked a woman who had two children
and an unemployed husband. The husband, a Ph.D. in philosophy, could not find steady work. He taught now and then, but
mostly stayed home to care for the children.

His wife, an art historian, was named Virginia. She was brilliant and attractive, and worked in an administrative job in the
department. She was the sole support of her family.

The head of the department was an overweight, middle-aged
man, unhappily married. He began an office affair with his
department's administrative supervisor, a woman in her thirties.
The affair, which everyone in the department knew about, gave
power to the supervisor. She began interpreting the department
to her lover, guiding his decisions and attitudes. She let it be
known, subtly, that when she spoke, it was with the authority of
the chairman himself.

The supervisor hated Virginia, the art historian, who was educated, good-looking, and vulnerable.

One day the supervisor sent an E-mail to Virginia. It said, "Who was Thomas Cole?"

Virginia knew perfectly well who Thomas Cole was, of course. For the sake of speed, she went onto a search engine on the Internet, found Thomas Cole, and copied a short biography which she sent to the supervisor:

> Thomas Cole was born in 1801 at Bolton, Lancashire in North-western England and emigrated with his family to the United States in 1818. During the early years Cole lived for short periods in Philadelphia, Ohio, and Pittsburgh where he worked as an itinerant portrait artist. Although primarily self-taught, Cole worked with members of the Philadelphia Academy, and his canvasses were included in the Academy's exhibitions.

> In 1825, Cole discovered the haunting beauty of the Catskills wilderness. His exhibition of small paintings of Catskills landscapes came to the attention of prominent figures on the New York City art scene including Asher B. Durand, who became a life-long friend and his fame spread. While he was still in his twenties, Cole was made a fellow of the National Academy.

And so on.

By return E-mail, the supervisor thanked Virginia. Then the supervisor went to the search engine herself, found the biography that Virginia had copied, printed it up, along with the E-mailed biography that Virginia had sent (the two items were of course identical)—and drafted a memo to the department chairman accusing Virginia of plagiarism.

The memorandum was inserted into Virginia's personnel file. Some weeks later she received formal notification from the university that a charge of plagiarism had been lodged against her.

On the advice of friends, she found a lawyer and filed suit. The money required to hire the lawyer drained her family's

already depleted resources. She won the suit. The accusation ᴏ
plagiarism was removed from her file.

But the department chairman and his lover now waged almost
daily office war upon Virginia, who could not afford to quit her
job, and of course could expect no further merit raises or other
signs of favor in the department. Virginia's health deteriorated.
Her nerves frayed. She began to rely on tranquilizers. Her life had
been poisoned. Why?

The story, which I heard from a friend of mine who tried to
help Virginia find another job, has the familiar feel of a certain
kind of modern office viciousness about it. The impulse to do
evil finds its expression in the places and situations at hand, even
in banal office jealousies.

Did the supervisor's malignant stunt rise to the level of evil?
Was it not perhaps merely a particularly dirty trick?

I sense, though somewhat faintly, the presence of evil in it.

There is first of all the cruelty of the act, and the gratuitousness of it. The accusation of plagiarism, not only totally
unfounded but utterly gratuitous, had serious consequences. To
be accused of plagiarism in the academic world is the equivalent
of being charged with child molesting; it is a virtually unforgivable sin. Virginia, as the supervisor knew, was both innocent and
vulnerable (evil enjoys expressing itself against the innocent and
vulnerable), because of the innocence and vulnerability of her
own children, whose home was endangered by the threat of their
mother's losing her job.

What convinced me of the evil of the act was the E-mail—the
offhanded innocence of the question ("Who was Thomas
Cole?"). People have implanted razor blades in apples that they
distributed on Halloween night to children trick-or-treating. The
E-mail had that touch of motiveless malignity, to use Coleridge's
expression. A boobytrap in the quotidian. You detect evil as
much by feel as by rational thought. In the midst of the Wash-

rea snipers' predations, one felt that evil gratu-
ised, covert element of evil glee.

...n the work of the very ordinary—the most ordi-
...y. It is a mistake to think that evil must emanate from people
of extraordinary cunning and even metaphysical brilliance—
characters like Iago. Instead, much evil is done by people as
small, as ordinary, as the supervisor. It is usually done precisely
because its authors feel so keenly their own smallness and ordinariness, and, it may be, wish to repair those defects in the only
way that small and ordinary minds can conceive to do the job: by
accomplishing something destructive. This is evil by way of Flem
Snopes—moral barn-burning.

The other evil, the grand, Shakespearean kind, the world-
historical evil, enacts itself on the public stage in large dramas of
war and genocide. But the chronic, daily form of evil is the sort
performed by the supervisor with her E-mail—not the mass
destruction of lives, but a common, unrecorded person-to-
person wickedness that goes on beneath the radar of history.

20

THE CONSOLATIONS
OF LITERATURE

I KNEW A WOMAN who suffered the sorrows of Job. Her son died by drowning on the night of his high school graduation. He had been drinking with his classmates at parties in New York after the graduation, and then they all went to Central Park. It was a hot night in early June. They decided to go swimming in the Central Park Lake. My friend's son swam far out, into the darkness, and his friends lost track of him, forgot about him in their general convivial drunkenness. He swam out into the blank of the night and after awhile, without a word, went into another dimension and was gone.

It was some time before the others realized that the boy was gone, and then they shouted and hooted, but were drunk enough themselves to imagine he might have simply walked off, gone home, passed out.

The next day the police dragged for his body in the lake. They brought him up in his rented tuxedo trousers.

That was the worst thing that happened. But the woman had been through much else. Her husband, a few years before, had told her that he had been living another, parallel life: He was gay, he said. He had a lover. He had spent years cruising gay bars and had found a man with whom he had fallen in love. He was leaving her to move in with his lover.

And so he did. The woman carried on alone, raising their son. The husband, a prep school mathematics teacher, sent child support money, and saw his son on weekends. The boy became depressed, smoked dope, drank. His father, with his lover, would take the boy out to dinner—the guys' night out—and the boy would drink too much and say things about "fags." Would make scenes, run out of restaurants into the night.

The husband's lover fell into a strange misadventure in the East Village one night—the details never did come clear—in the upshot of which, the lover was accused of murder. Someone died—I never understood who. The lover was there at the scene, in the middle of the night; cops came and arrested him.

And now the husband had a penniless lover in jail, charged with murder. The husband used whatever savings he had to hire a lawyer for his lover and help him beat the charge. The man was acquitted, and the husband was broke. And the lover left— packed up and vanished.

Not long after that, the husband began to suffer strange physical symptoms—odd pains in his backside, discharges of blood. He went to a doctor, and was diagnosed as having cancer.

The man, *in extremis,* returned to his wife, who took him back into their old apartment and escorted him to chemotherapy and nursed him through the nights that followed.

And it was at that point in the story that the boy graduated from high school and went to Central Park and swam floppingly out into the lake in his tuxedo trousers.

The woman told me the story—or part of it—one night at a dinner party, in one of those moments of intimacy when a stranger may confide painful secrets, as if partaking of a sacrament, as a sinner goes to confession and in the twilight of the little booth speaks through the grillwork to the gravely nodding priest in profile, the ear of God. I listened to the woman that night while sitting in the same attitude of nodding, thoughtful attention. Even the candles on the table seemed part of an ecclesiastical motif. She unburdened herself of evil. Now and then I would fill her wine glass, and my own (I was still drinking in those days), and the eight or ten other people around the table receded into the murmurous background—their faces animated, their hands gesticulating, one of the women now and then shrieking in laughter, but all of this occurring as if under water, in a different and subduing medium, a kind of slow motion.

We had started by talking about reading—about authors we liked to read. The woman understood perfectly what I meant when I said that there were certain writers I went to as steadying influences. I wanted to absorb their solidity, the confidence of their rhythms. I mentioned Edmund Wilson. I spoke of a different kind of morning energy that radiated from Emerson. In those years I read Emerson for a few minutes every day, as a priest resorts to his breviary.

The woman, whose name was Eleanor, said that Willa Cather had saved her life. I thought that was a turn of phrase, slightly extravagant, and so Eleanor said: "I began to read Willa Cather when I was having trouble—so much trouble that I would have lost my mind if I had not had something to hold onto. I would read Willa Cather very slowly. Her prose was so clear, so calm, so steadying, that I could read it for hours and find that I had gotten through some of the worst moments. Her writing kept me sane."

And then Eleanor told me about her son drowning in the lake, and about her husband's sexual apostasy, his lover and the murder and the cancer—the whole tragic soap opera. And over this real-life narrative of bad times there flowed the rinsing clarities of the prose of a writer dead for decades. It seemed to me that the action of Cather's writing upon Eleanor's anguished mind was itself sacramental—healing, the soothing touch of another mind upon one's own. There is much to be said for the consolations of literature.

In the years since that night when Eleanor told me about being saved by Willa Cather, I have thought about reading books as a response to evil. There is something to it—something of the old sense of enchanted words, of spells and priestly formulas *(apage Satanis!)* to keep off the bad things. Words are conjurations; there is a healing power in stories, if only because words take us away to other lives and places—the consolations of alternatives are, if only temporarily, a way of thwarting fate.

I am a romantic about the power of words, and think of Anna Akhmatova helping to keep Stalingrad alive during the terrible siege of 1942–1943, when cannibalism was so well organized that there was a black market in human flesh, by reading poetry (her own and Pushkin's) over the radio. I think of the dissident Russians in the Gulag, with their desperate word-love. Some, like Andrei Sinyavski, would write out remembered passages of the Bible, or Shakespeare, on scraps of toilet paper and conceal the passages in their shoes, to read from time to time, as comfort, as a burst of secret, saving grace in the exceedingly evil universe of the Soviet camps.

Once in Grenada, I talked to a politician who had been imprisoned by the Marxist regime for three years—held in a cell far underground, in solitary confinement. The politician said that he persuaded a guard to let him have a pencil, and he wrote out on toilet paper every passage of the New Testament he could remember, every line of poetry. It was words that kept him alive for three years, White told me. The words worked against the evil somehow. I envisioned the words as a kind of life-giving air bubble that sustained a man trapped in a tunnel, in the political and moral cave-in of his once orderly world.

Perhaps there is no point in being too reverent about books. I do not doubt for a moment that words also do the work of the devil. *Mein Kampf* was—is—a book. So is *The Protocols of the Elders of Zion.* Print may bring you terrible conjurations of lies: black magic, in something of the way that music, which is capable of Bach and Mozart, may also stir demons.

I am not sure that technology has made an essential advance upon the magic of written words. In bad times, television does not seem to me much of a consolation. A diversion, maybe, but a debilitating one. Television transforms the world into a bright dust of electrons—noisy, and vaguely toxic to one's own brain waves and peace of mind. Turn on the set in the middle of the night to check on news from the war, and your lingering dreams float out to mingle with CNN. Dreams are not an electronic medium.

I had a friend who was a magazine correspondent. One day during the American presidential campaign of 1984, we were flying as part of the press pool aboard Air Force One, which carried Ronald Reagan to Bowling Green, Ohio, where he was to address a student rally. I asked the correspondent, Bill Stewart, how he passed the time when he was living in Beirut and covering the Israeli siege of the city in 1981. The artillery bombardment was also continuous, gunfire was everywhere. He was confined to the inner rooms of his apartment, away from windows.

He laughed and said, "I had a VCR, and watched the entire video series of *Brideshead Revisited,* over and over again."

He went into Evelyn Waugh's parallel universe, a metaphysical neverland of Anglo Catholic scruples and dreamy Oxbridge homoeroticism. All of that got Bill through, all right—although of course the video would have been ineffective if his apartment had taken a direct hit.

I do not say that the Book of Job or the New Testament or the collected works of Shakespeare or Keats would have been effective either, in the event of a direct hit. But I would trust only words to have apotropaic power—the force to ward off evil. Why did the prisoners I have mentioned have such desperate faith in words? I think that the words represented a sort of prayer, flowing in the opposite direction. Prayer is customarily thought of as human beings addressing words to God. In the cases I am speaking of, it was God addressing words to human beings. The prisoners cherished words as tokens of divinity, as verbal communion (the word was made flesh—*hic est corpus meum*), as God's message that they had not been forsaken, even in the dark, hopeless places where evil had put them.

The consolations of literature are the consolations of God. It seemed to me then that it was through words that God made his most persuasive promises. Words enabled patience, enabled hope. Words, patience, and hope kept evil at bay.

And keeping evil at bay seems to be the best that we can do with it in this world, since we have no evidence that evil can be extinguished. When the serpent, as Thoreau observed, is pushed down at one hole, it will pop up at another. In the world now, evil pops up at many holes simultaneously.

Yeats wrote: "Words alone are certain good." Is it true?

The folklore of common sense claims that words are cheap and easy things, not to be counted on: the vaporings of politicians. The deed is everything. The act is the truth; words, on the other hand, skitter off into landscapes of hypothesis, where they may be true or false.

And yet it is precisely the capacity to frame hypotheses that gives to words their aspect of divinity: articulate language partakes of the process of creation, and is, I suspect, our best evidence of the existence of God. The alchemy of articulation—whereby all things become ideas, and ideas become things (that is, words) and time is annulled through the legerdemain of narrative conjuration—puts an ignition of divinity into the speechless lump of the world, the mud, the dead rock, the desolation. You may have life without language, but not thought, I would guess.

Science, mathematics, may conduct their business in codes and specialized symbologies, without recourse to ordinary language, but the soul cannot be a specialist; specialization damages spiritual integrity, which can be achieved only as it aspires to universals. Specialization unlocks secrets of the universe—makes rockets fly to the moon or nuclear bombs fall to earth—and sees to the heart of all, to find there metaphors of beer suds and strings, or the double helix. On the other hand, evil rather likes the blindnesses and bafflements brought on by specialization. Specialization involves an exclusivity and, it may be, a certain manic focus, that evil finds congenial.

But formulations of good and evil, I think, and formulations of God and human conduct, must be conducted in the language of the human experience. Language is what we have. Words are our universal medium of exchange—our communion, the way that our ideas touch one another and clash and grope their way forward. Words are our meaning. Good and evil arise out of words.

If some African tribesmen (Hutu, let us say, living in Rwanda) undertake to kill some people of a rival tribe (Tutsi), and proceed to do so, the business will have no communicable meaning until it is reported and described, and no moral meaning, it may be, until it is characterized in language as "self-defense," or "blood feud," or "civil disorders," or "mass murder," or "genocide." Merely to videotape the killings would not be sufficient. A person, seeing such videotapes, cannot tell another person about what happened without beginning to quantify and characterize.

But the good and evil we are discussing must always be brought back to the simplicities and clarities of the daily world. Good and evil are a human business that must be discussed in human language. Good and evil must be tested constantly by common sense, which is, of course—along with patience, humor, hope, love—one of the indispensable weapons against evil. Specialization claims aristocracies of knowledge that tend to ridicule common sense.

In other words, the knowledge of evil—the ability to recognize evil and to judge it—belongs to mankind in general. Such knowledge requires experience rather than education, and simple clarity of mind rather than speculative genius. The knowledge of evil, I'd guess, is encoded in the DNA—an instinctive recognition, a collective unconscious circuitry of taboo. That people in every age monstrously transgress the circuitry is precisely in keeping with the nature of evil. But people everywhere seem to share a certain rough consensus. Don't believe anyone who makes excuses for evil. "Father, forgive them, they know not what they do," may serve, may contain some element of truth, in the extraordinary circumstances of people crucifying God himself but not quite understanding the magnitude of the deed, or the nature of the Man being executed. In general, however, people know well enough. And in any case we cannot decently proceed without assuming—without demanding—that each of us, including the most ordinary, knows good from evil. You may choose to do evil, but don't plead ignorance. To do so is beneath human dignity.

21

Us and Them

A GRISLY STORY—the torture and rape and murder of a child, for example—might so shake a person, so enrage him, that no explanation short of the absolute of evil would seem sufficient; the word "evil" is the capital punishment of the moral world—the anathema, the excommunication, the unforgivable—and in the shock of the first news about such cases, one tends to reach for that uncompromising word, as a form of retaliation, a way of stating that such behavior is so beyond the tabooed zones surrounding our beleaguered decencies that the person guilty of such transgressions must be pronounced irreclaimable—that is, evil—and cast into an outer darkness that he has, in any case, chosen for himself: as Lucifer chose evil and hell and darkness. This reaction—a categorical rejection, the gag reflex of the system—proclaims a healthy moral immune system, I would guess.

And a healthy immune system is ruthlessly intolerant. It wants to kill the thing that seeks to do evil to it. Evil is the invader that must be repelled; if it is not repelled, the body sickens and dies. If God did not expel Satan, then God would become evil himself, would he not? He would be infected, and sicken, and die.

Theodicy wonders: How can there be a God who is 1) all powerful and 2) all good, while 3) evil exists in the world. You can have any two of those propositions, but not all three.

A troubling solution to that puzzle flickers through the mind: Perhaps God himself is ill.

The human immune system, as it projects itself into tribal forms, social forms, programs of law and justice, is by instinct most intolerant of evils committed against children. An instrument measuring the human sense of evil, on a kind of Richter Scale, would doubtless register the strongest shocks, the most powerful waves of revulsion, when confronted by gruesome, violent crimes against children. Such crimes come closest to being unforgivable. The deepest imperative of life—its survival and transmission to the next generation—has been menaced and offended. Life organizes a posse and goes after the killer, working on this premise: When a force exerts itself to kill the young and innocent who are the transmitters of the DNA, then that force is by definition evil, and must be destroyed. The future of the human race depends upon it. So a recognition of evil, and a revulsion against it, is no doubt programmed into our genetic coding, in the same sequence as our instinct to reproduce and protect the young.

In the eyes of those I spoke with during my informal survey— civilized people—I almost always saw that their primitive, protective ruthlessness, savage in its first arousal, made war in their minds with a softer instinct—installed at some later stage of evolution—that called for tolerance and understanding, even of such murderers. Their judgment of the matter changed before my eyes, and became a butterfly: The crime was monstrous, it was conceded; and yet, and yet . . . the person who did it was not evil, but "sick."

In this distinction, evil became medical instead of medieval. The diagnosis was more enlightened, it was thought. It is the difference between saying, "The man is a paranoid schizophrenic, driven by homicidal delusions," and "The man is evil." The difference, of course, relates to responsibility and punishment. The paranoid schizophrenic is himself a victim, to be treated and, who knows, even reclaimed. The evil murderer is satanic in himself and must like Satan be cast out.

What is one's moral default mode? The ruthless instinct of the immune system, which tends to be primitive and absolute? Or the instinct of tolerance and reclamation? Is the immune system's reaction merely savage, or entirely necessary? Is the instinct of tolerance merely feckless, the response of overprivileged people whose defenses have been weakened by their years of being, well, immune from evil? It is in rich Western democracies that the denial of evil is strongest.

Hitler's own default mode, of course, was the instinct of the immune system. His race theories, which were coherent in their own psychotic way, were almost entirely based on the most primitive premise of Us and Them—Us great, Them awful, Us clean, Them filthy, Us gods, Them vermin.

On October 3, 1943, at the height of the Nazis' mechanized annihilation—the "peak of production," in their industrialized conception of the work—Heinrich Himmler, in a sort of mission statement to his SS, an amazingly candid document, the most murderous evil couched in terms curiously ingenuous and weirdly self-congratulatory, laid out the case for the German immune system. It is worth quoting at some length.

"One basic principle must be absolute for the SS man," he said.

We must be honest, decent, loyal, and comradely to members of our own blood, and to nobody else. What happens to the Rus-

sians, what happens to the Czechs, is a matter of total indifference to me. What there is among the nations in the way of good
blood of our kind, we will take for ourselves—if necessary, by
kidnapping their children and raising them among us. Whether
the other nations live in prosperity or croak from hunger interests me only insofar as we need them for slaves for our culture;
otherwise, it does not interest me. Whether 10,000 Russian
females drop from exhaustion while building an anti-tank ditch
interests me only insofar as the anti-tank ditch gets finished for
Germany's sake. We shall never be brutal and heartless where it
is not necessary—obviously not. We Germans, the only people
in the world who have a decent attitude toward animals, will also
take a decent attitude toward these human animals. But it is a
crime against our own blood to worry about them and to give
them ideals that will make it still harder for our sons and grandsons to cope with them. . . . Our concern, our duty, is to our
own people and our blood. . . . Toward anything else we can be
indifferent. . . . I wish the SS to take this attitude in confronting
the problem of all alien, non-Germanic peoples, especially the
Russians. All else is just soap bubbles.

22

THE FACE'S SECRETS

AROUND THE TABLE SAT SCHOLARS from science and the humanities, enjoying their mid-morning coffee—a biologist, a historian of religion, a classicist from Oxford, a Nobel Prize-winning physicist, an historian-economist from Chile. Outside, a steady, early November rain pelted the Charles River. The scholars drifted upon the subject of whether a person's face discernibly reflects his moral character. Stalin was a monster. Should people looking at his face have known he was a monster? Should Harry Truman have seen it at Potsdam, rather than being reassured that Stalin looked indeed like "Uncle Joe," our resolute ally against Hitler?

Did Hitler's face reflect the monstrousness of his character. I thought not; I thought of certain close-up photographs that seemed to show eyes that were remarkably intelligent and a face one would have described as sensitive and simpatico. I thought of the picture of Hitler lovingly caressing his German shepherd dog at Berchtesgaden—his manifest tenderness and sentimentality. I thought of the scenes of the Führer accepting welcoming ceremonial flowers from children: a grotesque public show in the springtime-for-Hitler style; but if you did not know who Hitler was and what he did, you would not, I think, have detected the presence of evil in his face.

The classicist, whose own face was a perfect smiling mask of a certain Oxford type, argued that a person's character is manifest in his face. He said that, for example, "Ariel Sharon has a horrible, a monstrous face." He made a joke to the effect that Yassir Arafat "is not as bad as he looks."

The classicist thought that Harry Truman was a terrible judge of character, since at Potsdam he had missed the most important thing—the truth about Stalin.

We rambled on. I said that I think one sees what one is looking to see. I thought of Abraham Lincoln's singular face, in which history has learned to see a long-suffering, brooding nobility. At the time he was elected president in 1860, much of America—including gatherings very much like the one that rainy November morning in the university in Boston—beheld Lincoln and saw a coarse, ugly, ungainly backwoods buffoon, a knuckle-dragging ape in the cartoonist's version.

It did not seem at all to me that evil can necessarily be discerned in someone's face. On the other hand, I remembered Gitta Sereny's description of Franz Stangl, the Nazi commandant of the death camp at Treblinka—a man whom Jewish Nazi-hunters tracked down in Brazil after World War II and brought to trial in Germany for crimes against humanity. Sereny, a Hungarian-born author who had lived through the Nazi regime and wrote an extraordinary book about Stangl, called *Into That Darkness,* managed to interview the man at length in prison in Düsseldorf. Photographs of Stangl show a handsome face of a somewhat ordinary German kind—beefy but reasonably clean-featured, projecting a certain strength. But Sereny said that as she interviewed him—leading him back into memories of the death camp and the terrible evil that he had done there, presiding over the deaths of at least 900,000 Jews and others—his face became transformed, and monstrously disfigured. The evil he had done filled his memory, his mind, and hideously distorted his face—in the way that rage will sometimes seize a normally intelligent and even beautiful face and turn it ugly and menacing.

Faces change. They are never fixed—or rarely fixed (we do know some whose faces have become stone or wood, or else art-fully maintained façades). Most people's faces are capable of a considerable range and virtuosity. Dwight Eisenhower had a mobile and often charming face, with his famous smile and bright blue eyes. Yet Richard Avedon, the fashion photographer, captured Eisenhower's face one day in an expression of aston-ishing vacancy, his eyes canceled out like the eyes cartoonists used to draw, with X's on them, to tell us someone had been knocked unconscious.

The secret of the face lies in the mind at the moment that one looks upon it or photographs it—in its momentary animation or dullness. I would not trust my ability to read a face under any and all circumstances and deliver a pronouncement on whether this was a good or an evil face.

When I was a U.S. Senate pageboy in the early nineteen fifties, I frequently encountered Senator Joseph R. McCarthy of Wis-consin. I rode the Senate subway with him, and then went with him on the elevator up to the Senate floor. It was McCarthy in his prime days (if that is the phrase), or just at the beginning of the end for him. He was a heavy and untidy man, who wore rum-pled blue suits; his thinning hair was badly combed, and he impa-tiently brushed it back from time to time. The photographs of the time showed his saturnine glower, and if the photographer was acute, would catch the black bags under his eyes that betrayed his alcoholism—and catch as well the reddish piggy smudge in his hung-over eyes. And yet in the hundreds of times

I saw him moving through the Senate halls, greeting the startled and happy tourists (for he was wildly popular in much of America then), and even in his courteous encounters with other senators (even the ones trying to stop him, to censure him, including Flanders of Vermont), his was the face of kindness and affability, and as it seemed, unfeigned goodwill.

McCarthy's biographers have sometimes noticed this as well: That there was a part of him that was a genuinely nice guy, and that was astonished that people could think ill of him. At the age of 13 I was not much of a judge of character, but I would not have guessed, I think, on the basis of those encounters around the Senate, that Joe McCarthy was an ogre, and, as history has written him down, an evil and destructive man.

About McCarthy, this should be said:

He fought against evil (Stalinist Soviet Communism was incontrovertibly evil—and had, as the Venona decryptions of the 1990s show, infiltrated American life far more extensively than the enemies of McCarthyism would admit, then or now) and yet did so in a way that threw off its own sparks of evil.

I am always amazed that people discussing McCarthy's performance do not fasten quite quickly upon a central fact of the story, which is that Joe McCarthy was a catastrophic alcoholic. The phenomenon of McCarthy—his slovenly and slurring paranoia, his recklessness—becomes a fairly simple matter when you factor that in. Alcoholism is an occupying army that seizes the mind and then the life; McCarthy's mind and body were thoroughly poisoned by alcohol, which tainted everything he did—and destroyed whatever value his work might have had in combating a real danger. Whittaker Chambers judged that Joe McCarthy was ultimately an enemy to the cause of anti-Communism, and Chambers was right.

And yet here I have seemed to do what I have warned against. I have seemed to plead that McCarthy's behavior should not be judged evil because there is some other explanation—the same reasoning people might use to avoid describing, say, a mass murderer as evil because, after all, he was abused as a child. Well, I do not judge McCarthy to have been evil. He was history's equivalent of a drunk driver.

In any case, I mistrust the thesis that one can judge a person's evil by looking at his face. O. J. Simpson had a handsome, charming, open, good-hearted face, which was the reason that Hertz Rent-A-Car paid him millions of dollars to be its spokesman. If you had seen the earlier photographs of John Muhammad and John Malvo—quite beautiful faces, in the festive pictures we saw later—would you have picked them out as the Washington-area snipers, as men capable of killing so many people cold-bloodedly, as a sort of sport?

Before April 19, 1995, if you had seen photographs of Timothy McVeigh—a fresh, clean-cut American face, topped by a crewcut—would you have said to yourself you were looking at the face of a man capable of blowing up the Federal Building in Oklahoma City and killing 168 people?

When the trial of a monster comes around, it is usual to wonder how anyone so ordinary-looking could have done what he did. There is an element of disappointment in the process: the ordinariness defeats our expectations. Immensely horrible consequences should have immensely horrible causes. What do we make of this ordinariness? (It might be shrewder to ask whether evil is often the last resort of the ordinary—their way of distinguishing themselves.)

Hannah Arendt went to Jerusalem for Adolf Eichmann's trial, saw the drab little former bureaucrat, and proceeded to construct her somewhat misleading and unsatisfactory thesis about the "banality of evil."

Evil, in any case, is very good at disguises. Good wears its disguises as well.

I invited the scholars around that table in Boston to consider the case of Samuel Johnson, a good and wise man who had a notably ugly face. Does evil manifest itself in a person's appearance? Evil's disguises include beauty, nobility, charm. Is there any way to tell whether those appearances are deceiving? Or is it safer to assume that beauty, nobility, and charm are always chess moves—feints with ulterior purposes?

If evil were candid, presumably one would see in a face a quality of hatred, of death, of rage, of malice. Evil people cannot conceal themselves entirely. Where have I seen evil faces?

In the faces of people in a mob you often see unmistakable expressions of evil. You see something more alarming than mere collective anger. People who have joined a crowd of other people, and fused themselves into a mob, have abandoned individual conscience and moral judgment to some sort of enraged consensus. A high emotional temperature melts the individual minds into one. Beekeepers know something of the phenomenon. If, for example, one bee is accidentally crushed beside the hive, the dead bee emits a chemical that announces war to the entire population of the hive, and their collective purpose becomes attack and revenge.

A human mob reacts in much the same way. And may commit evil acts that individual consciences would have intervened to prevent—lynchings, for example. People in a mob may talk one another, by a kind of wildfire contagion, into committing extreme acts. If one shark reacts to blood in the water, some instinctive electricity fires through all the other sharks and they are abruptly a frenzied gang. I suppose the basic chemistry of the dynamic is little different from the chain reaction of the nursery: If one baby cries, then soon they all are crying. Nature is animated by a violent suggestibility. What acts at one moment as a valuable defense mechanism (defending the hive) becomes, a moment later, a species of hysteria and hatred. Human politics abounds with examples of behavior wherein an otherwise useful reflex turns hideous. Evil, the opportunist, exploits the mob's essential mindlessness.

Although essentially mindless, a mob can be directed. Mobs have leaders. A mob (wherein people can be led to do things they would never had had the courage or the viciousness to do on their own) is an opportunity. And truly outstanding demagogues know how to create their own mob—to turn the valve and light the spark and direct the blowtorch to their own political tasks. The mob becomes a tool.

In the breakup of Tito's old Yugoslavia, for example, a Communist party hack named Slobodan Milosevic saw the opportunity to consolidate old Serbian ethnic hatreds and paranoias, which Tito's autocracy had long kept under control, into his own powerful instrument—dreams of a Greater Serbia set aflame with hatred (notably against the Bosnian Muslims) and hissing nicely in order to serve the dream of a Greater Milosevic.

23

CLUB MED
FOR MONSTERS

"THERE IS NO VICE LIKE HATRED," writes Shantideva in a great eighth-century Indian treatise, *A Guide to the Bodhisattva Way of Life.*

Yet hatred is not one of the Seven Deadly Sins—unless it is covered under Wrath. Is hatred evil? The Old Testament is filled with hatred, for some reason, as it is suffused with wrath, notably God's. Is there a syllogism here (God-wrath-hatred) that leads to the proposition that God, being wrathful and hateful, may therefore be evil as well? No, God's wrath does not exactly equal hate, but rather, some kind of violently irrational disappointment, a paroxysm of divine heartbreak, emanating it may be from love, not hatred, and therefore not susceptible, one would think, to the charge of evil. Is God's wrath just? Well, His expectations were doubtless rather high, and therefore, his disappointments radical.

I attended a conference on the subject of hate—"The Anatomy of Hate"—in Oslo, Norway, convened by Elie Wiesel.

It was Wiesel's moral authority that brought together Vaclav Havel and Nelson Mandela, Jimmy Carter and François Mitterand, Günter Grass and Nadine Gordimer, Chai Ling and Li Lu, leaders of the democracy movement in Tiananmen Square— a remarkable collection of Nobel Prize–winners, professors, rectors, saints.

The hotel in Oslo, the SAS Scandinavia, seemed a perfect target for a bomb. You could not walk from elevator to lobby without bumping into three or four world-numinous figures. I kept finding myself a few feet away from Nelson Mandela, who became my favorite presence in Oslo. I sat just behind him during the conference sessions in the great hall; I rode up and down elevators with him. I was forever staring at the back of his head. Nelson Mandela was surrounded by an atmosphere of utter calm that I had never encountered—a stillness that seemed to me magic and profound. Does 27 years in prison make a man so calm? In the great conference room, sitting behind Mandela, I found myself so absorbed in his peacefulness that I no longer heard the speeches and responses. He glistened with a quality of purified light.

My mind kept cartooning the paragons. Günter Grass, that stolid, slovenly, joyless Teuton, slogged about this Valhalla of celebrity as if some huge gravity pulled him earthward—I guessed that the history of Germany that he had witnessed was gravity enough. Vaclav Havel, on the other hand, was an alert woodland creature, as canny and winsome as the Water Rat in *The Wind in the Willows*.

I kept running into Jimmy Carter—those glacial, comprehending eyes that emit a pale light, like cracked ice, and do not blink; a man in some inner conflict, unlike, say, Mandela: a provincial Georgia sweetness at war with whatever it was that so stiffened his neck and thrust his head forward—an arthritic, proselytizing, righteous turtle. You did not doubt, in any case, that Jimmy was a creature with a very hard shell.

A few years later, in the spring of 1998, *Time* magazine gave an enormous party to celebrate its 75th anniversary, inviting hundreds of famous people who had been on the magazine's cover over the year's to a blowout banquet given, improbably, in Radio City Music Hall, across the street from the Time-Life Building in New York. The Music Hall's seats were covered over with platforms, so that it became a sort of tiered ballroom, all glittering with the somewhat strange metaphysics of all these famous people reassembled out of their historical time and brought a little bizarrely together, all old differences, and even hatreds, annulled in a grand festive truce of celebrity, partying in the waxworks.

When the speeches ended, after several hours, there was an urgent break for the men's room. Streaming downstairs in their tuxedos to relieve themselves came an extraordinary parade: John F. Kennedy Jr., and Mickey Rooney, Henry Kissinger and Joe DiMaggio, Louis Farrakhan and Tom Cruise and Norman Mailer and Kevin Costner and Billy Graham and Kofi Annan and Mel Brooks. Mummified celebrity disconcerts the eye. The shock of recognition is a shock indeed, and there was an impulse all through the evening to squint at someone and wish to ask, "Didn't you used to be dead?" Jack Kevorkian was there, the doctor notorious for assisting people to commit suicide. I had the cruelty to wonder if he was there to look for clients. But the women displayed a certain gallant glamour—Lauren Bacall, for example, and Mary Tyler Moore.

But Leni Riefenstahl, Hitler's favorite moviemaker, also attended—physically unrecognized, a potent name from long ago, famous for her film *The Triumph of the Will*, Hitler's most artistic p.r. release. How does one make the right moral judgment about an artist whose work was not, people have argued, evil in itself, but whose dramatically sympathetic, Wagnerian images of triumphant Nazism at a Nazi rally in Berlin and, in her film *Olympia,* the 1936 Olympics in Berlin were at the time an instrument of evil, even if now the films are merely film school texts?

I speculated about the possibilities of celebrity as a detergent: Was it powerful enough to scour away evil on a night like this? In the lobby of the Radio City Music Hall before going in to the dinner, I stood talking with Elie Wiesel. Leni Riefenstahl walked by. Wiesel's face wore an expression of elegantly suppressed disgust. Then Minister Louis Farrakhan slid past, a sleek apparition. Interesting that the face of the has-been celebrity registers in the mind an instant before the name. You take in first the radiant energy of fame, and the fame is somehow enough—famous for what does not, in the interval of that instant, matter: You are captured by the fame itself, which is without moral content and gleams autonomously.

I wondered if Hitler would have been invited to the dinner, if he had been alive, or Stalin, or Mao, or Pol Pot; and wondered whether even they would have been treated, in the spirit of the evening, to those gazes of pleased wonder and fascination and privilege ("I can't believe that's . . . ") that people bestow when they see celebrity, even evil celebrity. I am sorry to say that I think they would. (A cartoon in *The New Yorker* got this perfectly: At a New York cocktail party a woman, dazzled and pleased, stands talking to a very tall, thin, bearded man wearing a turban; the woman exclaims: "Not *the* Osama bin Laden?!")

THE EMPEROR NERO entered his Golden House for the first time. He inspected the statue of himself, 120 feet high. He saw the enclosed lake surrounded by buildings that were designed to represent the cities of the empire. He admired the pillared arcade that stretched for a mile, the dining rooms paved with porphyry, the ceilings of gold and fretted ivory inlaid with jewels. "At last," he said, "I am beginning to live like a human being."

But eventually, Nero's armies revolted, and the Senate condemned him to be flogged to death with rods. Nero stabbed himself in the throat. Death spared him the fate of other toppled dictators, the haunted afterlife endured by Napoleon, for example. Exile is not necessarily a fate worse than death, but there is something poignantly ignominious in the spectacle of the once all-powerful turned out to graze on their memories, their paranoid introspections, in obscure pastures.

Napoleon's young aide-de-camp, General Gaspard Gourgaud, left a journal describing the Emperor's last years on St. Helena, a speck of British territory in the South Atlantic. Gourgaud's entries, unintentionally hilarious, record the great man's banality after he lost the thing that made him both interesting and, arguably, evil—his power.

"October 21 [1815]. I walk with the Emperor in the garden, and we discuss women. He maintains that a young man should not run after them. . . . November 5. The Grand Marshal [Montholon] is angry because the Emperor told him he is nothing but a ninny. . . . January 14 [1817]. Dinner, with trivial conversation on the superiority of stout over thin women. . . . January 15. I fetch the Imperial Almanac. The Emperor looks up the ages of his brothers. 'Josephine faked her age.' [He] looks at the names of the ladies of his court. He is moved. 'Ah! It was a fine empire. I had 83 million human beings under my government—more than half the population of Europe.' To hide his emotion, the Emperor sings . . . January 27. We read *Paradise Lost*. The Emperor wants to buy a cow, but where shall we keep it?" The imperial party acquires a cow, but someone turns it loose. "February 4. The Emperor is in a very bad humor, and full of the cow incident. At dinner, the Emperor asks [the coachman] Archambault, 'Did you let the cow get away? If you did, you will pay for it, you blackguard!'. . . His Majesty, in a very bad humor, retires at 10:30, muttering, 'Moscow! Half a million men!'" After dinner a few days later, the emperor remarks, "I should enjoy myself very much in the company of people of my own fortune."

What happens to strongmen when they are deposed? They do not all wind up as shattered as Lear on the heath. Napoleon was comfortable enough. He had a lady friend called Rosebud and spent much of his day soaking in his tub. But no doubt a peculiar loneliness descends upon an autocrat condemned to live out his days in exile.

At one time, an overthrown dictator almost invariably expired along with his power. But in the era of telephone and television (to keep track of how close the rebel army is) and helicopters (for quick extraction when the front door gives way), the world has from time to time seen an accumulation of leftover evil celebrities past their moment. Ferdinand Marcos settled in Hawaii. Baby Doc Duvalier moved to the French Riviera. Idi Amin made himself invisible in Saudi Arabia. The Central African Republic's Emperor Bokassa bought a home near Paris. They kept out of sight.

The task of brokering the departure of vicious autocrats sometimes involves this question: Since you wish to avoid violence, is it moral, and best for all concerned, to lubricate the skids with guarantees of safe passage to retirement (you can keep the Swiss bank account) in some comfortable country? Jimmy Carter used this technique to help ease out the Haitian General Cedras in 1994. If you do not provide such assurances, then the autocrat is liable to triple the guard and hold out indefinitely.

Is it moral to negotiate in this fashion? Is it right to give evil a golden parachute?

I had a mordant fantasy that all the deposed Big Boys of the world should be offered an opportunity to settle together on an island somewhere, in a sort of tropical retirement home, a Club Med for old dictators. The mayor of Honolulu once suggested settling Marcos, the old Filipino autocrat, on the island off Oahu that served as the set for the television series *Gilligan's Island*. I thought a better choice might be the Dry Tortugas, once the haven for pirates, an old prison island surrounded by shipwrecks, sharks, and poisonous dreams of sunken treasure. It seemed the right sunny-sinister atmosphere.

The dayrooms of mental hospitals were once famously supposed to be filled with Napoleons. The Dry Tortugas might be the same sort of place.

I entertained this Club-Med-for-the-evil fantasy back when the world was somewhat larger, when geography meant something, meant that it could isolate evil and insulate the world from it—back before the Internet had interpenetrated the world in such a way that evil men, even in the most extreme geographical exile, can pull electronic strings and dispatch their agents anywhere on the globe. But globalization means the globalization of everything—life in that other dimension in which both time and space are all but annulled.

This new world of the twenty-first century means an entirely new dimension of globally projected power, and therefore, pari passu, of globally projected evil. You cannot have one without the other.

There was a time when I believed that evil could not survive the sort of global scrutiny that satellite media coverage made inevitable. But that was a naïve belief. Evil can survive the scrutiny just fine; all it needs to do is to interpret the satellite images in its own way, for its own purposes. And satellite-Internet technology is not always a benevolent agent of the enlightened free market of ideas, ensuring the triumph of decency and the condemnation of wickedness wherever it is filmed and broadcast to the jury of world opinion. Alas, the technology adapts itself perfectly to the purposes of wickedness, so that a network of terrorists may be coordinated from a laptop with an uplink. It must be said, from the perspective of the antiglobalizers and anti-Westernizers, that technology also adapts itself perfectly to the wicked expansionist purposes of imperial consumer capitalism and its military dictatorship of the planet.

Does the technology represent a new form of civilization, or a new form of anti-civilization? We are locked in a very dangerous struggle, fought on a very, very small planet, over what all of this means.

I return to the coordinates of hate and evil at Oslo.

What is hate? At Oslo, Elie called it "a black sun." I thought the phrase gave hatred too much of a kind of literary prestige—like "white whale." "Black sun" sounded perversely attractive in the French decadent way, a bit rhetorical *("une civilisation à son dernier cri!")*, even though the phrase was sound enough if broken down: great consuming heat without light, heat emanating from the opposite of light (like that dim-lightbulb sun in Picasso's *Guernica*), and hate as a black hole that sucks all matter and life into it and transforms it to antimatter: hate as black fire in another dimension. No nourishment to be had from the Black Sun, no decency-charity-humor-love-forgiveness, but rather, death. I had an image of suffocation, and no exit.

But the good celebrities in Oslo found hate to be a subject that was oddly difficult to discuss. As evil is difficult to discuss. I suspected that the reason had something to do, first of all, with the fact that hate, again like evil, is simultaneously a mystery and a moron. It seems either too profound to understand, or else too shallow and stupid to bear much analysis—a cretin with a club, violent, repulsive, irrational, death's sidekick and accomplice. Hatred, like evil, is an intoxication; and intoxication can suggest either heady, even elegant ecstasies, or else a drunk in the gutter.

The delegates in Oslo were virtue's choir; they sang beautifully. If there was a hater among them, he kept it to himself. The only real controversy organized itself in a division between objectivists and subjectivists.

The subjectivists (poets and moralists) looked for the seeds of hatred within the human heart. The objectivists (economists, historians, lawyers) dismissed such vaporings and located the causes of hatred in the conditions of people's lives.

"Hard, visible circumstance defines reality," said John Kenneth Galbraith. In the past 45 years, he pointed out, no one had been killed, except by accident, in conflict between the rich industrial counties. In poor nations of the world, millions of people have died in struggles during those years. "Out of poverty has come conflict." Elena Bonner, the widow of the Soviet dissident Andrei Sakharov, stated the objectivists' case in an irritable outburst: "Moral concepts are lovely, but the key is governing these things by law."

Havel began by confessing an incapacity to hate—a suspect claim from most other men. "I look at hatred only as an observer," he said, and then proceeded to look at hatred as an artist does. He began with the psychology of individual hate: "It has a lot in common with love, chiefly with that self-transcending aspect of love, the fixation on others, the dependence on them, and in fact the delegation of a piece of one's own identity to them. . . . The hater longs for the object of his hatred."

Is that true?

"Hatred," Havel went on, "is a diabolical attribute of a fallen angel: it is a state of the spirit that aspires to be God, that may even think it is God, and is tormented by the indications that it is not and cannot be."

Havel described a typical hater: "A serious face, a quickness to take offense, strong language, shouting, the inability to step outside himself and see his own foolishness." I would have added, however, that those qualities of a hater—strength of conviction, seriousness of moral intent, passionate ideas about right and wrong, clarity of opinion—are indispensable in recognizing evil and combating it. Evil usually cannot be fought very well by people with a relaxed and tolerant attitude.

The subtitle of the Oslo conference was "Resolving Conflict Through Dialogue and Democracy." An excellent agenda. But the author Conor Cruise O'Brien reminded everyone that Neville Chamberlain's faith in dialogue gave the world the appeasement at Munich. As for democracy, Carter said: "Adolf Hitler and his Nazi Germany evolved from the results of free elections. We do not like to remember that."

But Hitler's cunning exploitation of democratic process does not mean democracy is an unreliable way of life, only that you need a tighter constitution, precisely to prevent the sort of usurpation that occurred Germany in 1933. Hitler came into power by a legitimate political route and then proceeded, in effect, to destroy the democratic ladder by which he had ascended.

What is the antidote to hatred? Education. Law. Justice. Charity. Love. The subject in Oslo was not exactly hate, but rather, evil, and its opposite, hope. Havel said he was neither an optimist nor a pessimist: "I just carry hope in my heart. Hope is not a feeling of certainty, that everything ends well. Hope is just a feeling that life and work have a meaning." Hope is the thing with feathers. Hope is the thing in diapers.

IS HATE ALWAYS EVIL?

Hatred savors of the violently negative, as rage does. But hatred is sometimes a survival tool, or even a motivated instrument of justice, as anger may be the weapon of righteousness against injustice. Is it evil to hate terrorists, murderers, child molesters? Is it evil to hate people who do evil? Is it wrong to be enraged at them?

Sometimes it is necessary to kill. Sometimes it is very difficult to kill. Soldiers going into battle are always conditioned to the thought that the enemy they will kill must be killed, even deserves to be killed, as our cause is just and their cause is unjust. Soldiers need a certain amount of hatred in order to do their work. Otherwise, a tenderness and hesitation may intervene. Soldiers should not pause to exchange family photographs. If they did, the war would stop, as it did during the spontaneous Christmas truce on the Western front in 1914. Good, says the sentimentalist, the pacifist. Good, says *Sesame Street*. But sometimes war is absolutely necessary—a war against genocidal peoples, for example, to get them to stop. And to pause and exchange family photographs with soldiers supporting an evil regime engaged in mass slaughter would be a fatuous and vicious indulgence. Hatred sometimes sustains justice and enables the soldiers of the just to do the killing necessary to stop the killing.

The task is to sort out who is just, and what is just. Each side in a war always claims to be defending the right. Each side always conceives itself to be the injured party. Each side represents itself as the Good engaged in combat against the Evil. In the Balkans, a region suffused with an atmosphere of evil, all parties—Serbs, Croats, Muslims, and subsidiary players—present themselves as victims of the others' evil.

And victims are supposed, in the clumsy moral theater of the tribes, to be innocent. A victim, of course, may be himself guilty of terrible evil, and usually us; the cycles of the *lex talionis*—atrocity and revenge chasing one another's tails—ensure the momentary purity of the victim/loser, whose tribesmen, waving his bloody shirt down the generations, will rush forth to butcher and decapitate the killer. And all through the cycles may be heard the wailed demands for justice.

But there is a universal misconception about justice—a metaphysical confusion that gives rise to all sorts of political delusions. The truth is that justice is not an absolute term, but a malleable idea, protean, flexible, changeable. Justice is at best a very distant ideal toward which different tribes aspire, moving by various, circuitous, and culturally determined routes.

The elders of the village may conceive that justice demands that a young woman found guilty of adultery be stoned to death. The good social order of the village requires such hard traditional discipline; it is our way, the elders say—our justice, the code we have to protect us against social disintegration. Our people are not given to speculative theory, but if we were, we would ask what horrors would ensue for all of us, the collective tribal organism, if we did not forbid, and punish, such crimes—if we allowed the males' seed to fire off irresponsibly, fertilizing any woman whom lust fancied, without the necessary contracts to honor the obligations of family and children. Sex is not casual, or even romantic. The procreative contract is the life and safety and future of us all. Endanger all of those, and you must be stoned to death—partly as a warning, but above all, in fulfillment of the collective justice we have agreed upon.

All civilized opinion howls when a woman is stoned to death in such a village. Barbarous! More evidence of the atavistic patriarchal injustice that has brutalized and enslaved women for millennia.

Which justice is the just one? That of the village or that of civilized opinion? The village, after all, has its own civilization, its working order. Terrible evil—death, slaughter, war—results when incompatible conceptions of justice clash with one another.

What is the struggle between Islamist terrorism and Western secular industrial democracy except the confrontation of incompatible ideas of justice—of good and evil?

"Justice" implies a world—an elaborately codified social and political arrangement, glued together by laws that are themselves often problematic. Huck Finn's great soliloquy deliberating whether or not to turn over the runaway slave Jim to the authorities is a brilliant illustration of the unaided natural mind groping its way toward a moral concept of justice. Huck's reasoning took him to the conclusion that he could not turn Jim in; he would defy white society's law and, as he says, go to hell, rather than betray his friend Jim.

24

SADE, COBAIN, AND THE PLEASURES OF EVIL

THE ROCK MUSICIAN KURT COBAIN, a heroin addict who committed suicide in 1994, kept a journal that recorded many diseased impulses, including the idea of cutting open babies' bellies so that he might "fuck them to death." The id of American culture is a repository of such stray depraved fantasies. Cobain's semiliterate, almost inconceivably stupid journals, full of the lumpen diabolism of the rock culture, record urges that distantly suggest the sort of ingenious depravities that the later Roman emperors went in for. Suetonius has a well-known passage about the Emperor Tiberius: "In his retreat at Capri there was a room devised by him dedicated to the most arcane lusts. Here he had assembled from all quarters girls and perverts, whom he called Spintriae, who invented monstrous feats of lubricity, and defiled one another before him. . . . He taught children of the most tender years, whom he called his little fishes, to play between his legs while he was in his bath. Those who had

not yet been weaned, but were strong and hearty, he set at fella-
tio, the sort of sport best adapted to his inclination and age."

In his diaries, published several years after he committed suicide, Cobain is found to have written as follows: "I like to make
incisions into the belly of infants, then fuck the incisions until
the child dies." One presumes not only that he did not treat
babies in this fashion but that the only violence of which he was
guilty was probably the taking of his own life.

Why such a loathsome entry in his diary? Perhaps he was
experimenting—somewhat childishly exploring the possibilities
of evil in himself. The entry seems to me to have been written in
the same spirit in which rock groups seek to name themselves
ever more outrageously and satanically—Megadeth, Anthrax,
Slayer, Grim Reaper, Cradle of Filth. Looking for the right name
for the group, of course, is always a commercial as well as an aesthetic venture: You want to find some ne plus ultra of badness.

The taste for satanic rock names originated in the unprecedented philosophy of forgiving and nonpunitive child-rearing
during the last several generations of parents. That sounds, I
know, like a reactionary's bromide, but listen. Children who
emerge from childhood with a sense of their own unconfronted
evil will seek to manifest it one way or another. They will dramatize their own sheer badness if their parents have not earlier disciplined and exorcised it, and thereby satisfied the child's powerful sense of justice—an instinct that the child quite often turns
against himself with a fierce impartiality and rigor. Parents, who
in the last several generations have come to be sentimentalists
with the conventional view of childhood's innocence and little
memory of the actualities of childhood, tend to deny their children the moral process that they need as they grow up, the disciplined rites of passage by which they learn to sort out the good
and evil in themselves.

Some parents' sentimentality has a dark annex. They abuse their children, so that the children's sense of their own evil becomes tragically confused. Overindulgence and abuse are two sides of the same coin—sentimentality. Sentimentality is an atmosphere in which evil often likes to do its work.

In any case, I suspect that when evil is unconfronted, or abusively confronted, in childhood, it may become an obsession in adolescence, and may simply arrest development beyond the adolescent stage.

Adolescence—a turbulent passage at best, and often a form of temporary insanity—is peculiarly receptive to evil. Adolescence runs to extremes, and what is more extreme than evil? For that matter, what is more extreme than adolescent love, or adolescent lust? Or adolescent self-pity? In adolescence, the fiercest thrust of procreative energy and potential violence inhabits the same flesh with moral inexperience and what is inevitably a vast ignorance of the world.

I take it in any case that nature intended adolescence to be a relatively swift passage that would end soon enough in disciplines of responsibility—food-gathering, child-rearing, the work of running an autonomous life. The affluent modern industrial world has of course prolonged adolescence—or else simply arrested development in the adolescent stage. The culture of rock music dramatizes the effect of adolescence hypertrophied, extended, and above all, commercialized. It has been the achievement of the consumerist West, from the baby boom onward, to turn adolescence into a vast market, a commercial phenomenon with a life of its own and with imperial ambitions.

If evil finds adolescence an especially congenial atmosphere in which to do its work, adolescence in turn finds evil to be an attractive aesthetic through which to express its rebellious impulses, its Oedipal fantasies, and its natural violence.

The entry in Kurt Cobain's diary was not intended to be public and commercial, like the satanic names that rock groups invent for themselves. One can surmise that in the fantasy, Cobain experimented with harnessing his own phallic pleasure to an act of evil. He chose to fantasize fucking a baby through incisions in its belly first of all because he instinctively saw that violence against children—against a baby!—must be the most reliable approach that human beings can take toward evil so absolute that even a psychologist or sociologist would have difficulty in explaining it away. As an outrage against human decency, I imagine it would be difficult to surpass Cobain's fantasy. His fantasy partook of the negative/creative ingenuity one finds in the monster emperors of late Rome—the talent for invention that Caligula brought to his depravity, for example. Certain Nazis brought touches of Lucifer's whimsy to what is—after all, after a while—the merely prosaic business of murdering people.

Kurt Cobain, in any case, was, on the evidence of his journals, a sort of idiot descendant of the Marquis de Sade. Cobain toyed with the idea of an ecstatic union of the principles of pleasure and evil—an alliance that is one of the more disturbing dimensions of the problem of evil. People would not commit so many acts of evil if they did not derive pleasure, sexual or otherwise, from at least some of them. Evil is sometimes awfully hard work—and might not be worth the trouble if it did not hold out the promise of some payoff, some unusual thrill. Sade derived pleasure from thinking about such acts, and writing about them, even if he was actually guilty of relatively few of the frenzied and sometimes hilariously loathsome acts he dreamed up.

No one wrote down more elaborate fantasies of this kind than Sade. The Rube Goldberg of filthy concatenations labored hard at dreaming up transgressions. In one succinct convergence of nastinesses, he wrote: "In order to unite incest, adultery, sodomy, and sacrilege, he buggered his married daughter with the Host." But Sade was not in the business of killing people. In the middle of the nineteenth century, the great French historian Michelet rendered this verdict: Sade, "professor emeritus of crime," represented the ultimate dead end of corrupt monarchy: "Societies end with these kinds of monsters: the Middle Ages with a Gilles de Rais, the celebrated child killer; the *Ancien Régime* with a Sade, the apostle of murderers." Not a killer, but the apostle of killers.

In the midst of a nearly hundred-year-long rehabilitation— actually a perverse literary canonization—of the man whom Apollinaire in 1909 called "the divine marquis," a debate has raged over the relationship between art and evil: Did Sade the apostle's work actually incite people to commit the evil deeds that he imagined and described; or was the effect of his writings, on the contrary, to be considered apotropaic, or cathartic, a kind of antidote, a release of evil energies through literary immunization? Simone de Beauvoir claimed that "Sade's eroticism doesn't lead to murder but to literature." Perhaps. But at the 1966 trial of the Moors murderers in Chester, England, the prosecutor referred to a collection of 50 books that the killers kept in a suitcase, including *Orgies of Torture and Brutality, History of Torture through the Ages, Sexual Anomalies, Cradle of Erotica,* Geoffrey Gorer's *The Life and Ideas of the Marquis de Sade,* and Hitler's *Mein Kampf.* The prosecutor read Sade's defense of murder as "necessary, never criminal," and referred to another quote: "Rape is not a crime, it is a state of mind. Murder is a hobby and a supreme pleasure."

Roger Shattuck, in his *Forbidden Knowledge,* brilliantly follows Sade's reputation through the course of the twentieth century. "His rehabilitation remains difficult to explain," Shattuck comments. "I attribute it more to an eerie post-Nietzschean death wish in the twentieth century. That death wish seeks absolute liberation, knowing it will lead to absolute destruction—

physical, moral, and spiritual. For some, apocalypse exerts a strong attraction."

In 1937, Aldous Huxley claimed that Sade represented "the philosophy of meaninglessness carried to its logical conclusion," and that "De Sade is the one complete and thorough-going revolutionary of history." Later, Jean Paulhan wrote of Sade's "unfaltering demand for the truth," and claimed: "His books remind one of the sacred books of the great religions."

Shattuck writes that during the 1930s, "the neo-Nietzschean philosopher Pierre Klossowski studied Sade's 'liquidation of the notion of evil' and his restoration of it in the notion of crime as a form of forbidden knowledge–'*crime-connaissance.*' Georges Bataille expressed outrage at the Surrealists' appropriation of Sade, for they had no conception of his truly excremental vision [a compliment is intended here, no doubt] and shirked the duty not just to imagine his excesses but to *practice* them. (Bataille had plans for trying out human sacrifice.)" By the 1960s, Yukio Mishima was writing a play called *Madame de Sade* that ended with the great man's wife announcing, "He is the freest man in the world. . . . He piles evil on evil, and mounts on top. A little more effort will allow his fingers to touch eternity. . . . He has created holiness from the filth he has gathered."

The motif of sinning one's way to God goes back at least to Augustine. But in the twentieth century's perverse literary celebration of Sade, the trajectory of that upward struggle is reversed, and the destination, rather than God, is the Satan of utterly disconnected self—a soul so isolated not just from God but from all human contact that the most violent cruelties barely manage to give physical pleasure or to disturb the spiritual rubble.

To mistake evil for freedom is a defining fallacy of the twentieth century, much employed by, among others, the authors of utopian schemes that became totalitarian hells. In the personal dimension, evil thrives upon indifference, and Sade's writing, suffused with fantasies of evil, turns indifference to another's pain into the principle of a radically disconnected individual's good. Freedom and pleasure expand and flourish in direct proportion to another's pain, suffering, and humiliation.

Writing is a powerful act; it has consequences. Powerful writing, such as Sade's, may have powerful consequences. To say so is not to argue for censorship: We are speaking here not of legal rights but of moral and metaphysical responsibilities.

The hell of self, acting out vicious fantasies on paper, may cause more evil than if it were acting out the fantasies in fact, inflicting the beatings and perversions on actual people. If the deeds were done in actuality, then their consequences would be restricted to the immediate objects of Sade's acts—the people being beaten and bled and sodomized and strangled; but as the fantasies were committed to paper and transmitted to millions of readers over centuries, the toxic daydreams proliferate, infecting one mind after another after another, down the generations. The First Amendment permits the writing and publication of such stuff, but that does not clear it of the charge of evil. Nor does the fact that it is written well, nor the protestations of critics glorifying Sade in order to work an agenda of *épater le bourgeois.*

The Roman playwright Terence's hospitable thought that "nothing human is foreign to me" may degenerate down the centuries to the error of thinking that if the human mind can imagine it, then it somehow cannot be evil—it is *human,* is it not? But Auschwitz was thought of, dreamed up—and by one of the most advanced societies on earth. Evil is very much the product of human thought and fantasy, and it seems a bizarre kind of double-jointed irresponsibility to indulge in evil fantasies and deeds and then claim, as Sade's apologists do, that they cannot be evil because they somehow represent the rebellious and untrammeled human imagination pushing the envelope of its own freedom.

The proponents of Sade's writing give him, and themselves, the fatal permission of irresponsibility. The refusal to take responsibility is one of the great gateways to evil. It is possible that that evildoing irresponsibility derives from an ancient human quarrel with God—men's perception that God himself, whom man would imitate if he could, does terrible things in an apparently irresponsible way: kills children wantonly, for example. The author of the world's evils—if God is the author—hides himself, irresponsibly. And so perhaps irresponsible human frenzies in the direction of supposed, unrestricted freedom have their origin in a perverse imitation of a God who is himself, well, sadistic.

It won't do. Precisely to the degree that God conceals himself or retracts himself or otherwise recuses himself from the human case, then human behavior, including evil behavior, becomes a human responsibility. To do good means to help other people in one way or another. To do evil means to harm other people. Sade's writings (the *acts* of his imagination) enact a thousand scenes in which a disconnected demonic self inflicts suffering upon others.

If no one had ever read Sade's writings, if, every evening, he had destroyed what he had written that day, would his writings still be evil? I would think not. They would be sad and repugnant, as indeed they are. But what makes them evil is precisely their infectious incitement of other minds.

The writings of Sade should be taught, if at all, as examples of the evil—the self-evil, as it were—that results from the vicious disconnection of life from the hard human work of love and compassion. The idea that love and compassion are bourgeois and therefore contemptible has animated much of the adulation of Sade. So, too, has a sort of diseased nostalgia for displaced aristocracy and its unbridled liberties—the lord's feudal license to abuse the peasants. Thus bourgeois intellectuals in their rebellion against the bourgeois performed a perverse glorification of Sade, the morally diseased aristocrat who seduced them to a vision of freedom as blind, vicious sexual frenzy and the infliction of suffering in order to stimulate an otherwise indifferent sexual appetite, for the divine marquis, was, despite all his lascivious exertions of mind, extremely fat and, according to much evidence, at least partially impotent.

25

GOURMETS AND
MONKEY BRAINS

Evil, SUBJECT TO BOREDOM, is forever concocting delicacies and refinements. Travelers in China have reported the cultish gourmet's ritual of dining upon the brains of a live monkey that has been imprisoned, immobile, below the center of the dining table, the top of its head exposed through a round hole in the table. The top of the skull is then removed and the diners use their chopsticks to dine upon morsels of the monkey's brain. A connoisseur's pleasure, made more exquisite, presumably, by the exoticism of the cruelty, and the onstage fatality at the table.

Is it an evil pleasure? Usually the animals that we eat are slaughtered offstage, and then sliced up, and grilled or stewed. Is the cruelty—the evil—somehow worse if we kill the animal at the table?

Part of our horror at the monkey-brain feast has to do with the fact that it is a monkey, our distant cousin, and not a sheep or cow or chicken. To torture and eat a live monkey seems near-cannibalism. And cannibalism is deeply tabooed, deemed evil among most human tribes—presumably because nature understands that if cannibalism were countenanced, there might be no end to it; cannibalism would add a practical dimension, a nutritional temptation, so to speak, to the already out-of-control habit that humans have of killing one another. We kill one another constantly in crime and war and car accidents and in our justice system, and doing so, do not experience a fraction of the instinctive horror we would feel if we killed people and then, instead of burying them, are them. Why such horror at the mere thought of cannibalism when we otherwise kill so casually, with relatively little remorse?

Among many peoples, cannibalism has been a religious rite or an homage to salin enemies. Among the "civilized," cannibalism causes instinctive recoil, as from evil. while other killing does not offend the sensibilities in anything like the same way. Is evil, in any case, to be judged by the sensibilities—by the instinctive revulsion we feel, rather than by some more objective, rational measurement? A good question: Is there such a thing as an objective standard of evil? Or is evil always registered in the emotions, the instincts—by a sort of moral sense of smell, a gag reflex? Is the degree of evil to be judged by the strength of the recoil, or at least by some, so to speak, aesthetic response?

We take it that killing another human being may be a paramount expression of evil—one of the dramatic ways that evil announces itself. Why is one form of killing more evil than another form of killing?

Because, I suppose, some forms of killing involve torture and cruelty. Is it more evil if the murderer takes pleasure in the deed than if he does not? If the killing is done merely for "business" purposes—as in a Mafia movie in which the Don, before he sends another gangster off for execution, tells the victim, "It's nothing personal, it's just business"; or as in a war when one army shoots its way through another army—does the practical reason for the killing absolve the killers of the charge of evil? It's murder, all right, but murder of a sort of anodyne variety; if it is evil, then it is something like necessary evil.

It is what might be called justifiable evil.

The concept of justifiable evil does not, perhaps, parse philosophically. It is inherently a slightly crooked business, since in order to talk yourself into it, you avert your gaze from the evilness and concentrate instead on rationalizing the thing. We indulge the idea of justifiable evil somewhere on the margins of our thinking, in terrain that angles sharply down a slippery slope. Genocidalists—the Nazis, for example—began by rationalizing the euthanasia of the most extreme cases of mental retardation, people whose "quality of life" was next to nil, for whom execution, though technically an evil, must seem an act of mercy. This was justifiable evil, a clinically conducted evil, which can hardly have given pleasure to those technicians called in to administer the gas in those first procedures (which were carried out by connecting a hose to the exhaust pipe of a truck and then feeding the hose into the closed rear of the truck, where the victims dumbly and obliviously waited). What did those technicians experience except a humane regret that such procedures were necessary—along with perhaps a private spasm of disgust that nature could produce such deformed human beings (there, but for the grace of God . . .), or alternatively, a sense, almost virtuous, of having performed a civic service?

Evil is often a matter of motiveless malignity—delicious to the evildoer precisely because of its gratuitousness. On the other hand, a great deal of evil, particularly in politics, thinks of itself as justifiable evil. The Nazis justified their exterminations as necessities of racial purification, preparing the ground for the thousand-year Reich. Pol Pot's Khmer Rouge justified its slaughters on the ground of cultural/ideological purification, stripping Cambodia down to Year Zero and a radically Maoist new beginning. It is fascinating that evil so often justifies itself as a necessary purification—the most extreme application perhaps of the no-pain, no-gain principle: Great new things can arise only from great conflagrations of the old.

Some evil arises from the impulse to cleanse; some from the compulsion to defile. "Cleansing evil" is one of the more toothsome ideas.

Cleansing evil, justifiable evil, arises no doubt from the need of all organisms to defend themselves—to throw off germs and dangerous viruses: To make the threatened organism clean again, to restore a primary integrity that has been lost to aliens. Evil in this model acts like a sort of (forgive me) high-temperature self-cleaning cycle in the oven: the crisis of cleansing evil—justified by the obdurate accumulation of filth over many years—becomes an ordeal by fire, and an instrument of rebirth. Only such a radical assault, says the justification, can break down the rotten, impure past, and put it to flight. The past is burned at the stake, reduced to ashes, as heretics must be burned, as heretical books must be fed to bonfires.

Revolutionary evil inclines toward the apocalyptic, cleansing mode of ideologically justified evil. Conservative evil, arising from entrenched autocratic power, tends toward gestures of thoughtless oppression interrupted now and then, out of sheer boredom, by vicious whimsy—"aristocratic" defilements of the sort that Sade made his specialty, or the theatrically evil displays of Nero and Caligula. Josef Stalin's style combined revolutionary "cleansing" (through his Gulag and his Great Terror, he purified the Soviet Union of millions) with brutishly ingenious personal sadism. He set the standard for dictators ever since, including

Saddam Hussein. Revolution and autocracy, of course, have almost always proven to be merely two stages in the cycle of power: An autocrat is a revolutionary who has settled in.

Revolutionary evil and autocratic evil are different expressions of the same thing: power. The distinction between the two may be the difference between, God help is, rational evil and irrational evil. "Rational evil"—or rationalized evil—has a raison d'être, political or philosophical or racial. Autocratic evil no longer feels the need to justify itself: Power is its justification.

Terrorism unites rational or pseudo-rational motive (a religious or nationalistic cause, for example, a collective grievance like Palestinian statehood or, at one time, Zionist statehood) with the menace of explosive irrationality (the Palestinian suicide-homicide bombers, or, in the 1940s, the Stern Gang).

Nazi evil made a travesty of the West's driving idea, Progress—and at one stroke, annulled it. With Auschwitz, all of Western achievement fell through a trapdoor into a filthy black abyss. It might be said that Hiroshima and Nagasaki performed a similar annulment of the Western promise—orgasms of technology's unintended consequences, leading in this case not to a black abyss but instead to a blinding white abyss: the nuclear blank.

Auschwitz was a factory to destroy lives. Its product was ash. The same might be said of Hiroshima, even though its purpose—its rationale—was ultimately to save lives (lives both American and Japanese, that would have been lost in an American invasion of the home islands). A judgment upon whether or not the dropping of the Hiroshima bomb was evil depends upon whether or not you accept that larger, life-saving explanation. The possible verdicts are, 1) Guilty; 2) Guilty, with an explanation; 3) Not guilty.

It is a truism that it is the victors who render the verdict in such cases. Those upon whom the atomic bombs fell cannot be expected to endorse the ruthlessly dispassionate arithmetic that balances their own 160,000-odd lives against the disputed number (one million Americans plus five million Japanese?) who might have been spared because the bomb so quickly ended the war.

After Auschwitz and Hiroshima, the idea of progress was never the same. Those events brought the snake into the garden of the Enlightenment, with its faith in progress as a force for good. They represented the terrible technological Fall. Thereafter, progress would never walk without its shadow, the danger of a terrible and decisive and apocalyptic regression.

Why should anyone be surprised? The works of human beings are always human, and there is no reason to expect that they would be exempt from the usual human attraction to evil. Garbage in, garbage out. Evil is our garbage, and our baggage.

There is no question, however, that "progress"—which we must now put into ironic quotation marks, signaling that it could go either way—changes, if not the nature of evil, then the possibilities of evil. The advent of nuclear physics made it possible to incinerate an entire city with one bomb. The decoding of the human genome makes it possible for human beings to accomplish great good (curing diseases, lengthening life, pushing the human life form down the road toward some better idea of perfection) and great evil (the possible abuses of cloning, for example, are endless). Human beings become increasingly important subcontractors in the work of Creation. Doing so, they assume greater and greater responsibility for good and evil. As John Kennedy said in his inaugural address, "Here on earth, God's work must surely be our own."

It is doubtful that the idea of progress can ever be restored to the innocent prestige of the Enlightenment. Progress now implies the danger of a simultaneous Endarkenment.

Technology is the theater of twenty-first century gnosticism wherein the possibilities of good and evil struggle against one another—benevolence and malevolence more or less canceling one another out, so far: technology giveth and technology taketh away. It saves lives medically and destroys lives militarily: as if the living planet were breathing—inhaling and exhaling, life and death.

Can it be that good and evil are merely the balance of nature? Or in any case a balancing act? That argues some higher purpose for evil, or at any rate a sociobiological justification for acts of evil—as when apparently vicious child-murders might be argued to have some hidden Darwinian objective farther down the line.

Perhaps. But suppose that all of the evil were suddenly removed from the earth. Suppose that the earth were composed quite suddenly of nothing at all but good. What would it look like? Would it be heaven? Would it be endurable?

War would cease. Cruelty and torture would be no more. Nuclear weapons would vanish. No more murder, or child beatings, or rapes. And so on.

What would be the consequences of a world without evil? Would anything be lost?

Look beyond the present crises (terrorism etc.) and think of evil as an ingredient in the human future. The Human Genome Project has uncovered God's hitherto secret blueprints. Bioengineers are in the process of trying to take over the firm and correct previous design errors.

Will they attempt to edit evil out of human nature? Will they arrange to make murder, rape, atrocity, genocide, hatred—all disappear, along with cancer and heart disease?

Can evil be engineered out of the world? If so, with what result?

It's an odd but essential question to ask: Can people live without evil?

Scientists working with artificial intelligence have a fantasy that eventually all of the contents of the human brain, a life, can be gradually emptied into a brilliant, nondecaying, stainless, deathless sort of robotic personoid. When the transfer of all the intricately nuanced matter of the mind and soul has been accomplished, the memories of the cells etched onto microchips, the human body, having been replicated in a better container, will be allowed to wither and die.

Will evil be transferred along with good, and installed in the new stainless-steel container? Or can the scientists sift the soul through a transforming cheesecloth and remove all the evil traces, the reptilian brain? Will the inheritance of Cain be left to wither and die with the human husk?

If so, will grace and love, evil's enemies, wither as well? Does good become meaningless in a world without evil? Do the angels depart along with the devils? If the stainless canister knows nothing of evil, will it think that Mozart sounds the same as gunfire?

It was just at the end of winter in 1996 that the 43-year-old scoutmaster, with an obsessive interest in guns, broke into an elementary school in Dunblane, Scotland, and opened fire.

But decency (which is Newtonian, by the way, and instinctively sees the fitness of an eye for an eye, revenge's Third Law of Motion) resists objective, clinical understanding of what might have prompted a man to murder the children. It's important to understand, of course, and it is primitive ignorance to reject whatever help science can give in forestalling repetitions of this kind of thing. Still, language that suggests mere dysfunction—some bug kicking the wrong wire in the brain—does not somehow . . . rise to the occasion.

Nor is there much comfort in thinking that such behavior results from some Darwinian maladaption. "Man has developed so rapidly," Loren Eiseley wrote, "that he has suffered a major loss of precise instinctive controls of behavior. So society must teach these controls. And when it does not, then the human arrangement breaks apart." In the trial of the Leopold-Loeb case in 1924, which was that era's prime specimen of tabloid micro-evil, Clarence Darrow argued essentially that crime (including the murder of 14-year-old Bobby Franks) was to be understood as a disease. A banal defense, but Nathan Leopold and Richard Loeb got off with their lives. What tends to get lost is this truth: The fact that evil may be a disease, which behaves like a disease, does not make it not evil.

Disturbing crimes call forth melodramatic generalizations. Nietzsche thought, "There are secret gardens in all of us. Which is another way of saying we are all of us volcanoes that will have their hour of eruption." Really?

The range and sequence of Nietzsche's metaphors is interesting—the secret garden (hidden and unlike Eden, covert, poisoned, like, I suppose, my hermit's cabin and the doll secrets beneath his floorboards) becomes, by surprise, a sudden violent public up-spewing of the hot guts of the earth—an eruption of hell into the upper air.

Is it true that each of us is a volcano waiting to erupt? And if it were true, would it mean that we all in some sense share the guilt, the original sin, an endemic poison of evil?

It must be said that anyone who does not know the difference between a person who kills and a person who does not kill has failed to grasp the first of civilization's house rules. That everyone is capable of murder, at least theoretically, but that most refrain from committing it is the start of social order.

Almost any definition of evil stipulates that crimes against children are uniquely satanic. The twentieth century and the early twenty-first have learned to recognize evil in the violent eruptions of nonentities: An insignificant man bursts out of his rented room into sudden, violent world prominence. Tiny cause, big effect, the social equivalent of splitting the atom. When nonentity murders innocence, an especially horrible fission occurs.

The murder of children always suggests a split that D. H. Lawrence discussed in his famous meditation on American literature: "Destroy! Destroy! Destroy! hums the unconscious." The killer of children wishes to annihilate the contrary impulse that Lawrence wrote of, the upper consciousness that urges, "Love and produce! Love and produce!"

26

THE LIMITS OF SILENCE

Evil—THE THEOLOGIAN'S *mysterium iniquitatis*—has always resisted explanation and analysis. Evil has so baffled modern attempts to understand it that many in the twentieth century came to the conclusion evil does not exist; some others—mostly writers about the Holocaust—threw up their hands, concluding that no mere political analysis of the Third Reich and the Holocaust—events that became the twentieth century's baseline of evil—was adequate to the actualities. Nor was any cultural, sociological, or psychological explanation quite persuasive. Something was always missing.

Some (Theodor Adorno and others) who thought hardest about Hitler's evil—including the most eloquent victims—decided at last, in a spirit of anguished paradox, that only silence is sufficient; that only silence can express the unanswerable metaphysical truth of that particular evil—or perhaps, by extension, the truth of any evil. The idea is that by a perverse physics of evil, truth decomposes into anti-truth, a black hole that sucks language into its unthinkable density and crushes all meaning.

Where are People of the Book to find the vocabulary to describe what happened at Treblinka or Dachau? Silence can merely point a mute finger toward the dimension of negation that lies beyond the frontier of the word. In the beginning was the Word. Perhaps the End means that the Word is extinguished.

But silence has its limits. Eventually, it becomes an irritating conceit. It gets to be an embarrassment—like a somewhat more elegant version of a prediction that the world will end on a certain date; a day or two or three afterward . . . and the world spins on.

Proponents of silence about the Holocaust were perhaps not quite serious anyway; they intended silence to be a kind of Munch scream—a protest without words.

Silence belongs to eternity. Human time abhors silence. We go on living, go on doing good and evil, go on trying to understand them through language, which is the only available medium for our philosophy and gossip. Science and mathematics may think in symbols of their own. But human behavior has no choice but to understand itself, and govern itself, through language. We know what we think when we find words. Language is the vessel that carries us, our home and spaceship, and outside its protection, there is no oxygen for us. Outside the dimension of language lies a void in which the human conscience cannot breathe. To abandon language is suicide. Evil relishes silence, as it delights in suicide, for silence, like suicide, expresses despair. Silence is the only thing death has to say.

So a mystical silence in the face of evil seems inadequate–especially if it becomes a prolonged silence.

The Holocaust has called forth certain ingenious articulations. Hannah Arendt invented her phrase "the banality of evil" because she sensed that such a paradox (who would call evil banal?) might modernize our sense of evil to explain Auschwitz, a phenomenon otherwise so shocking to previous experience and expectation as to push us over the edge into a lightless place where we cannot think or get our moral bearings. Arendt's phrase seeks to orient us to a new configuration of evil as elaborated politics, as follows: Politics appropriates the money to set up bureaucracy. The politics of the Third Reich organized its work through instruments as banal as Adolf Eichmann's bureaucratic routinization of death: production quotas, train schedules, paperwork.

Evil prides itself on its novelty, its inventiveness. But if you subject yourself to many stories of evil, one after another (murderous religious fanaticism blowing up infidels; tribal hatreds perpetrating slaughters; children murdering children for the fun of it; torture, rape, murder) you begin to sense that, for all their gory theatrical variety, they are essentially similar to one another. Can it be that all acts of evil are, at heart, alike? The French author Georges Polti postulated in 1916 that all the world's works of literature contain just 36 plots. If that is true, can it be that evil has even fewer lines of possibility?

Evil resembles its drooling cousin, pornography. Both evil and pornography, when witnessed repeatedly, become . . . repetitious. Pornography is not—necessarily—evil, but evil and pornography have things in common. Both of them become boring after awhile—to the witnesses, anyway; evil becomes tedious to torturers, and even (in the midst of pain and horror) to their victims. For all their intended atmosphere of excitement, even their higher claims to wild freedom, both evil and pornography partake of an unmistakable and distinctive moral deadness. (All the same things, incidentally, might be said of drug addiction—the diminishing flashes of illicit stimulation, the deadness at the center, the eventual tedium and exhaustion.)

But the Holocaust, the attempted industrial extermination of all the Jews of Europe (plus Gypsies and other inconveniences) seemed novel indeed—evil that broke new ground and for a time, at least, shattered the modus vivendi of good and evil. Here was a dimension of evil—a new ocean spread before stout Cortéz—to cause moralists to look at each other in a wild surmise. At Auschwitz, evil was thinking outside the box.

How was it to be understood? Could it be?

Arendt's insight was profound. Some Jews attacked Arendt's book *Eichmann in Jerusalem* on the somewhat irrelevant grounds that she seemed to be suggesting that some Jews collaborated in their own deaths. The important point that Arendt saw lay elsewhere, and has come to define more and more of human life. She saw that the virtual reality of Eichmann's bureaucratic manipulations—mere columns of statistics, lists—could create a new reality (in this case, a demonic one). Eichmann created a bureaucratic reality that effaced, superseded, and effectively annulled the human.

Movies today create and manipulate digital "realities." Much of the world's reality has become virtual—symbolic, electronic, and as ominously detached from the dimension of the human as were the lists in Eichmann's out-box.

Great evil can occur in the space between the actual and the virtual. Virtual reality—in video war games, for example—has an insidious way of persuading the mind, acclimating it, to the idea that, let us say, explosions and deaths are not really real. What occurs then is erosion of the moral sense of consequences. The mind is training itself not quite to believe that bullets are real, and therefore, that deaths from those bullets are real. The rigorous, crucial distinction between illusion and reality may begin to blur—one melting into the other.

Ultimately, I think Arendt's moral perception of Eichmann's office work as the "banality of evil" arose not from her faculties of political analysis but from a different quarter of her brain, from her poetic intuition.

Evil is something that we do not so much understand as feel. The painter, said van Gogh, paints not what he sees, but what he feels. Evil by definition defies understanding. If we understood it, we could not quite call it evil, for understanding implies that something is manageable, correctable. Evil prowls at the margins of our rationality—in the shadows, inside the treeline, like wolves. Now you see it, now you don't.

Often evil makes no sense at all. Sometimes, it has grand *raisons d'état*. What makes sense to the wolf may seem inexplicably wanton and savage to the peasant. What pleases the sadist torturer appalls the decent.

Much evil arises from perceived necessity. Euripides' Agamemnon confronts the necessity to sacrifice his daughter in order to appease the gods and bring winds to rescue his army, becalmed for weeks with ropes, sails, hulls rotting, and the men starving.

Calchas, the prophet of the army, cries, "The death of a girl will free the winds. Iphigenia, the King's daughter, must die."

And Agamemnon weeps saying (in Robert Lowell's translation): "The gods will curse me if I disobey this order. I shall be cursed if I murder my child, the love of my house, and stain my hands with her blood at the altar. Whatever I do will destroy me. How can I betray my ships and lose faith in the war? My soldiers are mutinous. They cry for winds, and care nothing for the blood of a child. The winds must blow. May all be well."

And a voice from the Chorus comments: "When the King accepted this necessity, he grew evil. Crosswinds darkened his mind, his will stopped at nothing. It pleased him to imagine the infatuation of his hard heart was daring and decision. Agamemnon wanted his ships to sail, and he was willing to kill his own daughter. . . ."

Much evil is done through perceived political necessity. Often it is a misbegotten perception, of course; the history of human politics teems with evils done—betrayals, tortures, slaughters, genocides—in order to advance career or cause or tribe. All political terrorism proceeds from a motive of perceived necessity in the service of career or cause. Terrorism is politics by other means—the politics of impatience. Democracy puts ballots into a box. Terrorism puts explosives there. Both aspire to political impact. Bad enough when the cause is something as secular and banal as national independence. When the necessity is ordained by the voice of the absolute, by God, or Allah, then terrorism loses its sense of proportion—loses whatever residual humanity it may possess (blow up some people, maybe dozens, but nothing too ambitious) and instead seeks destruction on an apocalyptic scale.

Evil necessity has its degrees, its moral calculus. Agamemnon measured the death of one girl, his child, against the larger necessities of his army. All fighting generals are forced to do such arithmetic. Ulysses Grant carried in his head an elaborate budget of carnage—a fairly sure sense of how many Union soldiers— and Confederates as well—would have to die in order for him to take Fort Donelson or Vicksburg or Richmond. (Grant, known in history as a terrible butcher, the world's first industrial warrior, actually had a lower kill ratio than Robert E. Lee; Grant, that is, sacrificed proportionately fewer men.)

Was Grant evil to send men into battle? The South thought so. But Grant won. He freed the slaves and saved the Union. He sacrificed men in horrifying numbers in order to accomplish what his sponsors, the U.S. government and the people of the Northern states, judged to be a cause worth massive sacrifice. A necessity. And Grant's battle casualties were, proportionately, lighter than Robert E. Lee's.

When the leaders of the Hutu tribe in Rwanda decided upon the necessity of eliminating the malign influence of the Tutsi from their land, they mobilized gangs that in only a few weeks, working mostly with machetes, killed 800,000 Tutsi men, women, and children. The slaughters—which the outside world judged to be so irrational, so evil in a *Heart of Darkness* way—made some sort of horrible tribal sense to the Hutu. To a European anti-Semite, Hitler's project also seemed to answer a necessity.

Evil often proceeds from motives that the perpetrators find to be perfectly coherent—to be, above all, perfectly righteous. The priests at the Aztec Temple of the Sun performed their necessary work of placating the sun god with human blood by opening the chests of tens of thousands of victims and ripping out their still beating hearts. Hard, necessary work. Auschwitz was hard work, too.

Evil crucially expresses itself through power—the raw energy of politics, good and bad. Caligula expressed the ideal extremity of power politics when he reminded his grandmother Antonia: "Remember that I can do anything I want, to anybody." The ultimate political power of course expresses itself in the royal prerogatives of life and death. Once, says Suetonius, "at a plenteous feast where there was great joy, he began all at once to laugh uncontrollably; and when the consuls seated by his side asked gently and with fair language the reason for his laughter, he answered, 'Why, for nothing but that with one nod of my head I can have your throats cut in an instant.'"

When Caligula became emperor, the people of Rome greeted him with joy and enthusiasm. He would preside over a new golden age, they predicted. He became, of course, a monster. His crimes were ruthless, imaginative, whimsical. Were they Satanic? Were they evil? Suetonius recorded that "he forced parents to be present at the execution of their own children. And when one father excused himself by reason of sickness, he sent a litter for him; another immediately after the heavy spectacle of his own son put to death, Gaius [Caligula] invited to his own table, made him great cheer, and by all manner of courtesy provoke him to jocoseness and mirth."

When he ordered someone flogged to death, he wanted the death prolonged: He said, "Strike so they may feel they are dying." On one occasion, he made a mistake in ordering a man killed; he had gotten the name wrong. "But it makes no matter," he said, in the spirit of a Kafkaesque or Stalinesque modernism, "for even he has also deserved death."

"Monster" is an interesting word that we may use to take some of the edge of the absolute off "evil." When we say monster, we do not quite mean a Satan, an embodiment of evil, but rather, something slightly less, halfway between the human and the demonic. Stalin was incontestably evil, I think, but perhaps more of a monster than a Satan—at least when compared with Hitler, who, though surely a monster, was something more than a monster. The subtle gray zones of evil. A monster, perhaps, is a horror of the natural world—a terrible cartoon of irresponsibility and depravity, the worst of bad human tendencies taken to gross extreme. A monster is a terrible product of the natural world. But a Satan seems to come from another dimension—from the supernatural.

Caligula is a monstrous figure. His behavior is monstrous, horrible—"diseased," as Suetonius says. Evil as well, certainly. But I doubt he had the full supernatural prestige of the satanic.

Power and freedom, the earthly desirables, the great positives of Western ascent—but also of ambitions originating somewhat to the east, like the Khan's Mongol hordes, for example—seem to be indispensable preconditions of evil. You must have the power to kill, and the freedom from conscience, the ruthlessness, to do it, even when killing as whimsically as Caligula did. Evil has a taste for the sinister.

I doubt that philosophy and theology bring us very close to an understanding of evil either. Evil tends to defeat explanation along the lines of earnest rational speculation, no matter how ingenious or erudite it may be. The conscious working mind tends, one way or another, to veer away from the awful truth, as if it cannot quite bear to look directly at evil, in the same way that the human eye cannot look directly at the sun—not for more than a flash, anyhow—without going blind.

The mind needs shade, and shades of meaning. It needs to get its bearings in the relative normal arrangements of the world, in sequences of cause and effect, for example—a world of predictable motive operating within a certain spectrum of known human behavior.

Evil is marked by audacity. It does not make sense—did the Holocaust make sense?—even though later, in retrospect, we might decide that it obeyed a Satanic logic.

Evil likes to dazzle—performing a black dazzle of negation—or to obscure itself in clouds of mystification. Evil prefers complexity, moral mazes, a sense of itself as the *mysterium*. Evil needs an atmosphere of inscrutability. It must perplex—must defeat expectation, must shock, and then must defy explanation afterward. That is evil's strategic dynamic.

Maybe.

When we draw back the curtain and disclose evil, there seem to be two possibilities: 1) Evil may turn out to be banal, as the Wizard of Oz, with the curtain drawn aside, was revealed to be a dumpy old man working the levers; or 2) Evil may be a more hideous secret than our worst or most ingenious imaginings.

27

THE ARGUMENT
FROM DESIGN

But if it is possible to map the human genome, possible to decode the secrets of human life, then might it be possible to decode the mystery of evil?

A few simple things may be said about evil.

Evil is a violation of trust.

Evil is not inert. It is a transaction, a human story—rape, murder, war, genocide, and millions of variant dramas.

And in most cases, evil involves a story.

Think of the devil's speculation about village brats who induce an unsuspecting child to lick the metal of an ice-cold axe.

The devil's interest fastens upon this vignette of relatively harmless malevolence. Why?

First, because a spot of viciousness in children always interests evil.

And second, because the game—so trivial in its consequences that it could not remotely be characterized as "evil"—nonetheless has the DNA of evil in it. Unless it is a merely immunizing touch of evil, it might, so to speak, grow up to be true evil. It is an almost invisible miniature of evil: The mainspring of the little drama is a violation of trust, followed by a nasty surprise.

Evil likes to work with booby traps. Satan in the Garden of Eden staged a cosmic moral ambush that induced Adam and Eve to commit the primal violation of trust: the first sin.

The Jews at Auschwitz thought they were being ushered into a large shower room. Roman Catholic priests who sexually abuse children repeat a motif of ambush and violated trust that dominates the history of evil. Evil favors a configuration in which power (adults, parents, priests, figures of authority) abuses the innocent and trusting young.

Third, evil is symmetrical—that is, stands in rough, long-term symmetrical relationship to the good. Rather than being a grotesque intrusion of the alien, of a foreign, malevolent something that shatters the integrity of an ideal, instead, evil belongs entirely to the symmetry and dynamic of human life—and is even indispensable to it.

There is a story about the nineteenth-century naturalist Louis Agassiz. When a student would come to his Harvard laboratories applying to study ichthyology with the great man, Agassiz would go to a shelf of his office and take down a jar of formaldehyde, from which he would withdraw a large dead fish. Placing the fish on a metal plate, he would hand it to the student with the words, "Study your fish."

The student would be instructed to sit in an adjoining room, with no texts and no instruments of any kind, and simply to look at the fish, to study it. Sometimes Agassiz would leave the student in there for hours.

The student at first would be mystified. But after a time, he would begin to do as he was instructed. He would study his fish.

He would stare at it, first on one side and then the other. And he would begin to notice, among other things, what?

First, the symmetry.

That the fish was a marvel of symmetry, a masterpiece of twinned features.

That the fish was completed by repetition: Two eyes, not one. Each fin with an answering opposite. One side of the fish repeated with sweet exactitude by the other side.

So what?

The student would go on to notice other things about the fish. The internal organs need not be twinned—a single liver would do, for example. But the individual creature overall—the package—would be relentlessly symmetrical. That completion depended upon symmetry. That anything less than symmetry means incompletion.

Why?

The pattern of symmetry—the rule of symmetry—in nature is profound. The universe seems to wish to attain the most symmetrical forms that are possible—and will always ultimately assume those forms and settle itself into the nest fashioned by its handsome and unbreakable laws. The symmetries of Agassiz's dead formaldehyde fish, still beautiful and elegant on the metal plate, are everywhere repeated, as if all life, color, event, and form were a Hegelian reverberation arising from universal call and response, positive and negative, port and starboard, man and woman, night and day. This is what theologians call the argument from design.

Music naturally composes itself in such reverberant symmetries—the intertwining of twinned motifs, a cluster of notes and then an answering cluster, an animal courtship of sound.

There exists in nature a universal species of longing that may be the animating dynamic of all this symmetry. The glove seeks its mate. Weight wants counterweight. The eye is instinctively binary, and if its mate is blinded, misses the dimension of depth. Crime cries out for punishment. Whatever is separate and incomplete stirs with a longing for its completion. Sex longs for the other. Mystery demands solution. Beginning craves end. Life journeys to the destination of death.

And good forms a symmetry with evil.

In Lurianic Kabbalism, that form of the kabbalah that dominated Jewish religiosity in the seventeenth century, "all existence presupposes a dialectical, twofold movement," according to the scholar Gershom Scholem. "Nothing comes into being by a simple one-way action. Everything subsists by the combination of retraction and emanation. The rhythm of the living God, like that of organic forms including man, can be described as a double process of inhaling and exhaling. . . . The double rhythm of regression and egression is at the root of everything that exists."

We are inclined to regard human affairs as chaotic, not symmetrical. The Newtonian model of a balanced and harmonious universe never had more than a theoretical application to history or society, it may be, and the twentieth century—Einstein, Freud, great slaughter—left an impression of disintegration, unreliability, randomness, everything but symmetry. Einstein's well-known line claimed that God does not play dice, but if not dice, it may be a game infinitely more obscure in its rules and probabilities.

And yet in the moral human sense, we live in a universe that is—nostalgically or ideally—ordered by an instinctive sense of justice and symmetry and the seemliness of right in its relation to wrong, and good as it stands against evil.

28

IT IS ALWAYS A STORY

THE ABSTRACTING MIND beats itself up against things like the subjective-objective conundrum.

As follows: What is evil? Something independent? A dark intergalactic cloud, an autonomous metaphysical force that would exist even if there were no human race to imagine it? Or is evil entirely the creation of the human imagination—without which, it does not exist?

People are inclined to ask, Do you believe in Evil? Or, Do you believe that Evil exists? In much the same way, they ask, Do you believe in God? Do you believe that God exists?

We set an absolute standard for evil—as God is supposed to be an absolute standard of good. And setting that absolute standard for evil (as if evil must be the coequal of God's good) usually places the bar impossibly high—or rather, impossibly low, in a black infernal abyss, somewhere at the moral latitude of Auschwitz. The natural if illogical result of such an absolute negative standard is to encourage people not to believe that evil exists at all.

Yet to say that evil does not exist seems foolish—and an obvious contradiction of what we see all around us, every day.

The trouble, as I say, is that evil tends to frame itself as a religious question, or a theological question. Odd. Why is it not a secular question, even a kind of scientific question, or a sociological question? Or an historical question?

Why not treat evil as historical fact? Try to locate evil in time—in relation to your own place in time. Reframe the perspective and see the question to be a matter of past experience and record. Do not ask, Does evil exist? But rather, ask, Has evil existed? That changes it slightly, at least for a moment.

A person who might deny the theological/religious/philosophical existence of evil in the present—or in the eternal abstract realm where universal ideas have their home—might, for a little while, be inclined to say, Well, of course evil has existed. We have seen it. In Hitler, for example. In Pol Pot. We have seen evil to be part of history. We have seen events in the past—genocides, for example, or smaller individual atrocities and massacres, or scenes of tabloid civic experience such as especially vicious murders, or unpublished, gratuitous horrors inflicted upon the innocent—that we cannot easily discuss or even describe without recourse to the word "evil."

But a hairsplitter in the back of the mind speaks up: Well, it depends on what you mean by "evil."

And with that, you find yourself being tipped out of history once more and tumbled through the mirror again, back into that timeless realm of religious or theological concepts—ideas that seem somewhat heavy and immobile, like statuary; or if these august ideations do move, they do so under constraint, like chess pieces that must obey arbitrary medieval rules of engagement.

In our world, paradoxically, evil, as an absolute or an abstract universal, lacks credibility. In the developed and comfortable

West, we cannot quite integrate or absorb the lurid, brutal universal into our self-image, into the way we think about ourselves and the secularized drama of our lives, even though the world, so much smaller now than it was a generation ago, presents us daily with behavior and tableaux that, if they are not evil, fall into some other category for which we have no name.

But retrospection shows us evil. For a second, we see it, intuitively and without reflection, simply by drawing on human experience. We know it is there, and has been there from time immemorial. We sense its presence, even if it is effaced by the elaborately protective systems and ideas in which we have settled our civilized selves. In a brightly lighted city, it is impossible to see stars and planets in the night sky. Our own bright, surrounding lights spare us the nightly contemplation of a beauty and mystery that is entirely beyond our understanding.

I think that for similar reasons, we sometimes have difficulty seeing evil, which, though not beautiful, is mysterious, and beyond the range of our vision.

The historical glimpse occurred when you asked, Has evil existed.

Now ask another question: Will evil exist?

When?

In the future. Any time in the future?

Certainly, you will answer. It is . . . human nature?

Suppose that Satan's axe cuts a tree somewhere in the universe, and no human is there to hear it fall: Does the axman exist? Does the tree exist? Does the tree fall? Is Satan in business for himself out in the cold dark where there is no life?

Or does evil need human life in order to exist? Is evil itself a life-form—a living moral organism? The organism of antagonism?

Is evil, indeed, something that lives—only—in the human heart, an Antichrist within, a sort of cancer? Does evil cease to exist if people cease to exist? Is evil merely—merely?—the creature of human imagination?

I think of speculation about evil as a walk through a vast haunted house—a castle, I guess it should be, since evil does have a medieval style—with endlessly intricate corridors and sudden trapdoors, and never as many answers as questions.

If the forms of evil (that is, the characters who do evil, the ways they do it, their technology, their dramaturgy, their costumes, their makeup, their horns, their shooting scripts) change, does the essence of evil change? Is it not always the same distinctive, powerful dark thing? Is it not the business of the forms to disguise the essence until, so to speak, it is too late?

But evil remains the *mysterium iniquitatis*—its core still maddeningly inaccessible.

Despite all the discussion down the centuries, the question returns, fresh and unresolved each time: Does evil exist? Or do we call it evil because we are superstitious, frightened, hateful, stupid?

Humane rationalists tend to call evil something else—a defect, a breakdown with comprehensible and therefore fixable causes—and to them the concept of evil is atavistic and barbaric, and "proofs" of its existence are merely anecdotal. If, however, you were present at Auschwitz, or Pol Pot's Cambodia, or Rwanda in 1994, you might have found the anecdotes persuasive.

In any case, I know this much: Evil is always a story. Evil is the indispensable stuff of stories, the agitation of conflict. Who has heard of a storyteller without resources of evil on his palette? Who has heard of God without some darkside Adversary? Everything is story, starting with the Big Bang, which was the primal once-upon-a-time. Everything after that—all history—is anecdote.

"All sorrows can be borne if you put them into a story, or tell a story about them," wrote Isak Dinesen. And Hannah Arendt, writing about Dinesen, remarked, "It is true that storytelling reveals meaning without committing the error of defining it, that it brings about consent and reconciliation with things as they really are."

Stories, I take it, are the key to passing back and forth through the looking glass—between the realms of chess-piece theological abstraction and the disorderly, complacent realm of present time.

I take it farther: Evil expresses itself in stories—or not at all. Evil is not an abstraction or principle, but is, rather, the world's narrative energy. Evil makes the world go round; goes round the world.

The proof of the existence of evil is in the stories about evil. More accurately, more to the point: The reality of evil is in the stories. And nowhere else.

29

THE LESSONS OF
MEIN KAMPF

A DISCUSSION OF EVIL tends to revert to Hitler, as baseline, as a negative paragon.

I had not read *Mein Kampf*. I knew what was in the book, I thought. Hitler dictated it to fellow prisoners Emil Maurice and Rudolf Hess while detained at the Landberg am Lech Fortress Prison in the spring and summer of 1924. Every historian of the Third Reich quoted from it in passing. I knew, in any case, about everything that came later.

What eventually emerged—the National Socialist movement, the Führer's new Germany, Kristallnacht, Polish blitzkrieg, London blitz, Holocaust, world war, twenty million dead—was so apocalyptic that Hitler's comparatively youthful rantings (he was thirty when he composed the book) seemed, in the scale of things, a seedling of history—premature, a curio, the monster's high school yearbook. Today, only historians—or neofascists bunkered up in the Bitterroot Mountains—read *Mein Kampf*.

An error of omission. I was born in September 1939, the month the Nazis invaded Poland. Hitler and Auschwitz gave me my moral formation through newsreels, through radio broadcasts and headlines, through the overheard conversations of adults. Hitler set the standard. Just as Munich furnished a cautionary paradigm in foreign policy, so Hitler—Satan as Charlie Chaplin, with his moustache and strut and glittering eye, comic and diabolical—became the model of world-historical madness—the *mysterium iniquitatis* gone global.

Evil has much to teach us. My answer to the dilemma of theodicy—the mystery of why a good God permits evil in the world—is that evil is our greatest and perhaps our only effective instructor. With so much instruction available in the form of evil, we should all be geniuses. Evil, in some strange way, is what keeps us in motion toward the unseen destination. Evil supplies us with the horrible incompleteness that we need. If we were perfected, then we would be motionless at last, and so would God. Is it blasphemous to say that evil is in some sense the primum mobile?

A moral danger, a sort of intellectual tragedy, has taken form over the years as the Holocaust has been remembered, analyzed, mythologized, suffered over in retrospect. The danger is that the Holocaust has become merely a genre, and a sort of moral bore. The danger is of atrophied meaning. One encounters this impatience with the Holocaust not only among anti-Semites and outright deniers, but also, unexpectedly, in Israel. Once in the 1980s when I was driving up the coast toward the (supposedly) demilitarized zone on the Lebanese border, my companion, an Israeli army officer whose father had died in 1948 while trying to convoy food and ammunition to Jerusalem, dismissed discussion of the Holocaust as being not only a bore but a symptom of weakness. Retrospective metaphysical anguish, he suggested, was the black hole into which the *Luftmensch* vanished. It was, he implied, not good for the Jews.

I saw his point—saw it with particular clarity when we arrived at the Lebanese border, where the sandbagged Israeli Defense Forces had been slinging rockets and artillery shells back and forth with Hezbollah. It was time, my companion meant, for the physics of the present, not the metaphysics of the past. The IDF soldiers had their hands full here. Most of them were very young. The boys and girls in their fatigues had an air of earnest campers. Their cheeks glowed with good health; their teeth were white and strong; their eyes were clear, and even dancing a little in the danger. One of the young men, as if to show off for visitors, or for the girls, argued, like a precocious kid, with his superior officer; the officer listened, then told the kid that he was right—the kid's suggestion made sense.

It was surely true that the generation of survivors from Auschwitz and the other death camps had, many of them, been through so much emotionally that their clocks had stopped, smashed up somewhere in the evil past, and they could not be entirely useful and responsive to the demands of present projects, new crises, new enemies.

I knew a colonel in the IDF who was born in Israel in 1946. His parents, both survivors of the camps, had met in Europe as refugees, and married, and made their way to *Eretz*, the mother getting pregnant along the way. They called him "our miracle child." But they soon gave him away to a kibbutz, to be raised collectively, more vigorously. The colonel's parents feared that they had too much death in them, too much past, and that their darkness would communicate itself to the miracle boy and shadow his new life. Let the horrid past stay buried in the past.

But what of "Never forget"? And "Never again"? And what of the hideous historical mirror-work in this scene: I am riding in the West Bank as a passenger in the car of a friend who is a Palestinian journalist. An Israeli checkpoint stops us, examines Jamil's papers, frisks a little through the car, then waves us on. When we have pulled away, Jamil says loudly, bitterly: "Heil Hitler!"

Tu quoque.

AND IT IS EXACTLY FOR THAT REASON—the poisonous *tu quoque*—that it is almost as big a mistake not to read *Mein Kampf* now, as it was in 1925, or 1933, or 1938 or '39, before it was too late. The point of reading the book is to study the play of evil's mirrors.

I read the book at last in the fall of 2001, when events raised the subject of evil again.

Go into *Mein Kampf,* and after a time, it dawns on you that you are in the presence, full flower, of the method and technique and text of evil. This is not the high school yearbook, but the masterplan, the architect's drawings. This is the metaphysic of cunning. Having thought the project out in considerable detail, all Hitler needed were the contractors, the plumbers and electricians and laborers, the Heydrichs, Eichmanns, and Speers.

Curiously, some historians have condescended to *Mein Kampf* as a vulgar, loutish performance, as if, in presuming to write a book, Hitler had profaned the profession of letters and had, therefore, to be sneeringly dismissed by the civilized people who are the guardians of books. How could the man who burned books be admitted to the company of authors? How could it be admitted that he had written a book of such . . . power? That was the subliminal judgment.

Mein Kampf is vulgar enough, and explosively vicious, all spittlespray and venom. Such hatred. Such contempt. Such cunning. But it is also a dark education—a textbook for evildoers and by its weird moral optics, a premonition of all that was to come.

Think of drawings that show the way that an image passes through the lens of the eye and is inverted as it arrives upon the back of the retina. It is up to brain and optic nerve to sort reality out and put the image right-side up again, so that a man standing before you has his feet down on the ground and head up in the air, and not the other way around.

In *Mein Kampf,* Adolf Hitler, war veteran and budding politician, gives the reader a lucidly—ruthlessly—inverted universe. It is the universe of evil: things upside down, a trick of black magic.

THE WEATHER in the fall of 2001, after the attacks, was unnaturally warm, almost until Christmas. People who went to Ground Zero spoke of the fires still flaring and smoking, and of the smell (the smoulder of electric wires compounding with the nebulous agitated powder of concrete and human flesh and bone), and of the unexpected scale of destruction—of the deconstruction, the great towers rubbled.

That fall, in several essays for *Time* magazine, I used the word "evil" to describe the attacks. So did President George W. Bush, who, it seemed to me, wished to signal to terrorists and Islamic zealots that he was as willing as they to use uncompromising vocabularies. Bush spoke repeatedly of "the evildoers." His use of the word "evil" was not aimed only at terrorists; he aimed to draw Americans away from relativism and to frame the struggle against terrorists in absolute terms.

I think that Bush, as a leader mobilizing public opinion, was wise to speak of evil. But I found my mind snagging and lingering, as it often has, upon the word and its implications—upon the meaning of evil.

30

What Nachtwey Sees

Each age gets its own evil. What's evil now? The questions are always there, just out of focus, flicking in the corner of the eye.

In the corner of the eye, I often see that distinct contemporary evil captured in the photographs of James Nachtwey, one of the two or three best photojournalists of the last century. Nachtwey has come away from El Salvador, Guatemala, Lebanon, the West Bank, Sri Lanka, Afghanistan, Chechnya, Somalia, Sudan, Rwanda, Kosovo, with that elusive awfulness caught on film—fear, hate, adrenalin, the surreal unexpectedness of evil danger when it arrives, say, in a public square: soldiers suddenly chambering around, a woman's face just at the instant she begins to comprehend. Nachtwey catches the obscene smear of blood, the postures of bodies in violent death. His lens, by some mysterious intuition, sees into the heart of evil moments.

In the age of Stalin, Hitler, Mao, the distinctive evil was the totalitarian police state that murdered its people and took away their freedom. Then came Third World genocides in Pol Pot's

Cambodia and in Rwanda. And after that the brutal disorders in all the places where Nachtwey has worked, and still later, with the millennium and after, the maturity of international terrorism and September 11. Nachtwey, who was in his apartment at the South Sea Seaport on Manhattan's East Side the morning the World Trade Center was struck, rushed to the scene with his cameras and nearly got killed in the collapse of the second tower. His pictures of that morning have a riveting, apocalyptic quality. Nachtwey is a rare artist who rises to the occasion of evil, and sees it clearly.

Great evil is never exactly an accident. But evil sometimes likes to work by falling dominos of inadvertence.

Here is a row of dominos:

In the late spring of 2002, India and Pakistan unsheathed nuclear weapons and pointed them across the borders at one another. Terrorist raids in Kashmir—a parochial business— threatened to touch off a war that could kill as many as 20 million people. From a tiny acorn grows the mighty oak: a mushroom cloud. The world works on a logic of disproportions. It takes only the infinitesimal diddling of an atom to accomplish mass death.

If evil can be measured by counting bodies (not a bad way to make an estimate, though evil does not always like to equate quantity with quality), you begin to think that the twenty-first century may usher evil into a new dimension. In a nuclear exchange of—what?—an hour or less, India and Pakistan might kill as many people as Stalin eventually destroyed in 20-odd years of dogged, ingenious brutality.

The world has been through nuclear terrors before, during the Cold War when think tanks projected megadeaths in a spirit of grim machismo: Herman Kahn's realpolitik.

But the human imagination of apocalypse has changed somewhat. Cold War projections assumed that any use of nuclear weapons by the United States or the Soviet Union would result in global apocalypse. During the Cold War we envisioned the use of nuclear weapons as the immediate path to extinction. At the end of *Dr. Strangelove,* the whooping cowboy American B-52 pilot rode the nuke out of the bomb bay to its target. The rest was post-apocalyptic silence.

Today we do not think in terms of the global big bang. What is novel and dangerous in the twenty-first century's emerging dimension of evil is that what we call mass destruction has become thinkable—even provincial.

India and Pakistan are not superpowers that have matured into a stability of mutual assured destruction and therefore, of what, in the last age of nuclear anxiety, became mutual forbearance. The new nuclear franchisees are threadbare regional powers whose trigger fingers are wired to the primitive part of the brain where religious hatred lives. As one of Saul Bellow's characters remarked, different people may inhabit different centuries. Our problem today is that the small, interlocked world lives in real time and cannot survive a moral and cultural gap of centuries between these different people.

Still, it is a world of regionalized apocalypse: The use of nuclear weapons has come to seem, for those of us not directly in the impact zone, a survivable horror—just an incalculably more awful species of endurable terrorism. Death will be massive, but the world will go on. September 11 has led Americans to think a bit this way. Besides, if you visit Hiroshima now, you see no evidence of August 8, 1945, except for a lush memorial park, and a museum, and that one blackened building with its skeletal dome—the prefecture—that was allowed to stand as a token of that morning's apocalypse. The rest of Hiroshima is human bustle amid garish corporate logos done in neon.

The prospect of regional nuclear exchanges leads us to see the future as a Hobbesian mess that will go on and on, the world, day

by day and region by region, growing dirtier and dirtier with violence and radiation and religious hatred: mankind soiling itself
with evil, but never quite managing its own destruction.

Ultimately, the world survived the Cuban missile crisis and the
rest of the Cold War 1) because it was lucky, and 2) because the
leaders of the superpowers were equipped with superegos; they
were inhibited precisely by the horrific possibilities of their
power to do the unthinkable. The danger now is that the leaders
of impoverished and religiously inflamed populations are
tempted by their power to put themselves on the map by doing
the unthinkable. They have too much id, and too much ego, but
not enough superego.

31

THE QUEST FOR PURITY

Evil takes the outward form of hygiene—of good housekeeping.

Genocide expresses itself in this way. "Ethnic cleansing" means that territory ends up "cleaner" than before—the death squads, like good political housemaids, having scoured off the unwanted human dirt and grime. "Ethnic cleansing" implies an ideal state of tribal purity—cleanliness—that is sullied by alien people. It demands restoration, the undoing of those wrongs that corrupted the tribe. The authors of genocide frame the mission in heroic, nostalgic terms—a bloodbath to recapture, when it is ended, an ideal golden state that exists in tribal myth, in the collective pseudo-memory.

Thus Hitler's enterprise evoked a sleazy *volkische* Wagnerian prehistory, lurid and banal and stunningly vulgar. Slobodan Milosevic's Greater Serbia drew upon collective memories from before the Battle of Kosovo (1389). Genocidal evil quite often tries to rationalize itself along these lines, as an appeal to some

Shinto in the tribal blood—what Lincoln, with infinitely more humane intention, referred to as "the mystic chords of memory."

Lincoln used that phrase to appeal, not to evil, but to the "better angels of our nature." He spoke in the midst of the American civil war. The South, defending the evil of slavery as necessary for its way of life, had concocted for itself a mythic cavalier past, a golden ideal in which it managed to accommodate happy, simple-minded slaves, the loyal darkies living under the protection of genteel grandees, their natural masters.

Odd that so much evil emanates from the discrepancy between the daydream of a golden age and the disappointments of the present. It is one of the great lessons of evil that it flourishes in the subjective self-righteousness and grievance of a highly developed victim-culture. Germany after the Great War and the Versailles Treaty was such a culture. The American South before, but especially after, the Civil War, steeped in its fetid nostalgia, became a nightmare of bigotry and night-riders, a backwater of ignorance and poverty.

What makes Israel/Palestine so dangerous is that both peoples cherish a sense of aggrieved nostalgia for the land that each claims at the expense of the other. It is almost impossible for two different peoples' dreams of the past to be reconciled, to live with one another. Each people speaks of past disasters that cut it off from its past glories and happiness.

I think sometimes of quintessentially American moments of evil, and locate them in a certain whip-mean implacably homicidal something that D. H. Lawrence was getting at when he wrote, in his essay on Fenimore Cooper, that the average American is "hard, isolate, stoic, and a killer." In *Huckleberry Finn,* this trait appears in the person of the colonel in a small town along the Mississippi who is chivvied by the town drunk one day—the drunk standing outside the colonel's handsome house and hurling insults. At length, the colonel emerges, and in clean, disdainful terms, informs the drunk that he has until one o'clock to cease his howling and insults; if he does not do so, the colonel will kill him. The warning issued, the colonel turns and closes his door.

The drunk of course keeps up his baying, and at exactly one minute after one, the colonel emerges from his house and shoots the man dead in the street.

I find that an indelibly American moment. Why? The raw pitilessness of it combined with a ruthless sense of lawless justice, and the implicit self-confidence of the executioner that he has the right to act as he does. I connect it always to a scene in the autobiography of Frederick Douglass, when Douglass was young, on a plantation in Maryland, and watched as an overseer started to whip a slave. The fieldhand, to escape the whip, runs into a nearby creek. The overseer stands on the shore and calls to the slave to come out, and warns him, in the same authoritative tones as the colonel, that if he does not come out, he will shoot him. The terrified slave remains in the creek; the overseer coolly shoots him dead, and his blood reddens the water.

Both scenes (one fictional, one autobiographical) have for me a certain American eeriness. I find that in a rather different way, the evil done by Andrea Yates in Houston—drowning her five children that morning after her husband had gone to work—also suggests a quality of spooky isolation erupting suddenly in violence. It's the sheer disconnection that seems so American, I think—although that may be an American's optical illusion and perhaps the same could also be said of evils committed in other parts of the world. I associate that disconnection and isolation, in any case, with something in the conditions and history of my own country—a loneliness turned mad. Joan Didion caught this sense of America sometimes in her essays on southern California—the atmosphere of the snake in the mailbox, of the Manson gang prowling like coyotes in the canyons where a city has unnaturally intruded.

Truman Capote captured this in his book about the Clutter murders in Kansas, *In Cold Blood*. Rootlessness and a certain freakishness—that shallow American freedom and the metaphysical bewilderment that goes with it. Cormac McCarthy gets it in his stunningly violent novels about the Southwest—gruesome savagery performed with a strange calm and detachment. Francis Parkman gives it a stranger, different air of the detached, of sheer foreignness, in his descriptions of Iroquois and Mohawks torturing the French Jesuits who insisted upon trying to save their souls. One priest, who survived his captivity, described how, when he was bound and tortured in a Mohawk village, a brave seized his hand, and assessed each of the fingers, as if he were examining croissants at a bakery, and then called over a five-year-old boy, gave the boy a knife, and instructed the boy to cut off one of the fingers. Which the boy obediently did.

In *Slaughterhouse Five,* Kurt Vonnegut records a fantasy that all the bombs of World War II, and all bombs that fell on Dresden, could be magically recalled by running the film of history backward, so that the bombs would leap up out of the earth and recombine in midair and ascend into the bomb bays of the planes that had dropped them, and the planes would reverse themselves in the air and, flying backward, return to their bases, and presumably all bullets would return to their muzzles, leaping out of the flesh that they had struck so terribly, so that the wounds would close up by magic and the body return to its former wholeness, and all would be well.

Vonnegut's fantasy might more usefully have been applied, I would think, to Auschwitz and Treblinka—reverse the film on those—recall the smoke that went up to heaven from the chimneys of the crematoria, recombine the bodies of the six million, and restore them to their homes and families.

Can an evil act be rescinded? No. But it may sometimes be transformed, turned into a lesson, or into some other good. Evil, though usually seen as an inexplicable anomaly (gratuitously malevolent, Satanic, an autonomous wickedness), is, even at its worst, a part of the symmetry of history and human nature.

Caught in the grip of evil, you do not see it in such dispassionate terms. Even as a witness of evil, you are profoundly involved: The spectacle of evil makes painful demands upon the observer's senses, nerves, faculties of understanding and judgment. (Evil also overwhelms the evildoer, though in a different way—so that even he is usually inarticulate about what he has done.)

It is part of evil's strategy to shock the nervous system and moral instruments of those who witness it. That sense of shock accounts for evil's mystique of glamorous inexplicability: The trauma of evil tends to disable the capacity for rational judgment—tends to inject itself directly, sensationally, into the center of the brain, bypassing reason and language.

But if we view evil at a reasonable distance, it is possible to think of it as part of a larger ecology.

Although those suffering from the viciousness of their fellow men can be only remotely comforted by the thought (I would not attempt to persuade a survivor of Auschwitz on the point), evil is ultimately indispensable and creative, a part of the world's energy. It is one necessary half of a cosmic exchange. Good and evil are matter and antimatter. Even the unthinkable eventually recedes into the soil and fertilizes new history.

This fairly simple and sane view has a distinguished pedigree in some Eastern religions. In the West, clarity about evil has tended to be obscured in doctrinal complexities, in forests of dense theological nicety and ecclesiastical politics; efforts at symmetry have tended to be suppressed as heretical (Manichaeism, Gnosticism, Albigensianism, and so on).

Time is meaningless without the punctuation of events. Evil is the great agitator of events. Evil makes things happen; so does good, which makes its living—defines itself and perfects itself—by responding to evil.

It is not extravagant to say that without evil, history ceases—or rapidly winds itself down to a sort of immobile paradise, a neverland where, for example, the evil of death does not exist. In short, it becomes Eden, back where we started. Stories began with the expulsion from the Garden and are a struggling forward motion through time.

Time has no meaning except in stories. Stories measure time. In the beginning was the Word; the purpose of the Word is to record the stories and seek their meaning.

Without evil, there is no time.

Without violation, there is no trust. Without trust, there can be no violation.

Without evil, there is no symmetrical definition of the good. In fact, there is no good. Without valleys, no mountains, and vice versa. All moral meaning—although we may be disconcerted to think it—depends upon the existence of evil.

It is not the direct action of transformation—as of caterpillar into butterfly—that gives evil its meaning. It is rather a much broader chemical response, the dialectic of good and evil in the human heart, that is important. It is not so much that evil is transformed directly into good, as that evil acts as foil and antagonist in the theater of the world, and without evil, you have no drama, that is to say, no life perhaps worth living.

32

THE FOXES LOSE HEART

THE ENLIGHTENMENT HAS BEEN squandering its prestige for the last century or more in a murderous irrationality that keeps pace with progress and uses the tools of technology, such as nuclear bombs and other weapons; to the extent that the world's problems, in the face of such destruction, seem more and more hopeless, the foxes have been losing heart. At dusk the dark forms of the trees melt together, and the future looks like One Big Thing of forest.

More religious temperaments—including, to some extent, my own—already have a hedgehog's inclination to see the One Big Thing—the forest, the aggregate. If, as Freud said, there is an "oceanic" instinct to yearn for God, there may be a similar tidal pull to "believe in" evil. I find it difficult, in any case, to think about Dunblane, for example, without using the word evil.

The leap from fox to hedgehog means that instead of speaking of the world's evils, you speak of its evil. You take a considerable journey in going from the plural to the singular—as breathtaking, in its way, as the leap from polytheism to monotheism.

If we may speak of evil in the titanic singular (which conjures up a sort of negative monotheism—a monodiabolism), then what exactly is it? Is evil organized and conscious and endowed with malevolent intelligence and will—a sort of immense corporation with headquarters in hell and countless devils in the branch offices and Satan presiding as CEO—the model as Christianity has traditionally conceived it? How does this evil behave? What are its policies? What is its mission? Who sent it? Who or what is responsible for evil? Does it have a life of its own, quite apart from the realm of the human?

What does evil do when it is not practicing its practical jokes upon the human race? Is there evil in the Crab Nebula, Mu Camelopardelis, Orion's Belt, the Milky Way?

Or is evil entirely the projection, here on earth, of what is dark in human nature?

Is evil a substantial force or, on the contrary, an absence or absent-mindedness, a negative, the retraction of God from his creation? Is evil to be seen as a sort of routine deterioration in the condition of things, as if God's creation, however splendid, were constantly in need of maintenance and repair?

Would evil exist in a universe from which human beings were absent? Male Kodiak bears eat the cubs toddling down from their winter dens. Is that evil behavior in the tabloid class (if bears had tabloids), or is it sociobiology, is it mere animal behavior? Why do such acts by humans have dire moral meaning, theological significance, while among animals, they have none? What sermons about mankind's inherent evil would we inflict upon ourselves if human males were in the habit of seizing and eating newborn babies on their way home from the hospital?

And suppose that we assign psychological or sociological meaning to similar acts that human beings do commit. Are the perpetrators exonerated by the sheer fact of explanation *(Tout comprendre, c'est tout pardonner)*?

And yet if evil is seen from a reasonable distance (if it is possible to achieve a reasonable distance from evil), is it plausible that evil might be part of a larger ecology? That evil might be . . . necessary?

In 1757, Samuel Johnson wrote a short and savagely dismissive review of a book called *Free Inquiry into the Nature and Origin of Evil*, by a man named Soame Jenyns. The Johnson scholar W. Jackson Bate has written: ". . . it is hard to believe Johnson would have bothered to focus on [Jenyns's book] such an array of artillery had not its glib optimism—the old argument that evil is an inevitable part of the picture, that it helps good to shine out by contrast, that the suffering of the individual helps out the larger good—been expressed within the drama of deistic or 'natural' religion rather than of Hebrew-Christian teachings. . . . The luckless Jenyns, hoping for philosophic 'detachment,' imagines 'superior beings' who could regard us—regard our struggles with each other and the conditions of life generally—as we do the lower animals." So Johnson, pushing Jenyns's argument, responded:

He might have shewn that these hunters whose game is man have many sports analogous to our own. As we drown whelps and kittens, they amuse themselves now and then with sinking a ship, and stand around the fields of Blenheim or the walls of Prague, as we encircle a cock-pit. As we shoot a bird flying, they take a man in the midst of his business or pleasure, and knock him down with an apoplexy. Some of them, perhaps, are virtuosi, and delight in the operations of an asthma. To swell a man with a tympany is as good sport as to blow a frog. Many a merry bout have these frolic beings at the vicissitudes of an ague, and good sport it is to see a man tumble with an epilepsy, and revive and tumble again, and all this he knows not why. As they are wiser and more powerful than we, they have more exquisite diversions, for we have no way of procuring any sport so brisk and so lasting as the paroxysms of the gout and stone which undoubtedly must make high mirth, especially if the play be a little diversified with the blunders and puzzles of the blind and deaf.

Samuel Johnson's contempt is formidable; but I am not certain he was right; or that Bate was correct in dismissing the idea of a sort of cosmic collaboration between good and evil—a necessary struggle indeed, in which evil stimulates not only good, but history itself.

33

CZERNIAKOW'S CHOICE

WHAT DO WE MAKE of the suicide, on July 23, 1942, of Adam Czerniakow, the abundantly decent man who was the first head of the Warsaw ghetto's Judenrat, the Jewish Council?

What exactly was the meaning of Czerniakow's death? He swallowed cyanide in his office on the day after the Germans began mass deportations to the death camp at Treblinka. Did a humane, civilized, and hopeful man mean—quite accurately—to signal to other Jews in the ghetto the hopelessness of what lay ahead? Was the suicide an act of fecklessness, of weakness, of narcissistic despair?

Or did Czerniakow mean, in the most dramatic way available, to instruct his people that his own way with the Germans (he had spent nearly three years heroically temporizing, making deals with the SS, trying to mitigate the evil occupation in hope it would eventually end) had failed—and that something unprecedented and unimagined lay ahead, something he had only just now understood?

Czerniakow's story is in my mind a case study in a discussion of how to cope with political evil, and of when and how to draw lines against it. And it is an elaborate cautionary tale about the uses and the pitfalls of hope. I find myself drawn with great affection and pain to Czerniakow, and at the same time slightly mystified by him.

I think sometimes that the real struggle in the world may not be between good and evil but rather, between hope and evil. Hope seems more active and creative than the somewhat nebulous "good." Hope aspires; good has arrived. Good, like God, lives outside time; hope keeps people alive, moving forward, inside time. As long as hope remains healthy, it is a match for evil; about good, no one can be so sure.

But in the Warsaw ghetto, the perverse German evil learned to manipulate Jewish hope, and to turn it into a Nazi tool of management. It was hope—the faintest, most tantalizing, vanishing glimmers of it—that led the victims on from day to day. Surely the worst is over now, they told themselves, against the mounting evidence, unable to repress the deepest need of human nature. They won't take me. They need me at the Többens factory. This new identification card will keep me safe. Hope, grasping at straws, deflected, day by day, the full, unillusioned despair that, when it came later—too late—roused the ghetto to armed resistance.

The story began on October 12, 1940—on Yom Kippur, a little more than a year after Hitler's invasion of Poland—when the Nazis decreed the establishment of the Warsaw ghetto; 400,000 Jews would be confined in 1.3 square miles, roughly the size of New York's Central Park. A once thriving Jewish community, the largest outside of New York City, was sealed in, like Poe's character in "The Pit and the Pendulum," squeezed incrementally by humiliation, poverty, hunger, cold, starvation, an epidemic of typhus, tuberculosis, marauding Nazis who murdered on a freelance basis, and at last, mass systematic deportations—the hopeless trudge to the Umschlagplatz (transshipment station) at the end of Zamenhof Street and the trains to "resettlement," which meant to death camps like Treblinka.

Warsaw's Jewish Historical Institute assembled a collection of personal records (available in English translation as *Words to Outlive Us*). Most of the writers of these accounts are unknown. Many of their records, scribbled in Yiddish or, more often, Polish, were found in attics and basements of the ruined city after the war. Some of the stories are unbearable to read. *The Diary of Anne Frank* was a poignant solo piece for cello. This collection performs a work of full orchestral anguish.

Themes, sometimes of immense moral complexity, thread through the scraps and diaries. There are more than enough glimpses of what might be called the sporting beast—for example, an SS officer's execution (sardonic, satanically playful, summary) of a young Jewish mother with a baby on her shoulder, to whom the officer had, a moment before, given a loaf of bread. Or this, recorded by an anonymous woman: "One day a small Jewish boy was killed on Biala Street as he attempted to pull a carrot lying in the gutter on the Aryan side through a hole in the fence. A German spotted him, inserted his gun in the hole, and killed the boy with one well-aimed shot." One Samuel Puterman writes: "One officer drove a small sports car. This gentleman would zigzag down Leszno Street, firing all the while at pedestrians. It was a game." Through such scenes runs a vibration of Caligula's boast: "Remember, I can do anything to anyone"—the pleasure that power takes in its own vicious freedom.

Still, there was that fatal vein of hope. A dental technician named Natan Zelichower analyzed it: "The Jews did not believe in their own extinction. At the very center of their 'spiritual refuge' sat God, who, having led them through the Red Sea, would surely knock down the walls of the ghetto. . . . The Germans [might] eliminate a few thousand, or, let's say, tens of thousands, but surely not half a million people. Logically speaking then, since not everyone inside the ghetto was doomed, each person had a chance of escaping alive." For Zelichower, the hope—seductive and fatal for others—actually proved justified: He went from the ghetto to Buchenwald, where he was liberated in 1945.

The diaries show from new angles the moral complexity—or immoral complexity—of those Jews who served in the SP, the Jewish police that did the bidding of the Nazis in exchange for promises of immunity. There are fascinating passages on Adam Czerniakow, the first head of the Judenrat. Czerniakow, a decent man dedicated to his people (who sometimes mocked him and sang nasty ditties about him), illustrates among other things the dangers of mere meliorism, of trying to negotiate with evil. Czerniakow worked like a dog to mitigate a horror that could not be mitigated. When he at last understood the terrible dimensions of the German ambition, on July 23, 1942, after the Nazis demanded he sign a Judenrat order purporting to request that the Germans start "resettling" everyone "to the east," Czerniakow excused himself from his SS masters for a moment, and swallowed the cyanide pill.

At a distance of 60 years, one wonders what exactly to make of that suicide. An act of weakness? A confession of failure? Or a warning to his people of what was to come, expressed in the terminally eloquent language of suicide?

34

HOPE

PUMLA GOBODO-MADIKIZELA is a South African psychologist who served on her country's Truth and Reconciliation Commission, set up under the leadership of Bishop Desmond Tutu in an effort to prevent the overthrow of apartheid in South Africa from turning into an orgy of retaliation and revenge.

In her book called *A Human Being Died That Night: A South African Story of Forgiveness*, Gobodo-Madikizela writes with lovely clarity and directness, and therefore with great moral force. She built her book around the interviews that she conducted in the mid-1990s with the man known in black South Africa as Prime Evil—Eugene de Kock, for many years the commander of the state-sanctioned apartheid death squads responsible for torturing and executing members and sympathizers of the African National Congress. De Kock is serving a 212-year sentence for crimes against humanity.

Beginning in the fall of 1997, Gobodo-Madikizela interviewed de Kock for a total of 46 hours. They talked in a small interrogation room of a prison in Pretoria. The guards shackled de Kock and chained him to the metal stool that was bolted to the floor of the room, and they provided to Gobodo-Madikizela a chair on wheels, so that she could roll herself quickly out of range if de Kock were to lunge for her. De Kock might as well have been Hannibal Lecter.

But de Kock surprised the psychologist. He made an appeal to the TRC to meet with the widows of several black policemen from a place called Motherwell—men whose execution he had arranged, blowing them up with a remote-controlled bomb in order to silence them and prevent their testifying against the white death squads.

De Kock said that he wanted to apologize to the widows, and that he wanted to do so privately. The widows' lawyers agreed to the meeting. Two of the widows, Pearl Faku and Doreen Mgoduka, came to the prison and talked to de Kock.

A few days later, Mrs. Faku told the psychologist: "I was profoundly touched by him." The women said they felt that de Kock, a monster of mythic repute in black South Africa, had astonished them by communicating how deeply he felt his own remorse and their own pain at what he had done to their husbands.

Mrs. Faku said, "I couldn't control my tears. I could hear him, but I was overwhelmed by emotion, and I was just nodding, as a way of saying, yes, I forgive you. I hope that when he sees our tears, he knows that they are not only tears for our husbands, but tears for him as well. . . . I would like to hold him by the hand, and show him that there is a future, and that he can still change."

The psychologist wondered: was de Kock deserving of the forgiveness shown him? Was he too evil—"Prime Evil"—to be worthy of the forgiveness Mrs. Faku and Mrs. Mgoduka had offered him? Was evil intrinsic to de Kock, and forgiveness therefore wasted on him?

Gobodo-Madikizela wondered, "If showing compassion to our enemies is something that our bodies recoil from, what should our attitude be to their cries for mercy, the cries that tell us that their hearts are breaking, and that they are willing to renounce the past and their role in it?"

The psychologist's mission, as a member of the Truth and Reconciliation Commission, was not merely spiritual, but also practical and political: "How can we transcend hate if the goal is to transform human relationships in a society with a past marked by violent conflict between groups?"

T. S. Eliot asked one of the most pertinent questions of the twentieth century: "After such knowledge, what forgiveness?" After what de Kock had done, forgiveness seemed beyond the resources of human nature.

Gobodo-Madikizela explored the dynamics of forgiveness as a kind of instrument of public health. The task, she said, is to redefine an understanding of atrocities and "see them as something that is, like evil in the self, always a possibility in any political system that has emerged from a violent past. There are countless examples in history of government by people who have risen out of oppressive rule to become oppressors themselves."

There is no bromide as fatuous and false as the thought that to understand everything is to forgive everything—one of the founding inanities of the *bien-pensant* incapacity to deal with evil in the world. Gobodo-Madikizela thought more deeply about these matters. She knew among other things that forgiveness is less a matter of understanding than of a more profound motion of the heart—a grace and transcendence.

"Motion of the heart" is the right phrase: Forgiveness permits all parties to lay the past at last to rest and to proceed with a new beginning, uncontaminated by the infections of past wrongs, by thoughts of grievance and revenge. The great achievement of forgiveness is not so much that it absolves the one forgiven as that it cleanses the one who forgives.

Forgiveness is possible only if the person who has done evil is truly repentant and remorseful. De Kock apparently was.

When Gobodo-Madikizela talked to him about his meeting with
the two widows, "his face immediately fell, and he became visi-
bly distressed. I could hear the clatter of his leg chains as he
shuffled his feet. . . . There were tears in his eyes. In a breaking
voice, he said, 'I wish there was a way of bringing their bodies
back alive. I wish I could say, "here are your husbands,"' he said,
stretching out his arms as if bearing an invisible body, his hands
trembling, his mouth quivering, 'but unfortunately . . . I have to
live with it.'"

Then something unexpected happened. The black psychologist writes that she was so moved by his pain and remorse that,
"relating to him in the only way one does in such human circumstances, I touched his shaking hand, surprising myself."

That impulsive gesture startled and disconcerted Gobodo-
Madikizela—startled both of them. The hand she touched—his
"trigger hand," as he later informed her with a sort of savage
ruefulness—was one that had done very considerable evil to
Gobodo-Madikizela's people over a period of years. Her black
hand touched his white hand—an impulsive gesture of solidarity
and compassion that at the same time made an almost electrical
connection, charged with implication. A black presumed to comfort the former white master, their roles reversed. A black
woman in authority touched a white man in chains. If this was
the territory of the Beatitudes, in which the first shall be last and
the last shall be first, it was also a surreal moment in which the
ghost of the forbidden reappeared. Good put its hand on evil's
hand, just for a moment.

And so the question that troubled Gobodo-Madikizela was
whether, in that gesture, she somehow became implicated or
identified with evil, or whether, conversely, she, as the representative of apartheid's victims, had bestowed a sort of blessing
upon the evil hand. Did she have a right to do that—the old
Wiesenthal question?

The moment plunged her into confusion; she was relieved when, a moment later, the prison guard informed her that her time was up for that day. "But as I drove out of the prison toward Johannesburg, I started to feel a great sense of anxiety and despair. During my drive, I suddenly broke down in sobs."

She thought about it. "Hard as the memory of having touched him was, the experience made me realize something I was probably not prepared for—that good and evil exist in our lives, and that evil, like good, is always a possibility. And that was what frightened me."

One of the two or three indispensable tools for dealing with evil is the knowledge—simple enough, even banal—that evil, like good, is always a possibility. But the mind, having said that, rebels at the banality, the inadequacy of the thought that we are all sinners and that there but for the grace of God, go I: To say that seems to imply that somehow de Kock and others who do evil things are less guilty of evil, since everyone has the capacity to do evil. The line of thinking seems offensive to everyone who precisely does not do evil, but rather, resists the temptation to do so. If evil is a radical choice, why trick it up as a kind of accident? Why extenuate the responsibility and make evil deeds seem a matter of chance?

De Kock seemed to repay the woman's kindness sadistically, when he told her, next time they met in the little interrogation room: "You know, Pumla, that was my trigger hand you touched." She recoiled in anger and confusion.

"In touching de Kock's hand, I had touched his leprosy, and he seemed to be telling me that, even though I did not realize it at the time, I was from now on infected with the memory of having embraced into my heart the hand that had killed, maimed, and blown up lives. . . . I was engaging a man who still carried evil with him. He wanted his evil to be real to me because it was still real to him."

The morning after he told her about the "trigger hand," Gobodo-Madikizela lay in bed, "it dawned on me that I could not lift my right forearm. . . . It was the same hand with which I had reached out to offer consolation to de Kock, and now it had gone completely numb. . . . For a long, anxious moment, it felt disabled, grounded, as if placed on probation for engaging in a prohibited act."

I liked the complexity—the forward motion—of Gobodo-Madikizela's reflections on this business. She kept taking her mind to the next hill, and seeing new landscape. After her arm went temporarily numb, she did not accept her own predicament as the last word. Instead: "De Kock, I came to see, seemed also to be wrestling with the implications of the 'touched' hand; he too was struggling to comprehend what being touched meant." She speculates that he communicated his anxiety about the gesture of the touched hand by unconsciously "splitting off" the hand: "That cannot be me. It was my 'trigger hand' that killed." Distancing himself from and casting away the evil part of his body was an effort at self-preservation. But it was also an illustration of how fragmented he was—a person broken into bits struggling to achieve some sense of wholeness.

Then Gobodo-Madikizela crested another hill: "I was aware of a disintegration happening within myself. I was struggling with the part of me that made it possible to identify with de Kock—the evil de Kock."

Identify? How? The discussion of evil is filled with landmines and boobytraps of this kind. For her to fear she might "identify" with the evil de Kock implies that the only real defense against evil is not to understand it—not to be capable of an act of imagination that would allow you to trace the plausible origins of evil acts and to see ("identify") that any human being, even you yourself, might be led into such acts.

But Gobodo-Madikizela pushes beyond such artificial problems. "It didn't matter. Watching de Kock struggling with his past was what mattered. It gave me a sense of hope that he was in some emotional pain about the things he had done."

She returns interestingly to the motif of hands. She looks—for the first time, carefully—at de Kock's hands: "His fingernails were surprisingly neatly manicured. The nails were clean and white, with tidy symmetrical edges. One might even have been persuaded to call his hands beautiful. . . . For a moment, it struck me that the line separating good from evil is paper-thin."

In 2001, F. W. de Klerk, the last white president of South Africa, gave an address at Harvard's Kennedy School of Government; Gobodo-Madikizela was there, and during a question period asked de Klerk about de Kock's bitter statements that some of the blame for his crimes lay with the heads of the apartheid government.

De Klerk shot back: "My hands are clean!"

During the Vietnam era, the poet Robert Lowell wrote sardonically about the American war: "My eyes have seen what my hands have done." De Kock lost count of how many people had died at his hands. But when Gobodo-Madikizela asked him his worst memory of his cross-border death squad raids, he recalled one morning driving back from an operation in which he killed some members of the ANC's armed wing. He began to notice an odd smell on his body. The smell grew worse and worse, an acrid smell that he first thought was a normal smell of discharged gunpowder but which he decided, more and more, was a smell of death.

"It was like the taste of metal in the mouth, the smell of blood all over my body. I couldn't get it off." De Kock stuffed his clothes into a plastic bag and threw them out. He took four or more long showers. But the smell persisted.

The psychologist says that as de Kock described this scene, "his gestures had become extreme; he motioned in an exagger-

ated way, his eyes bulging, pulling at his arms as if he were struggling to remove something attacking his flesh, something unde-
tachable from his skin."

Gobodo-Madikizela saw a man struggling with guilt, "a
shadow that would not leave him. . . . A human being died that
night in the murder operation. This reality seemed to stand
between us. At that moment, I thought I saw a man finally
acknowledging the debt he owed to his conscience."

I THINK THAT the opposite of evil is not good, but rather,
hope—a more kinetic and practical thing. Evil, God knows, is
energetic, and needs to be opposed by something more vigorous
than "good," which, as John Milton found when his Lucifer
turned out to be far more interesting than God, is blandly undra-
matic, a sort of Unitarian vanilla. Hope, on the other hand, is
goodness in a tight spot, and ambitious to improve things.
Robust hope creates new realities, and is, as Aeschylus said, the
thing that exiles feed on. Hope is the primary energy of the will
to live, the will to survive.

Rely on hope.

Rely, simply, on love.

INDEX